# Spirits of
# America

# Spirits of America

## America

Intoxication
in Nineteenth-Century
American Literature

Nicholas O. Warner

University of Oklahoma Press

Norman and London

This book is published
with the generous assistance
of the Mellon Foundation.


Library of Congress Cataloging-in-Publication Data

Warner, Nicholas O., 1950–
Spirits of America: intoxication in
nineteenth-century American literature / by Nicholas O. Warner.
p.  cm.
Includes bibliographical references and index.
ISBN 0-8061-1873-3 (cloth: alk. paper)
1. American literature—19th century—History and criticism.
2. Drinking customs—United States—History—19th century.
3. Drug abuse—United States—History—19th century.
4. Drinking of alcoholic beverages in literature.
5. Alcoholism in literature.
6. Drug abuse in literature.     I. Title.
PS217.D75W37     1997
810.9'355—dc21        97-11225
CIP


Text design by Cathy Carney Imboden. Text is set in Usherwood Medium.

*To three young spirits of America:*
*my children,*
*Natalie,*
*Katherine,*
*and*
*Gregory*

Sobriety diminishes, discriminates, and says no; drunkenness expands, unites, and says yes. It is in fact the great exciter of the *Yes* function in man. It brings its votary from the chill periphery of things to the radiant core. It makes him for the moment one with truth. Not through mere perversity do men run after it. To the poor and the unlettered it stands in the place of symphony concerts and of literature; and it is part of the deeper mystery and tragedy of life that whiffs and gleams of something that we immediately recognize as excellent should be vouchsafed to so many of us only in the fleeting earlier phases of what in its totality is so degrading a poisoning. The drunken consciousness is one bit of the mystic consciousness, and our total opinion of it must find its place in our opinion of that larger whole.

—William James, *The Varieties of Religious Experience*

America is the only legal country which admires the breaking of rules, provided this action is of an exceptional order.

—Jean Cocteau, *Diaries*

The road of excess leads to the palace of wisdom.

—William Blake, *The Marriage of Heaven and Hell*

# Contents

# Acknowledgments

Just as my subject intersects with many different areas of human experience, so too this book has drawn on many different sources of information and assistance. Financial help at various stages came from Claremont McKenna College, and I extend my thanks to former Deans of the Faculty Gaines Post, Jr., and Ralph Rossum, as well as to the current dean, Anthony F. Fucaloro, for their support. I also thank Claremont McKenna College's Gould Center for Humanistic Studies and its director, Ricardo Quinones, for a generous summer research grant and for sponsorship of three exemplary student research assistants, Hilary Smith, Rubaina Azhar, and Jumana Abu-Ghazaleh. For a Graves Award in the Humanities that helped to bring this book to completion, I am grateful to Pomona College and the American Council of Learned Societies.

An earlier version of chapter 2 originally appeared in *Literature and Altered States of Consciousness,* edited by Evelyn J. Hinz, a special issue of *Mosaic: A Journal for the Interdisciplinary Study of Literature* 19, 2/3 (Summer/Fall 1986). A portion of chapter 8 appeared in *Beyond the Pleasure Dome: Writing and Addiction from the Romantics,* edited by Sue Vice, Matthew Campbell, and Tim Armstrong (Sheffield: Sheffield Academic Press, 1994).

The following people, representing a wide array of disciplines in the humanities, sciences, and social sciences, shared ideas or provided information that made my task easier: Carol B.

Brener, Carol Carney, Dr. Ralph M. Crowley, Daryl De Nitto, Lyle W. Dorsett, Bill Grant, David Greenberg, Gayle Greene, Dwight B. Heath, Jonellen Heckler, Denise Herd, Timothy Hickman, Sally Joranko, Jenijoy La Belle, Charles Lofgren, D. G. Myers, Peter Nardi, William Novak, James T. Sweeney, Vincent Virga, Dan Wakefield. Particularly valuable have been the suggestions of Lawrence Buell, Hennig Cohen, Frederick Crews, Herbert Lindenberger, and Robert Tracy. Also helpful were staff members at the institutions where I did most of my research: the Huntington Library, the Houghton Library at Harvard University, the New York Public Library, and the Alcohol Research Group in Berkeley.

The manuscript benefited from the insights of Audrey Bilger, Langdon Elsbree, Roger Forseth, Ricardo Quinones, and Michael Riley, who all read and extensively commented on various portions of it. Clayton Koppes and William Norris were at once rigorous and unwaveringly supportive, as always, in discussing this project with me and in sharing perspectives from their own respective disciplines, history and sociology. Thomas B. Gilmore, Jr., and Robin Room, who read the entire manuscript, offered many useful suggestions that found their way into the final text. For unfailing efficiency and resourcefulness, I salute Kimberly Wiar, senior editor at the University of Oklahoma Press.

Various members of my family contributed in no small way to the completion of *Spirits of America*. Susan Bailey, Harriet Bailey, and Margaret Bailey kindly allowed me use of their homes during early rounds of research, as did Raymond and Judith Hanselman. But for more acts of support, both tangible and intangible, than I can begin to enumerate and that I can never forget, I thank Donald and Claire Warner and Vitaly and Magdalina Beldin.

I offer a special toast to Robert Fossum, whose superb editorial skills are equaled only by the generosity with which, over the years, he has listened, read, reread, argued, and advised. His counsel and friendship have played a sustaining role in this project from beginning to end.

Above all I wish to thank Sarah Pratt for her incisive scholarly insight, for her help with translations from the German, and for her seemingly boundless patience and good humor during my long addiction to this book. What my work and my life owe her is incalculable.

*Spirits of America*

# Chapter 1

# Introduction

## The Varieties of
## Intoxicated Experience

In a memorable scene from the film *Casablanca,* the American saloon keeper, Rick (played by Humphrey Bogart), sits at a table with the evil Nazi Major Strasser and the amoral but engaging prefect of police, Captain Renault. Exuding oily malevolence, Major Strasser turns to Rick and menacingly asks, "What is your nationality?" "I'm a drunkard," is the laconic reply. "That makes Rick a citizen of the world," quips Captain Renault. A facile witticism, designed merely to smooth over a tense social situation, Captain Renault's comment speaks also to a much larger issue: to the truism that intoxication, in some form or other, knows no geographic or ethnic boundaries.[1] But, like many truisms about the universality of human nature or behavior, the observation that drunkenness occurs the world round masks a host of cultural complexities and national differences.

Certainly in the United States—whose national anthem itself originated in a drinking song—intoxicant use has assumed vivid and distinctive patterns. Both as symbols and as physical realities, alcohol and drugs have long possessed remarkable importance in American culture. And American literature amply reflects this fact, from the eloquent sermons of the Puritans to the most avant-garde productions of contemporary fiction, poetry, and drama. My topic here is one particular aspect of that literature—the critically neglected but extraordinarily rich depiction of intoxicant use in the antebellum period, with occasional glances beyond the Civil War in the interests of continuity and contrast. The book examines the importance of intoxication as a symbolic issue for Americans of the time, showing the extent to which literature itself was often associated by the powerful temperance press with intoxication, which in turn became an emblem of supposedly literary values, as opposed to values of the emerging industrialist-capitalist nation. I am particularly interested in the ways that literary and social discourses of intoxication mesh and diverge from one another in this period, when questions of intoxicant use, abuse, and abstinence reached unprecedented—and, to many modern readers, unbelievable—levels of intensity and influence.

Surprisingly, few literary studies have examined the topic of intoxication. In fact, *Spirits of America* is the first book-length study of drinking and drug use in nineteenth-century American literature.[2] Throughout the book, my chief aims are to clarify the ways that individual writers accept or challenge society's dominant attitudes toward alcohol and drugs; to extend our sense of antebellum writers' thematic concerns; and to demonstrate the importance and complexity of an unduly neglected aspect of nineteenth-century American writing.[3] In exploring this issue, we will discover that antebellum authors often reveal a profound ambivalence about intoxicant use that dovetails not only with a similar ambivalence in their society but also with a deeper, long-standing conflict in American culture. Often expressed in terms of intoxication and sobriety, this conflict tends to appear in parallel sets of opposing values or forces, such as pragmatist and dreamer, repression and desire, rationality and imagination, self-control and abandonment, disciplined conformity and recklessly defiant individualism.[4]

Although every writer we examine condemns some aspect of intoxicant use—and some condemn intoxicants entirely—a major strand in antebellum literature runs counter to the temperance movement's pervasive influence, endowing images of intoxication with positive, redemptive qualities. As we will see, this positive strand is connected to British romanticism, to ancient traditions associating poetry with wine, and to the supposedly distinctive American values of individualism and democracy. In many significant instances—mainly in the work of Ralph Waldo Emerson, Emily Dickinson, and Edgar Allan Poe, but also in parts of the work of Herman Melville, Nathaniel Hawthorne, James Fenimore Cooper, Elizabeth Drew Stoddard, and even the temperance activist Louisa May Alcott—intoxicants can console, aid, illuminate, and empower human beings, as well as distort and destroy them. For some writers, the positive evaluation of intoxicants goes no further than a hearty appreciation of the "good Creature of God," to use Increase Mather's famous phrase. For others, intoxicants ultimately evoke the realm that, though invisible to what Poe called "the sober eye of reason," is nonetheless real, possessing its own coherence and truth.[5]

"Apollo found that he could not live without Dionysos," wrote Friedrich Nietzsche (34,89).[6] A similar sense of the validity and even the necessity of the irrational informs the most complex and compelling visions of intoxicant use in antebellum literature. But this appreciation of Dionysos's gifts includes an unflinching awareness of their dangers, for the generous god of wine and joyous celebration can also exact a horrifying vengeance. At one end of a single continuum lie visionary perception and expanded consciousness. At the other lie the ravages of alcoholism and addiction. This continuum, in all its pathos, humor, and complexity, provides the abundant theme to be examined in this book.

The thematic abundance I mention stems partly from the unquestionable and well-known power of intoxicants to affect such fundamental aspects of human experience as behavior, perception, and consciousness. But it also stems from the remarkably different contexts and motivations for intoxicant use. A simple sip of wine can in different situations signify celebration or disease, religious ritual or sensual indulgence, macho prowess or spineless ineffectuality, timid conformity or swaggering rebelliousness.

These distinctions reflect the wide-ranging symbolism and

cultural variability—the "meaning-fullness"—of intoxicant use. Focusing specifically on drinking, for example, the influential alcohol researcher E. M. Jellinek notes that for millennia the "profound meaning" of alcohol use has taken many forms. Instead of viewing alcohol "solely in a negative or tension-reducing aspect," many cultures treat drinking "as positive and reinforcing," as something that not only reduces tension but bestows power. Frequently associated with disease and death, alcohol nevertheless functions as a "divine" fluid with symbolic links to such "life-giving substances" as blood, water, and milk, as well as to fertility, virility, and social identification (Jellinek, "Symbolism," 852).[7]

This symbolic richness is most apparent with regard to alcohol, which Erich Goode, in his authoritative *Drugs in American Society,* calls "the universal intoxicant." But as Goode reminds us, all aspects of drug use, including substances other than alcohol, are intimately tied to ideology and culture and depend "as much on irrational cultural factors as on . . . objective properties" (Goode, 5). Thus not only are various forms of intoxicant use fraught with significance beyond their psychobiological effects, but this significance shifts in relation to sociocultural context. Drinking and drug use are far from being unitary entities with fixed, universally accepted definitions. Rather, such things as drunkenness, addiction, alcoholism, "recreational" versus "medical" drug use, mode of drug ingestion, and even intoxicant choice assume highly symbolic, emotionally charged meanings that can vary dramatically between and within different periods, nations, and cultural groups.[8]

One need not be a proponent of American exceptionalism to recognize the long-standing and intense cultural significance of intoxicant use in the United States. Already in 1832, Nathaniel Hawthorne described America's "predilection for the Good Creature" as a "vice, to which . . . we have a long hereditary claim." Nearly a century later, the pioneer historian of Prohibition, John Allen Krout, wrote that "from the day in 1642 that William Bradford confided to his journal his astonishment at the growth of drunkenness, the use and abuse of alcoholic beverages has been an important factor in determining the characteristics of American life."[9] Nor has this history revolved around alcohol alone. Although we often think of the 1960s as that period when drugs erupted into the national consciousness, the truth is that drug use in the United States, like the consumption of alcohol, "has a long history and touches many basic American attitudes and tastes." Just as heavy drinking seemed to be turning antebellum America into an "alcoholic republic," so too "excessive opiate use in the nineteenth century was not considered 'un-American' but 'peculiarly American.'" By the turn of the century, the United States had developed a relatively large population of addicts that, though decreasing after 1900, continued to exceed "the per capita rate in other Western nations."[10]

It was also in the early twentieth century that the long-standing struggle between pro- and antitemperance factions (or "drys" and "wets") went into a crescendo that climaxed in Prohibition, that "noble experiment" that has loomed so large in modern American history and folklore. Indeed, reference to Prohibition reminds us that two of our constitutional amendments relate to drinking—a telling indication of the importance attached to intoxicant use in our society (Moore and Gerstein, "Introduction," 3).

In more recent history, the power of alcohol and drugs to provoke controversy has manifested itself in many ways: in the evocative associations (good or bad) of the sixties chant, "Turn on, tune in, drop out"; in the notorious fashionableness of cocaine in the seventies and early eighties; in our perennial "war against drugs"; in the proliferation of Alanon and MADD chapters; in our fascination with "addictions" and "codependencies" of all types; in the need of the Democratic candidate for president in 1992 to reassure American voters that, although he had smoked marijuana at Oxford, he didn't inhale.

Antebellum America's heavy drinking patterns were fostered by numerous factors: Old World drinking traditions brought with the colonists; economic pressures that led to increased production of alcoholic drinks; the difficulty of maintaining the freshness of (as we now say) alternative beverages such as water or milk. Even ideology entered the picture, as colonial taverns were often regarded as seedbeds of democratic sentiment, and bourbon was celebrated as a patriotic, "all-American" drink because of its manufacture from a native American grain: corn (Lender and Martin, 54; Rorabaugh, 35, 63–64, 91). But some commentators have perceived a yet deeper link, not only in earlier times but throughout our history, between American drinking habits and the nation's general cultural situation, as described in John W. DeForest's novel, *Kate Beaumont*. Here the protagonist's brother, Tom, explains American culture in terms anticipating Leslie Fiedler's description of a "self-declared and self-celebrated Whiskey Culture":

> As to America, I Hurrah for it, of course. We can whip the world, if we could get at it. But when it comes to palaces and picture-galleries and that sort of thing, by Jove, we're in the swamps; we're just nowhere. We haven't anything to show. What can you take a man round to when he travels amongst us? The only thing we can offer to pass the time is just a drink. . . . And that's the reason, by Jove, that we're always nipping.[11]

These comments may amount to no more than an alcoholic version of Henry James's famous lament about the "thinness" of American culture in his biography of Hawthorne. But a growing body of sociohistorical research suggests a strong cultural predisposition to alcohol (and other drug) abuse in America. As several important studies have shown, societies characterized by rapid demographic, economic, and social change, as well as by ideals of extreme individualism and self-reliance—that is, societies like that of the United States in the antebellum period (and numerous periods thereafter)—tend toward high rates of intoxicant abuse, especially through alcohol.[12] Basing his conclusions on theoretical and applied cross-cultural drinking studies, the historian Norman Clark writes that "morbid drunkenness is common in those societies . . . where every man is expected to make it on his own, . . . to be achievement-oriented and splendidly self-reliant" (Clark, 33–34), a statement of obvious relevance to American ideals and notions of cultural identity. From the early nineteenth century on, historical, economic, and cultural factors in the United States have inadvertently fostered that "inducement to drunkenness which seems to rise naturally in an individualistic society" (Clark, 33). The great irony here is that intoxicant abuse departs from and even violates those values of self-reliance and individual responsibility that early became enshrined in American culture. By another stroke of irony, to become intoxicated is to defy standards of sober conduct by making oneself incapable of satisfying those standards. In a sense, the "drunk" invalidates the game of achievement by becoming incapable of even playing it. Thus drunkenness can simultaneously represent the failure to measure up to sacrosanct American standards of individual responsibility and the rebellious rejection of those standards.

But American culture has long tolerated, often even celebrated, this "failure" that, from another perspective, looks like individualistic defiance. From Washington Irving's Rip Van Winkle to Finley Peter Dunne's Mr. Dooley to the sympathetic lushes of contemporary film and television (e.g., *Arthur* and "Cheers"), Americans have produced a rich vein of humorous, lighthearted treatments of drink (less so of drugs), often depicting drunkenness admiringly or at least forgivingly. Particularly popular in the nineteenth century were comic celebrations of alcohol as a form of rebellion against hearth, home, and housewife, as in G. W. Harris's tales of the jovially inebriated Sut Lovingood, or the humorous portrayals of warmhearted drunks in Edward Harrigan's popular plays. The best known of all such characters, of course, is the legendary Rip himself, who defies all principles of sobriety and responsibility to emerge forgiven and victorious at the tale's end. His triumph was even more emphatic in the long-running stage version of the story, in which Rip, having gained his wife's permission to drink, takes a sip of liquor and winks knowingly at the audience as the curtain goes down (Fiedler, *Re-*

*turn,* 62). Despite the influence of temperance ideals, there has long been a strong affection for the figure of the drunkard throughout American literature and folklore, such as the lovable drunks mentioned above, or Mark Twain's images of the "fragrant town drunkard" in *Life on the Mississippi* or of the harmless Muff Potter in *The Adventures of Tom Sawyer.* In Twain's case, of course, such affable drunkards as Muff are offset by the violent Pap, one of literature's most horrifyingly volatile instances of drunken brutality. But even Pap's drunkenness is turned to (admittedly grotesque) comic effect more than once. When, for example, the naive new judge gets Pap to sign a temperance pledge and provides him with a beautiful room in which to stay, Pap promptly proceeds first to fall off the wagon and then off the porch. His room is so thick with the fumes of liquor that when the judge and others come to "look at it," says Huck, "they had to take soundings before they could navigate it." Later, Pap reveals an unusual method for gauging the amount of liquor he has left, telling Huck that he has "enough whiskey . . . for two drunks and one delirium tremens."[13]

The contradictory patterns described above accord well with America's historic, deep-seated ambivalence toward intoxicants. As David Pittman explains in the introduction to his classic anthology, *Alcoholism* (1967), unlike societies that are either more permissive or more prohibitive regarding alcohol use, "probably in American society one finds the prototype of the ambivalent culture. The American cultural attitudes toward drinking are far from being uniform and 'social ambivalence' is reinforced by the conflict between the drinking and abstinent sentiments co-existing in many communities. . . . Drinking pathologies in American society are perpetuated by cultural attitudes that veer toward asceticism and hedonism" (8–9).[14]

Other studies have reaffirmed Pittman's conclusions. For example, in their magisterial overview of temperance and prohibition history, Paul Aaron and David F. Musto point out a "pervasive ambivalence" present even at "the root of the 18th amendment and its enforcement statutes," which resulted in the paradoxical situation where "possession of liquor illegally obtained was un-lawful" while "the act of drinking was maintained as privileged" (159). Similarly, the historians Mark Edward Lender and James Kirby Martin conclude that contemporary American attitudes toward intoxicants continue a historical pattern of debate, ambivalence, and wild fluctuation (190–95).

It remains to note that when sociologists refer to American ambivalence regarding intoxicants, as opposed to the more consistent national attitudes of some countries, for example, Italy, Spain, and Israel, they do not mean that no Americans hold un-ambivalent, definite views of drinking or drugs. Rather, they mean that (a) the United States does not possess a coherent, unified national attitude toward intoxication or intoxicant use but presents instead an often confusing plurality of disparate, at times sharply conflicting attitudes; and (b) relatively high numbers of individual Americans do in fact feel considerable ambivalence about the intoxicated state and about specific intoxicants. Thus ambivalence, as used by social scientists describing intoxicant use, and as I will be using it here, may be rooted either in sociocultural inconsistencies—which some might feel should be more accurately termed "ambiguity"—or in conflicting attitudes within the individual mind (Room, "Ambivalence," 1062). While nineteenth-century New England tended toward temperance (and temperance there often meant abstinence), the frontier fostered a tradition of heavy drinking; the same upper-class teetotaler who would never dream of darkening a saloon doorway might eagerly embrace opium; moderate drinkers concerned about public drunkenness might, like one Kansas community, choose to "vote dry and drink wet."[15]

---

For several reasons, the study of intoxicants in literature makes a good fit with the antebellum period—or as good a fit as, to use Lawrence Buell's term, the "necessary evil" of literary periodization will allow.[16] Most obviously, there is the alcohol binge that lasted from the 1790s until about 1840, as well as the increased perception of an opium problem in the 1840s (Lender

and Martin, 196; Morgan, *Drugs,* 6). Related to this increased intoxicant use are the "brutally rapid" social changes and attendant tensions that antebellum Americans experienced (Aaron
and Musto, 134–37), as well as the development of those ten-
sion-producing ideals of individualistic achievement discussed
earlier. But three other issues related to intoxication in antebellum literature require fuller attention. These are the temperance
movement, the influence of British romanticism, and the long-
standing tradition (related to romanticism) of the Dionysiacally
inspired poet. These three issues will converge in yet another
important aspect of our theme—a virulent culture war between
the temperance movement and the antebellum literary intelli-
gentsia.

Although my topic is neither temperance nor the voluminous
body of literature it produced, the concerns of this movement—
"without question the most popular American mass movement
of the nineteenth century"—occupy a significant place in antebellum culture (Bernard, 337).[17] In fact, temperance's period of
greatest legal effectiveness prior to Prohibition coincided exactly with the years 1851–1855, the chronological heart of the
American Renaissance. The first of the prohibitionistic Maine
Laws was enacted in 1851, and by 1855, similar bans on liquor
appeared in twelve other states (Lender and Martin, 45).

Modern intellectuals have tended to dismiss temperance as
a manifestation of repressive Victorianism, a strain of the "rural-
evangelical virus" so eloquently pilloried by Richard Hofstadter
(290). But as Jack S. Blocker and others have demonstrated, the
notion of temperance supporters as grim backwoods killjoys ignores both the reality of alcohol problems in U.S. history and the
considerable presence of urban, progressive elements within the
temperance movement. Temperance advocates were not simply
a mass of pietistic, thin-lipped puritans bent on eradicating everyone else's pleasures. Many temperance supporters and leaders
were moderate, enlightened, progressive-minded people genuinely concerned about a problem that seemed to impinge on
every facet of their lives (Blocker, "Introduction," 4). Supplement-

ing these views, Susanna Barrows and Robin Room suggest that the modern stereotypical image of temperance stems partially from "a generational reaction against Prohibition and temperance concerns," which in turn resulted "in a scholarly distaste for dealing with what were seen as misplaced and bigoted concerns" ("Introduction," 3).

Nevertheless, elements of fanaticism and moral meddlesomeness increasingly crept into the temperance cause. In its earlier stages, temperance reform was essentially "assimilative," characterized by sympathy for the drunkard and the drinking poor. But by the time of the Civil War, another major component of the temperance movement had developed: "coercive" reform, which viewed the drinker as an enemy of respectable society and which stressed legal prohibition rather than moral suasion. It was this side of temperance—"the hammer of reform," in Stephen Crane's vivid phrase—that eventually became what Joseph Gusfield calls the "dominating theme of Temperance" and that led to the familiar, negative stereotypes of puritanical prohibitionism.[18] It was also mainly this coercive variety of temperance against which many American authors protested. But temperance, in whatever form, also struck many a responsive chord in our literature. Whether individual American writers in the nineteenth century blessed or damned it, one thing is certain: temperance remained an unavoidable part of the society in which they lived and wrote.

One feature that temperance supporters shared with their opponents was a tendency to invoke their own Americanness and to impugn the Americanness and patriotism of the opposition. Temperance pronouncements often drew parallels between American independence from Britain and independence from drink; thus John Pierpont's song, "Jonathan's Declaration of Independence" (sung to the tune of "Yankee Doodle," no less), explicitly identifies the title character's freedom with the throwing away of his "grog" (Krout, 253). Independence Day celebrations became particularly popular occasions for comparisons between temperance agitation and revolutionary activity, and the year 1826, marking a half century of America's existence as a nation, witnessed a flurry of elaborate analogies between the causes of abstinence and independence (Rorabaugh, 193–94). In 1833, the famous abolitionist Theodore Grimké fused Christianity, patriotism, and temperance into a single, by no means uncommon formula when he asserted that "the Temperance Reformation is peculiarly Christian, *AMERICAN*" (quoted in Perry Miller, *Life,* 86).[19] The very name of a temperance organization like the well-known Washingtonians served to connect a popular national icon, and thus the national identity that that icon represented, with temperance. The Washingtonians' nationalism, lampooned by Poe, is evident in their founding, when the members originally considered calling themselves the Jeffersonian Temperance Society before appropriating the name of the first president (Chidsey, 18).[20]

This sense of a special link between temperance and the United States reflects the notion, already present in prerevolutionary times, of the United States as a unique civil and religious entity—a "city upon a hill," in the famous metaphor from John Winthrop's sermon, "A Modell of Christian Charity" (1630) (100). The same idea informs the opening words of Cotton Mather's *Magnalia Christi Americana* (1702): "I WRITE the *Wonders* of the Christian Religion, flying from the Depravations of *Europe,* to the *American Strand*" (89). In specific connection with drinking and temperance, the idea of America's special spiritual quality—its status as a kind of second promised land—appears vividly in the 1673 pamphlet, *Wo to Drunkards,* by Cotton's father, Increase Mather. Himself a defender of drink as a "good Creature of God," the elder Mather castigated the abuse of that good creature as a sin that became particularly reprehensible on New England's holy soil: "What? To be a Drunkard in New England. . . . [I]s this Sin now become Common in New England? The Lord Help! Will you be sinners in Zion? Will you be fools in Israel!" (45).

But the partisans of temperance held no monopoly on appeals to patriotism or national identity. As we have seen, early in the nation's history, drinking became linked with independence and democracy, and even a particular beverage—bourbon—became invested with patriotic sentiment. In literature, the poet Royall Tyler exemplified such attitudes by uniting anacreontic and patriotic subjects in formats that were popular, widely available, and utterly respectable, for example, poems sold as broadsides or published in newspapers and special issue periodicals on such occasions as Independence Day. In "Anacreontic to Flip," printed in three different publications in 1794, Tyler praises flip's all-American ingredients—New England rum and maple sugar. In "Convivial Song," printed as a broadside to be distributed on July 4, 1799, and reprinted in several newspapers, Tyler gave his vinous theme a political twist. The first stanza sets the tone for the whole:

> Come fill each brimming glass, boys,
> Red or white has equal joys,
> And fill each brimming glass, boys,
> And toast your country's glory.
>
> (27)

Successive stanzas offer toasts to various American heroes and subjects. The then president, John Adams, earns special praise, ironically, because Adams's own temperance makes it possible for the average citizen to abandon *his* without fear of molestation: "the Sage of Quincy . . . guards us while we're drinking" (Tyler, 104).[21]

Tyler's conjunction of anacreontic delight with Republican virtue may strike us today as odd or merely quaint. But only a few years after these poems were published, the national anthem itself provided an indirect form of such a conjunction. Now endowed with all the emotional trappings of officialdom and sanctified sentimentality, "The Star-Spangled Banner" took, as its melody, the jaunty air of "To Anacreon in Heaven," a transatlantically popular drinking song. Nor was there any sense of impropriety in this; in 1814, the first sheet music issue of "The Star-Spangled Banner" explicitly identified the tune as "Air, Anacreon in Heaven." So did numerous subsequent issues, although by the 1850s, whether because the melody's original source had faded from memory, or because of temperance sensibilities, or both, the link between anthem and drinking song no longer regularly appeared.[22]

Perhaps it was because this link had all but vanished that, during the heyday of temperance legislation (the first half of the 1850s), *Cozzens' Wine Press,* a monthly journal edited by vintner Frederick Swartout Cozzens, proudly reminded Americans that their national anthem's melody was that of a once-beloved drinking song. The *Wine Press*'s discussion of "The Star-Spangled Banner" furthered this journal's general program of providing information of interest to wine connoisseurs and presenting convivial drinking as a positive activity in the best American tradition; the *Wine Press* regularly encouraged growth of wines in the United States, presented wine-related anecdotes and literary passages, and persistently portrayed temperance reformers as fanatical, irrational, undemocratic, and un-American. The April 20, 1855, issue even implied that the prohibitionist atmosphere of the times was in direct conflict with the Declaration of Independence and attacked the current prohibition law in New York State as being based on three assumptions that obviously contradict American notions of individualism and self-determination:

> First, that punishment is the road to virtue!
> Second, that no man can be safely trusted with control over himself.
> Third, that the governor is superior to the governed. (81–82)[23]

Some opponents of temperance carried their activities well beyond the scope of a journal like *Cozzens' Wine Press,* going so far as to form *antitemperance* societies. And on at least one occasion the tensions between dry and wet factions even led to "a pitched battle" between drinkers and temperance supporters who were staging rival Fourth of July celebrations (Rorabaugh, 193).

From our contemporary perspective, this polemicizing and politicizing of temperance may well appear ludicrous. But the controversies surrounding temperance in the antebellum period were serious matters to many Americans, including American writers—as serious, substantive, and controversial as questions of abortion, environmental protection, and homosexual rights are to us today, and revealing many of the same tensions in American society.

---

Less pervasive in society than temperance, but of considerable importance to literature, was a distinct intellectual trend in Europe and America during the early 1800s. From the beginning of the nineteenth century, or, as it has been called, "the age of intoxication," intellectual and artistic interest in the alteration of consciousness through psychoactive drugs (of whatever kind—opium, laudanum, alcohol, ether) dramatically increased (Logan, 81–94). As Suzanne R. Hoover writes (regarding Coleridge's experiments with nitrous oxide), "the nature of consciousness was to become one of the most explicit and intense concerns of the nineteenth century" (26). Similarly, Leon Chai draws our attention to the "Romantic emphasis upon mind and consciousness" in both British and American literature (11). As part of this larger interest in consciousness and its expansion beyond the boundaries of logic and empiricism, the intoxication theme in antebellum literature blends in with one of the major intellectual currents of its time.

The exact nature of this blending, however, requires closer attention, for intoxication does not merge indissolubly with the vaster issue of heightened or illuminated consciousness. Most of the major authors I discuss would probably agree with William James that "drunken consciousness is one bit of the mystic consciousness, and our total opinion of it must find its place in our opinion of that larger whole" (13:307). But that "bit" usually remains distinct from the higher state of "mystic" consciousness. Hence the notion of "two wines"—one sublime, one mundane—infusing antebellum literature, most strongly in Emerson and Dickinson, but also in Hawthorne, Poe, and Melville (especially the later poetry).

Romantic writers often celebrate wine for its pleasing qualities and poetic associations. But at times they reject literal wine as a paltry substitute for the truer wine of art, poetry, or intense spiritual experience. Addressing this issue in a notebook entry of 1808, Samuel Taylor Coleridge writes that humanity "before the Fall [was] possessed of the Heavenly Bacchus"; in our fallen world, however, only "the Bastard Bacchus [of artificial intoxication] comes to [our] Relief" (3:entry 3263). The concept of a superior spiritual wine as opposed to an inferior earthly one appears vividly in Keats. The notion is jovially expressed in "Hence Burgundy, Claret and Port," and rapturously in "Ode to a Nightingale," where the longing for vinous intoxication gives way to yearnings of a more sublime nature:

> Away! away! For I will fly to thee,
> > Not charioted by Bacchus and his pards,
> But on the viewless wings of Poesy,
> > Though the dull brain perplexes and retards.
> > > > > (Keats, 527)

This bifurcation between physical and spiritual wine or intoxication appears not only in romanticism but also in a long religious and philosophical line that includes Increase Mather, Philo, and, ultimately, the Bible: "Be drunk, but not with wine; stagger, but not with strong drink," (Is. 29:9); "be not drunk with wine . . . but be filled with the spirit" (Eph. 5:18).[24] In practice, however, literal and spiritual intoxication can blur all too easily. The heavenly Bacchus and the bastard Bacchus, to use Coleridge's terms, are not always easily distinguishable. There is, to be sure, an undeniable difference between having a drink and having a mystical experience of expanded consciousness. But there is also an undeniable connection between them, reflecting the widespread sense of relation between literal intoxicant use and a more metaphorical, spiritual form of intoxication, as this book's opening epigraph from William James suggests.[25] Thus the notion of "two wines" can lead to two quite different assessments of literal intoxicants; they can be denigrated as vulgar counterfeits of the true sublime or celebrated as humble yet nonetheless genuine avatars of intoxication on a higher plane. As we shall find, the divisions and intersections between spiritual and physical intoxication that are apparent in British romanticism reappear with subtle persistence in the work of the authors examined here.

A more familiar part of the British romantic legacy to American literature is the emphasis on the artist as an outsider and rebel. Often this figure is a visionary who has drunk the milk of a paradise far different from the bland, convention-ridden, "middle-class paradise" scorned in William James's essay, "What Makes a Life Significant" (10:153). Though published in 1899, James's article attacks an antiromantic ideology whose seeds were already beginning to sprout in the antebellum period. For it was then that, in the words of Paul Johnson, "a nascent industrial capitalism became attached to visions of a perfect moral order based on individual freedom and self-government" (Johnson, *Shopkeeper's Millennium,* 141). It is well known that during the nineteenth century, American society became increasingly bourgeois, both in the Flaubertian and the Marxist senses of the word. This fact is strikingly reflected in the changing role of liquor, which went from being "a builder of morale in household workshops, a subtle and pleasant bond" between master and worker, to being a symbol of working-class rowdiness and undisciplined dissolution (Johnson, *Shopkeeper's Millennium,* 60). For writers questioning this developing middle-class ethos, the imagery of intoxication (and sometimes intoxication itself) served as a vehicle for their alienation from a supposedly philistine, unimaginative social order. This syndrome is evident all the way from Hawthorne's dreamy artist-tippler, the hapless and helpless Owen Warland, to Hemingway's and Fitzgerald's Prohibition-defying sophisticates to the grittier, drink- and drug-using antiheroes of the Beats, Charles Bukowski, and William Kennedy, among many others. Already in the antebellum period some significant authors—for example, Emerson, Dickinson, Poe, Hawthorne, Melville—used images of intoxication to suggest individualistic defiance of tame convention. Thus from a very early date, the antibourgeois strain so evident in American literature easily absorbed intoxication as a significant motif.

Underlying the above discussion is the implication of romanticism's contrast with eighteenth-century literature, especially in its neoclassic and Enlightenment dimensions. As far as intoxicant use is concerned, the eighteenth century provides a substantial body of literary material, including, as I have argued elsewhere, what is probably the first literary depiction of the modern concept of alcohol addiction.[26] But eighteenth-century authors generally do not follow the intoxication theme either into the symbolic realm or into the dimmest reaches of consciousness. That territory has usually belonged to romantic and modern literature. However, like so many other aspects of its break with eighteenth-century rationalism, romanticism's versions of visionary intoxication look back to earlier traditions.

The romantic image of the visionary poet continues an ancient link between artistic creativity and an inspired madness whose closest analogue has long been intoxication.[27] This tradition, which I will call Dionysian, is important to my topic in two ways. First, its emphasis on nonrational perception parallels, in varying degrees, those works of romantic American literature in which intoxicant use possesses a visionary or transcendent dimension. Second, this tradition became a major reference point in the culture war (referred to earlier) between "temperance" and "literature." Our understanding of alcohol and drugs in American romantic writing will benefit from a consideration, in turn, of the Dionysian literary tradition and of the cultural conflict I mention. The concept of the poet as Dionysially frenzied or drunken, inspired by a "furor poeticus," gained wide currency in romantic literature and art. Specifically invoking Dionysian myth, Johann Gottfried Herder, for example, traces poetry's origin to the "ancient dithyramb, . . . a raving inspiration of the Bacchantes who, struck by the lightning of the wine, with foaming mouth sang of the birth and deeds of its inventor."[28] In English romantic poetry, the artist as inspired visionary finds its most potent exemplar in Coleridge's "Kubla Khan":

> Weave a circle round him thrice,
> And close your eyes with holy dread,
> For he on honey-dew hath fed,
> And drunk the milk of Paradise.

Though at odds with neoclassicism's ideal of the poet, Coleridge's visionary figure is far from new, tracing its roots all the way to Plato's *Ion*. In the English tradition, this image of the poet has the authority of Shakespeare himself, in the famous passage on poetic creation from *A Midsummer Night's Dream:*

> The poet's eye, in a fine frenzy rolling,
> Doth glance from heaven to earth, from earth to heaven,
> And, as imagination bodies forth
> The form of things unknown, the poet's pen
> Turns them to shapes, and gives to airy nothing
> A local habitation and a name.
>
> (5.1.12–16)

In *The Shepheardes Calendar* (1579), Edmund Spenser more specifically associates the poet with Bacchus, the Roman variant of Dionysos, and even manages to reconcile the usually opposed figures of Dionysos and Apollo:

> Who euer casts to compasse weightye prise,
> And thinks to throwe out thondring words of threate;
> Let powre in lauish cups and thriftie bitts of meate,
> For *Bacchus* fruite is frend to *Phoebus* wise.

In classical times, the poet-wine association is widespread, finding its best-known formulation in Horace's claim that no poems written by water drinkers can attain immortality. Ultimately, this tradition stems from the myths of Dionysos, out of whose worship both comedy and tragedy are traditionally said to have sprung.[29]

The Dionysian tradition I have just outlined possesses a long and venerable history. But the relevance of the Dionysian concept to my project goes even further than my discussion of that tradition indicates. In its traditional sense, "Dionysian" refers to Dionysos, the wine god, and, of course, to intoxication. By extension it indicates the nonrational, the ecstatic, the spontaneous. We generally understand the Dionysian to imply opposition to rationalism, control, and materialism and to nonspontaneous or highly scripted, conventional modes of being and behavior. But "Dionysian" can also suggest the *recognition* of the power and benefits of the nonrational, which in turn lends itself easily to expression in terms of intoxication. Thus in this book, a Dionysian perspective means neither dissipation nor drunkenness but rather the view that Dionysian qualities must be acknowledged and accorded a place in the individual and in society.

This issue of acknowledgment lies at the heart of that most crucial of all texts dealing with the Dionysian, Euripides' *Bacchae.* The debate in that play between Dionysos and Pentheus centers not on drunkenness versus sobriety but on the question of recognition—on Dionysos's demand that his power and divine identity be recognized, lest that power destroy those who deny it. Thus it is that the aged Teiresias describes Pentheus, Dionysos's opponent and self-appointed spokesman for reason, sobriety, and order, as being himself insane (*Bacchae,* 203). When Pentheus scornfully defies Dionysos's claims to worship, Teiresias demonstrates the proper response to Dionysos by inviting Cadmus to join him in paying "due service / To Dionysos, son of Zeus" (*Bacchae,* 203). Teiresias worships Dionysos not in a frenzy of mindless revelry but in tribute to the awesome power of the god, whose irrationality or "madness" must be incorporated into the psyche that would be truly balanced. A curiously parallel concept emerges late in Plato's *Laws,* where wine can play a beneficially cathartic role and even help the psyche to achieve equilibrium between its diverse components, establishing that sense of healthy balance called *sophrosyne.*[30]

Unlike Teiresias, the repressive and repressed Pentheus, obsessed with rational control, is driven mad by Dionysos, becoming the very thing that he most fears. The fate of Pentheus illustrates the point, eloquently articulated by the classicist E. R. Dodds, that "we ignore at our peril the demand of the human spirit for Dionysiac experience. For those who do not close their minds against it such experience can be a deep source of spiritual power and *eudaimonia*. But those who repress the demand in themselves or refuse its satisfaction to others transform it by their act into a power of disintegration and destruction" (xiv).

Much of *The Bacchae* can be seen as an ongoing debate between Dionysos and Pentheus, in which the latter repeatedly condemns the god and his followers as mad, bad, and dangerous to the state. An analogous debate existed in antebellum America (some might say that it has never really ceased). On one side of this debate we find what I call the party of Pentheus: supporters of that cluster of moral, economic, and cultural views that we loosely term the "Protestant work ethic." Key values for the party of Pentheus included industriousness and industrialization, common sense, efficiency, capitalism, and, as the basis on which all of these rest, sobriety. On the other side of the debate we find the party of Dionysos, constituted chiefly by writers and others with literary affiliations who resisted the onslaught of temperance. Of course, many writers could not be described as members of the Dionysian party. Nevertheless, the authorial class as a whole was perceived as hopelessly "wet" by temperance leaders. This view was also fostered by writers evoking the poetry/ wine links described earlier and by such well-known sources as the "Noctes Ambrosianae" of *Blackwood's,* an English publication with a large American following.[31] For the party of Dionysos, key positive terms and values included poetry, romance, imagination, art and the artist, and tolerance or even celebration of intoxicant use.

As all this suggests, temperance touched on many more issues than the literal imbibing of intoxicating substances. In their emphasis on social control, and their twin condemnations of indulgence in intoxicants and literature (which for them was merely another form of intoxicant), such apostles of abstinence as Lyman Beecher revealed a Pentheus-like desire to restrict not only Americans' drinking habits but their thinking habits as well. Among such temperance leaders, and increasingly among spokesmen for the supposedly typical American values of practicality, business, and common sense, writers and even literature itself were often associated with intoxication, which became a metaphor for the corruptive nature of much imaginative writing.

The antiliterary stance of the capitalism-cum-temperance ideology finds wonderfully blatant expression in an 1849 editorial piece from the *New York Herald*. Using the death of the notorious Edgar Allan Poe as its point of departure, the *Herald* lashes out at an entire class of America's citizenry: its writers. Claiming that "hard drinking is the besetting sin of our fine poets and romancers," the article goes on to equate the writing class with the drinking class:

> A majority of them [literary authors] are so weak and helpless, that they need more the aid of Father Mathew than the worst loafers of the rum holes. Vanity, self conceit, contempt of honest labor, combined with a flighty imagination, and certain stray portions of intellect, do the mischief. Common sense— the basis of all usefulness and success in life—they have not, and despise it as beneath their ethereal fancies. As a class, they cultivate music, poetry, and the fine arts; but, rejecting common sense, they naturally take to the bottle. It is only your men of common sense . . . plain practical, every day men . . . that succeed. . . . Hard knocks and common sense have superseded poetry, rum, and romance. (Quoted in Pollin, 132)

Of course, the split here described between common sense and "poetry, rum, and romance" has less to do with the drinking habits of actual writers than with a set of attitudes that fostered a sense of the writer/artist as a misfit—like the addict or drunkard. The *Herald's* parallels between idle poet and idle drinker could not be more obvious. As one modern scholar of drug use observes, the "work ethic was foremost among the national values which addiction seemed to threaten. The addict was depicted as a non-producer, a parasite"—as, all too clearly, was the writer (Morgan, "Introduction," 20).

The *Herald*'s parallel between writer and drunkard typifies what Burton R. Pollin has called "the conflict between the man of 'plain practical common sense' and the 'poets and romancers' of 'flighty imagination' and 'stray portions of intellect'—a conflict increasing in America up to the present" (Pollin, 132). This split was not, to be sure, limited to America. Alfred Kazin, with perhaps only slight exaggeration, has noted the "cleavage between the artist and capitalist society that runs all through the history of modern Western literature" (*Native Grounds,* 18). In the nineteenth century, however, many American writers seemed especially sensitive to this split. Their sensitivity very likely stemmed from the outsider's status that early accrued to our writers. As Larzer Ziff observes, there are a number of ways that "a culture's major writers could themselves become outsiders, at least in point of view. . . . In traditional societies the artist had a well-defined place and spoke from within it. But his place in American society seemed to be either no place or the marketplace." The American writer was, thus, often "a native-born outsider" (*Literary Democracy,* 262).[32]

No place or the marketplace—by the mid-nineteenth century, this seemed to be the only choice for a number of American authors. Unless they became journalists, many writers occupied the role of native-born outsiders.[33] Drink in particular became associated with the supposed rebelliousness or outsider quality of the writer, whether expressed in life or art. A profound suspicion of the arts characterized much temperance writing about the inflamed imaginations of poets and drunkards alike, neither group fitting in comfortably with the burgeoning capitalistic development of the United States. In fact, temperance ire was often directed less at immorality than at the inefficiency of drunken or hungover workers. Drinking, and especially the more lassitude-producing drugs like opium, violated the Protestant work ethic of American culture.[34] By the 1830s, Americans had "created a new culture that appears to have enabled them to prosper amid the upheaval unleashed by the Industrial Revolution. . . . Central to the new culture were the subordination of emotion to rationality, the postponement of gratification, and an orientation toward the future" (Rorabaugh, 212).

In the emphasis on industriousness as opposed to idleness, and on disciplined restraint as opposed to unbridled emotion, not only authors but their readers were linked to intoxication in surprising ways. Nowhere is this clearer than in the writings of the eminent temperance leaders Lyman Beecher and Jonathan Townley Crane, who were, ironically, the respective fathers of two important, if very different, novelists: Harriet Beecher Stowe and Stephen Crane. In his autobiography, Beecher treats imaginative literature itself as a form of intoxication. "Reverie," he writes, "is a delightful intoxication into which the mind is thrown," a statement that on first reading might seem like high praise. But such romantically inspired misprision could occur only with readers who, like myself, have been conditioned by the imagination-celebrating discourses of romanticism. Beecher's subsequent statements make his meaning all too plain. Reverie, it turns out, is nothing less than "extempore novel-making. I knew a person who was wont to retire into this garden of reverie whenever he wished to break the force of unwelcome truth. I told him he must break up the habit or be damned" (Beecher, *Autobiography,* 2:430).[35]

Later in the century, the father of Stephen Crane applied Beecher's once-popular dictum about alcohol to the reading of fiction: "Touch not, taste not." Further echoing Beecher in his condemnation of the dire effects of drugs, drink, and fiction, Reverend Crane went on to warn his audience that habitual novel reading "creates a morbid love of excitement somewhat akin to the imperious thirst of the inebriate" (Crane, *Popular Amusements,* 124, 143). To any contemporary reader, the message would have been obvious: between the pages of a novel lurked dangers equal to anything contained in the whiskey bottle or laudanum vial.[36]

Crane's and Beecher's attitudes parallel numerous other temperance pronouncements on the evils of writers and their disreputable productions. Writing in the 1830s, for instance, Edward Hitchcock, temperance advocate and professor of chemistry at Amherst College, lamented the fact that "the distinguished poets of ancient and modern times, have devoted their most captivating numbers to the praise of Bacchus." Hitchcock then blames "literary men," both in their writings and their lives, for condoning that moderate drinking "which is, in effect, a license to intemperance" (Hitchcock, 42–43).

Byron was an especially favorite temperance target throughout the nineteenth century. In 1830, William Goodell asked,

"Why is it that sober reasoning is well nigh banished from our Senates? . . . Why is it that history and biography have lost their interest and charms? Why are they displaced by quixotic romance and demoralizing fiction? Why are the classic models of the last century delivered to the moles and to the bats, while the ravings of insanity are admired? Why has the inspiration of the poet degenerated into the vagaries of derangement? Lord Byron will answer. He confessed that he wrote under the influence of distilled spirits. Here the disgusting secret is developed. Authors drink and write: readers drink and admire." (Quoted in Rorabaugh, 199–200).

In 1843, the second edition of Ralph Barnes Grindrod's *Bacchus,* a British volume dedicated to American temperance workers, featured a long section entitled "The praise of inebriating liquors by poets, a fruitful source of intemperance" (112–14). Grindrod's longest, most bitter fulminations were reserved for Byron. Nearly forty years later, in 1880, G. W. Samson lamented Horace's and Byron's "pictures of pleasure in the wine-cup," but tried to salvage the English poet from complete condemnation by confidently, if somewhat short-sightedly, announcing, "They have but half read Byron, who only revel in his *Don Juan.* . . . [T]he poem that will outlive his age, is *Childe Harold*" (266).[37]

These and dozens of similar statements about the links between high culture and low morals proliferated in nineteenth-century America, foreshadowing the obsession with a "cultural elite" in our own time. At times, so vehement were attacks on writers that intemperance and literature became virtually interchangeable terms. One might even wonder if drink was not more guilty by association with literature than the other way around. Putting this situation to humorous use, Herman Melville joked in a letter that a "dreadful rumor" was circulating about his seaman brother, Tom: not that he had taken to drink, "oh no, but worse—to sonnet writing."[38]

In opposition to these temperance views, many writers seemed to champion the party of Dionysos, either overtly or in details of rhetoric and tone. Not that American writers presented a united front regarding intoxication and temperance. Just as there is no monolithic, single cultural meaning assigned to drink and drugs, so too there is no single "party line" regarding the temperance movement and its attacks on the literati. Often inconsistency and vacillation characterize a single author's attitudes, while temperance influenced even those writers hostile to its ideology and tone. Though frustrating to the scholar's rage for order, complexity, contradictoriness, and even confusion are part of what gives our topic its multifaceted, provocative power.

---

Provocative, powerful, pervasive: these are some of the qualities that I have argued are inherent in my theme. Yet, as I have observed before, few scholarly works address the literary depiction of intoxicants; among those few, the earlier studies in particular tend to be either apologetic or dismissive. Thus, in a serious, thoughtful essay on drinking in Shakespeare's plays, Émile Legouis sounds positively embarrassed by his topic, a "seemingly humble question" that amounts to no more than "the mere scum and froth of [Shakespeare's] genius" (115).[39] And Edward H. Rosenberry seems needlessly condescending in his otherwise superb analysis of Melville's humor in his references to Melville's drinkers as "tosspots" (*Melville,* 18,20). Recent scholarship has fortunately become both less tentative and less dismissive in dealing with intoxicant use, although intoxication in the *text,* rather than in the *author,* is still represented by only a handful of studies. Three studies out of this handful are particularly important to my own work, not so much as specific sources, but as examples of the kind of sensitive literary analysis that can be brought to bear on this still vaguely disreputable theme. These are Alethea Hayter's *Opium and the Romantic Imagination* and, more recently, Thomas B. Gilmore's *Equivocal Spirits* and John Crowley's *The White Logic* (see note 2). Hayter's book differs from mine in its exclusive focus on opium and (except for a chapter dealing with Poe) on British and European romanticism. Gilmore and Crowley deal mostly (entirely, in Gilmore's case) with the twentieth century and emphasize alcoholism, with Gilmore treating British as well as American authors and primarily applying the perspectives of Alcoholics Anonymous to the texts he discusses. Crowley focuses on the medicalization of alcoholism in relation to modernism. These are valid and valuable approaches, but they obviously differ in various ways from my own treatment, with its national and temporal emphasis, attention to both alcohol and drugs, and use of social history.

Precisely because intoxicant use is so much a function of culture, I combine close analysis of individual literary texts with historical perspectives on alcohol and drugs in the United States. In so doing, I have tried to fit my approach to my materials rather than bend my materials to fit into preconceived slots. As a result, I have drawn not only on various critical perspectives but also on a wide range of sociohistorical studies of drinking and drug use as well as on nineteenth-century periodicals, temperance pamphlets, medical manuals, and treatises on addiction that, though supplementary to my purpose, have provided a valuable background for my reading and thinking about literary depictions of intoxication. While incorporating these nonliterary perspectives into my own frame of reference, I concentrate on the texts studied as works of art, not as samples of sociological evidence.

Because of its greater acceptance in American society, and hence its more common appearance in literature, alcohol receives more attention here than drugs. But for several reasons it has seemed desirable not to limit my discussion to either drugs or alcohol alone. Such a split would be arbitrary, even clumsy in the case of writers like Emerson and Dickinson, where intoxicated consciousness is the main concern: the particular intoxicant is generally unimportant. There are also times—especially in the work of Poe and Alcott—when the contrasts between alcohol and drugs merit, even demand, comparative discussion. Moreover, drugs and alcohol have often been linked in the history of temperance and prohibition: as David F. Musto points out in his study of narcotics control, *The American Disease,* "Alcohol . . . cannot be easily separated, either in its effects or as a target for legal control, from the antinarcotic campaign which paralleled the drive for national liquor prohibition" (xiii). And, in our own day, researchers and treatment specialists are increasingly concerned with multiple drug use.

"It is remarkable how many people . . . immediately and unwittingly transform the word 'alcohol' into 'alcoholism' when they are told the subject matter one is studying."[40] What Dwight B. Heath says of alcohol studies in anthropology is equally true for studies of the intoxication theme in literature. Where most discussions of intoxicants in literature emphasize drinking or drug *problems,* my own interests lie as much with neutral or positive intoxicant use as they do with abuse. Thus *Spirits of America* is concerned with the multivarious cultural significance of alcohol and drugs—*for good or ill*—in antebellum literature.

The writers I discuss are those in whose work intoxicants appear with some frequency, whose depictions of drinking and drug use seem particularly suggestive, and whose work lends itself well to examining the relationship between literary and social discourses of intoxicant use. Consequently, I ignore some major authors in whose work alcohol or drugs do not figure prominently. Thoreau, for example, writes infrequently of intoxicant use, as does Whitman, apart from texts like *Franklin Evans* or "Reuben's Last Wish" which, as temperance fiction, lie outside the purview of my purposes and interests here.

As the preceding comments indicate, sociohistorical considerations are crucial to my approach. In organizing the book, however, I have found it more efficient to employ an authorial-thematic rather than chronological structure; the sequential neatness offered by pure chronology in this instance would, alas, belie the often wayward paths that my topic follows. In chapter 2, Emerson, as so often, establishes many of the basic questions to be addressed by other American writers. The chapters on Dickinson and Poe present distinctive variations on the problem in Emerson, especially regarding the Dionysian dimension of intoxicant use as a mode of transcendent and/or apocalyptic experience. To each of these three writers, the romantic interest in heightened perception and consciousness is especially relevant, as is the notion of a universal human "quest for paradise" that often assumes the form and imagery of intoxication. The fifth, sixth, and seventh chapters concentrate on three other major authors—Cooper, Hawthorne, and Melville—who espouse surprisingly compatible ideals of vinous conviviality. No superficial matter, this conviviality assumes substantial philosophical dimensions in each writer, but with Hawthorne and especially Melville going far beyond Cooper in their sense of intoxication's darker ironies and symbolic associations. In chapter 8, the literary politics of gender take center stage. Illustrating the constraints on female discourses of drinking and drug use in the antebellum period, this chapter also charts the shift away from those constraints near the turn of the nineteenth century.

The framework I employ here grew out of the need to organize a vast, often recalcitrant topic. From the "sociological" dimensions of that topic has come the intersection of literary and sociohistorical perspectives that informs my approach. But the field of intoxication in American literature is capacious enough, and as yet untilled enough, to admit many more approaches: studies of single authors, of alcohol or drugs alone, of subcultures characterized by different intoxicant choices, of American literature compared with that of other countries. A phenomenon that has delighted and plagued human beings for so many centuries, in so many different guises, does not exhaust easily.

# Chapter 2

# God's Wine and Devil's Wine

## The Idea of Intoxication in Emerson

> If another simile may be allowed, another no less apt
> is at hand. Wine is the most brilliant and intense ex-
> pression of the powers of earth—it is her potable
> fire, her answer to the sun. It exhilarates, it inspires,
> but then it is liable to fever and intoxicate too the
> careless partaker.
> —Margaret Fuller, on Emerson's *Essays,* First Series

Although it gave no indication of his future poetic achievement,
the drinking song Emerson wrote for his freshman class supper
at Harvard strikingly anticipates the motif of intoxication that is
so prevalent in his later work. Already in 1818, when he was fif-
teen years old, the future author of "Bacchus" invoked the god of
the vine in such rollicking stanzas as the following:

> In the hall of Minerva, Philosophy's Shrine,
> Recitations we've offered the goddess divine;
> In the temple of Bacchus we'll finish the day,
> And libations to his plump divinity pay.[1]

Poetically insignificant as such lines are, they mark the beginning of a long chain of intoxication imagery running through
Emerson's lectures, sermons, journals, essays, and poems. This
concern with intoxication ties in with the burgeoning interest in

the subject throughout the period in which Emerson lived. Emerson's own interest is particularly appropriate when one considers the importance, discussed in the previous chapter, that has often been attached to intoxicant use and nonuse in American society. However, apart from discussions of wine imagery in the poem "Bacchus" and occasional references to intoxication in biographies and criticism, there has been no systematic examination of this topic in Emerson's work as a whole.[2] In this chapter I wish to clarify Emerson's concerns with the links between what James called "drunken consciousness" and "mystic consciousness" and to explore the underlying tension between fear and fascination in Emerson's thought on the intoxicated state. This fascination is evident in Emerson's use of intoxicant imagery even in contexts in which there is ostensibly little, if any, connection to either literal or symbolic intoxication, temperance, or related subjects. But so attuned was Emerson to these issues that even when his topic is not the altered consciousness as such, he often couches his ideas in terms of intoxication or intoxicating substances. And, as we will see, Emerson shares a significant affinity with the ambivalence that has often characterized American attitudes toward intoxication. Thus, once again, Emerson proves himself to be a truly "representative man" in American culture.

The range of Emerson's attitudes toward intoxication generally covers three related areas: temperance, literal drinking or tippling, and symbolic or spiritual intoxication. However, while physical and spiritual forms of intoxication often diverge sharply for Emerson, the two are not always mutually exclusive but blend into one another on a continuum of experience. This is especially true when Emerson blurs the distinctions between these kinds of intoxication by applying literal intoxication imagery to experiences of intense spiritual elevation. As is so often the case with Emerson, here too we find a suggestive rapport between his views and those expressed elsewhere in American literature, as if Emerson's own musings and writings on intoxication had distilled a spirit infusing many another American pen.

It is not surprising that Emerson, grandson of a distiller and author of the unabashedly anacreontic song mentioned above, should have felt a certain resistance to the increasingly strident voices of the temperance movement in antebellum America (Rusk, 3). Yet Emerson was too much a child of his time not to recognize temperance as one of the central concerns of the intellectual and religious milieu in which he grew to maturity. That milieu was, of course, strongly tinged by the spirit of reform, which "merged temperance with goals as diverse as school reform, abolition, and women's rights" (Lender and Martin, 64). Emerson's birth in 1803 (the same year in which morphine was discovered) coincided with the first stirrings of a reform renaissance that, over the next few decades, would lead temperance into the front ranks of nineteenth-century social causes and give rise to a powerful antiliquor movement. As a result of these efforts American consumption of alcohol sharply declined. For although temperance had preoccupied some Americans in the seventeenth and eighteenth centuries, it was only in the nineteen century, particularly in the 1830s and 1840s, that the temperance movement gained the momentum necessary to render it one of the most potent political and social forces in the land. Carrying their passion for temperance beyond that of earlier advocates of moderate drinking, many temperance leaders of Emerson's day, such as the Congregationalist minister Lyman Beecher, author of the widely distributed *Six Sermons on Intemperance,* vigorously demanded total abstinence from all alcoholic beverages. That attitude was at first associated with more evangelical, revivalist denominations, such as the Methodists, but the temperance cause, even in its teetotal form, rapidly permeated all segments of American society.[3] Thus in 1834 Emerson could write in his journal, "What concerns me more than Orthodoxy, Antimasonry, Temperance, Workingmen's party, & the other Ideas of the time? Is the question of Temperance pledges a question whether we will in a pestilence go into quarantine?" (*JMN,* 4:343).[4] This statement clearly indicates the magnitude of temperance as an issue on the nineteenth-century American social and intellectual horizon.

That temperance was indeed one of Emerson's serious concerns by the 1830s is evident from the frequent allusions to it in his sermons, early lectures, and journals. Throughout these writings, temperance has two basic, often quite separate senses. The first of these is temperance as the historical reform movement flourishing in Emerson's lifetime. The second is temperance as a more inward, private quality, an ideal of personal moral conduct. In 1834, the same year in which he included temperance among the "ideas of the time" that preoccupied him, Emerson entered into his journal a passage that cannot help seeming ironic in light of his grandfather's trade: "If you ask me whether I will not be so good as to abstain from all use of ardent spirits for the sake of diminishing by my pint per annum the demand & so stopping the distiller's pernicious pump, I answer, Yes, with all my heart" (*JMN*, 4:354). The sentiment expressed here rings with all the ardor of a temperance advocate and identifies Emerson as one of the increasing number of Americans cutting down on or completely forgoing the consumption of alcoholic beverages. But the statements immediately following in the journal entry qualify this ardor and simultaneously reveal both the famous Emersonian individualism and an ambivalence toward the methods and style of the temperance movement. After voicing his opposition to the "distiller's pernicious pump," Emerson asks, "Will I signify the same fact by putting my name to your paper? No. Be assured, I shall always be on your side in discouraging this use and traffic. But I shall not deprive my example of all its value by abdicating my freedom on that point. It shall be always my example, the spectacle to all whom it may concern of my spontaneous action at the time" (*JMN*, 4:354). What bothers Emerson here, then, is the issue of the pledge, its status as a symbol of the abdication of individual choice and of external pressure to be virtuous out of contractual obligation. With the temperance movement's basic ideology he seems to have no argument.

Some four years later, however, Emerson's sympathy with the temperance cause seems to be wearing thin. In an unexpectedly forceful journal entry for 1838 he writes, "I hate goodies. I hate goodness that preaches. . . . Better indulge yourself, feed fat, drink liquors then go strait laced for such cattle as these" (*JMN*, 7:31). Temperance movement sanctimoniousness still rankled Emerson five years later, as we see when he complains that "temperance is a plume, a feather in the cap; this ostentatious glass of cold water & dry raw vegetable diet that makes your blood run cold to see, is not the joyful sign that they have ceased to care for food in nobler cares, but no they peak & pine & know all they renounce. . . . Is it not better they should do bad offices & be intemperate so long as that is their ruling love? So at least they should not be hypocrites" (*JMN*, 7:279). Writing of temperance again in the essay "Heroism," Emerson praises the hero who does not rail against wine, tobacco, or opium, who does not love temperance for its "austerity," but rather for its "elegancy" (*CW*, 2:150). This point recalls a journal entry of 1834, which asks, "Does not Aristotle distinguish between Temperance for ends & Temperance for love of temperance? Each of these virtues becomes dowdy in a sermon. They must be practised for their elegance. The virtuous man must be a poet & not a drudge of his virtues, to have them perfect" (*JMN*, 4:385). In "Heroism," Emerson's hero is just such a poet of his virtues, taking the approach of the Indian apostle John Eliot, who "drank water, and said of wine,—'It is a noble, generous liquor, and we should be humbly thankful for it, but, as I remember, water was made before it'" (*CW*, 2:151). It was not this spirit of calm moderation but rather the earnest humorlessness of so many temperance crusaders that Emerson must have had in mind in what has probably become his best-known statement on the temperance movement—his lament that temperance zeal had deprived travelers, in this case Emerson and his companion, Hawthorne, from enjoying the sociable comforts formerly found in American taverns. "Then again," Emerson tells his journal, "the opportunities which the taverns once afforded the traveller of witnessing & even sharing in the joke & the politics of the teamster & farmers on the road, are now no more. The Temperance Society emptied the bar-room; it is a cold place. H. tried to smoke a cigar, but I observed he was soon out on the piazza" (*JMN*, 8:273).

The brand of temperance that "emptied the bar-room," that required abstinence pledges and fought fermentation to the death, was clearly an uncongenial one to Emerson. As the nineteenth century went on, the temperance movement, for all the justice of its many concerns, became increasingly dominated by elements inconsistent with Emerson's ideals and style. Although often "feverish and anti-intellectual," many temperance groups also "encouraged people to subordinate emotions to rational, institutional processes," to postpone gratification, and generally to adhere to narrowly middle-class, capitalistic values (Rorabaugh, 208–09). In sharp contrast to this negative, forbidding temperance is the life-affirming quality Emerson praises in "Heroism"— the temperance that does not "denounce with bitterness flesh-eating, or wine-drinking, the use of tobacco, or opium, or tea, or silk, or gold" (*JMN*, 2:15). It is this form of temperance that Emerson refers to when he says, "Hang out your temperance, my friend, like an amulet" (*JMN*, 4:68), that he praises in his sermons, and that he attempted to observe throughout his own life.

Just as Emerson distinguished between two types of temperance, so he distinguished between two kinds of actual drinking— the light, measured consumption of alcohol, on the one hand, and heavy drinking or inebriation, on the other. Anyone as favorably disposed to the good-natured temperate living Emerson described in "Heroism" would obviously disapprove of the riotous drunkenness that, despite the temperance movement's efforts, was all too common in Emerson's time—even if it was sometimes better to "indulge" than to be numbered among the "goodies." Any instance of intemperance was "all waste of time" (*JMN*, 8:14), and Emerson sardonically observes in his journal that "there is this to be said of drinking, that it takes the drunkard first out of society, then out of the world" (*JMN*, 16:19). Yet even with regard to moderate alcohol use, Emerson seems to be pulled in different directions, now indulgently tippling, now denying wine's beneficial effects, now praising wine, now lamenting its high cost, both moral and financial. At the age of twenty, for instance, Emerson observes that "now as ever, maugre all the flights of the sacred Muse, the profane solicitudes of the flesh, elevated the Tavern to a high rank among my pleasures" (*JMN,* 2:179). And, despite his regret in March 1832 at having spent "$20 in wines & liquors," the entry for September 9 of the following year, written on shipboard, describes "much wine & porter" as the "amusements of wise men in this sad place" (*JMN,* 4:4, 238). Two days later, he adds, "I tipple with all my heart here. May I not?" Still, some eight years after this, Emerson wistfully confesses that wine continues to produce not the vivacity he desired but rather the opposite effect: "I drank a great deal of wine (for me) with the wish to raise my spirits to the pitch of good fellowship, but wine produced on me its old effect, & I grew graver with every glass. Indignation & eloquence will excite me, but wine does not" (*JMN,* 8:41).

Indeed, it is psychological anesthesia, not excitement, that Emerson associates with drinking when he writes that men drink to shield themselves from the harsh ugliness of reality: "men want wine, beer, & tobacco to dull or stupefy a little the too tender papillae.... The edge of all objects must be taken off.... Drop [thy eyes] to the floor, & do not see every ugly man that goes by" (*JMN,* 11:255). This view, while hardly a celebration of drink, is sympathetic to drinking as a means of protecting the "too tender papillae." But in the the 1847 version of the poem "Monadnoc," alcohol becomes distinctly more negative, as Emerson bluntly associates it with an undesirable stupor in his description of a Monadnoc inhabitant as the "dull victim of his pipe and mug" (Allen, 486).

As the foregoing examples suggest, at its best, alcohol for Emerson is but a crude substitute for the "immortal meat" of Pan that Emerson praises in "Monadnoc" and that leads to a sublime alteration of everyday consciousness, to an unearthly "intoxication" described in celestial, mythical terms.

I will give my son to eat
Best of Pan's immortal meat,
Bread to eat, and juice to drain;
So the coinage of his brain
Shall not be forms of stars, but stars,
Nor pictures pale, but Jove and Mars.

(*W,* 9:71)

At its worst—in the torpor of drunkenness, for instance—alcohol betrays the mind, and drinking becomes a pathetic travesty of more sublime expansions of the spirit. But because of their power to alter consciousness, wine and drinking can be apt symbols for such expansions and, in fact, take their place among Emerson's favorite, most frequently used metaphors for intellectual and spiritual transcendence.

The exact nature of this transcendence has been so well charted that, as Hyatt Waggoner observes, it is "too familiar to need further repetition" (Waggoner, 67). What is of more immediate concern here is the way that wine and its consumption become symbols for a kind of consciousness expansion that has nothing to do with alcohol, except that alcohol's effects on sense perception and mood, as well as its time-honored association with poets, make it a perfect image of the heightened imaginative condition that Emerson praises and seeks.[5]

Emerson explicitly distinguishes between literal and symbolic or spiritual wine, between coarse intoxication through alcohol and a finer intoxication akin to Plato's "furor divinus," at the end of the essay "Circles": "Dreams and drunkenness, the use of opium and alcohol are the semblance and counterfeit of this oracular genius, and hence their dangerous attraction for men" (*CW,* 2:190). This distinction surfaces again in the powerful journal entry of 1846 (repeated, with some modification, in "Poetry and Imagination"): "O Bacchus, make them drunk, drive them mad, this multitude of vagabonds, hungry for eloquence, hungry for poetry, starving for symbols, perishing for want of electricity to vitalize this too much pasture; &, in the long delay, indemnifying themselves with the false wine of alcohol, of politics, or of money. Pour for them, o Bacchus, the wine of wine. Give them, at last, Poetry" (*JMN,* 9:441). But the most famous expression of this distinction between different kinds of wine and intoxication occurs in that passage from "The Poet" where Emerson writes that "poetry is not 'Devil's wine,' but God's wine" (*CW,* 3:17). Like the journal entry beginning "O Bacchus," the passage from "The Poet" sounds at first like a panegyric to the various intoxicants beloved of poets: "This is the reason why bards love wine, mead, narcotics, coffee, tea, opium, the fumes of sandal-wood and tobacco, or whatever other procurers of animal exhilaration" (*JMN,* 3:17). But Emerson's seeming admiration for such substances quickly modulates to a warning about their dangers, as he calls them "quasi-mechanical substitutes for the true nectar" that lead to "dissipation and deterioration." It is as if Emerson, at the beginning of this passage, feels enamored of the sensual intoxicants he describes, but no sooner has he begun to list them than he exhibits what Joel Porte has called his "old ambivalence about letting himself go" (*Representative Man,* 311).

In "Bacchus," by contrast, the distinction between the two wines comes at the very beginning of the poem in a definite, unambiguous command: "Bring me wine, but wine which never grew / In the belly of the grape" (*W,* 9:124). Throughout the entire poem, Emerson uses physical intoxication imagery to suggest the decidedly spiritual, nonphysical excitement for which the artist longs. Indeed, the visionary intensity of the poem, with its passionate affirmation of imaginative transport, has led Harold Bloom to observe that the poem is "misnamed"; what Bloom means, presumably, is that the poem's title should be "Dionysos," after the original Greek god of the vine, not his secularized, somewhat debased Roman variant (Bloom, 299). But is "Bacchus" really misnamed? While it is true that, in the words of R. A. Yoder, "the Orphic Dionysus is . . . not the god that traditionally passes as Bacchus," Emerson's poem, for all its "insistent spiritualising" of Bacchus (Yoder, 98, 101), retains an element of strong physicality and even a jaunty joviality of tone that befits the festive, merry god whose title the poem bears.

Pour, Bacchus! the remembering wine;
Retrieve the loss of me and mine!
Vine for vine be antidote,
And the grape requite the lote!

(*W,* 9:127)

Furthermore, here and elsewhere Emerson associates the inspiration and imaginative freedom of the poet with a celebratory, even lighthearted quality, for all the grand sublimity of the poet's vision. Without denying the profoundly passionate, Dionysian aspect of Emerson's thought, we can see that Bacchus, as a convivial, cheerful version of the god of wine, has his place in Emerson's thought as well as Dionysos. Indeed, Bacchus even seems more appropriate than Dionysos for the Emerson who writes that poetry is the "gai science" (*W,* 8:37), who links intoxication with the spirit of joyous union with the natural world in poems like "Berrying," Mithridates," and "To J.W.," and who, in the essay on Persian poetry, praises Shakespeare's Falstaff by saying, "A saint might lend an ear to the riotous fun of Falstaff; for it is not created to excite the animal appetites, but to vent the joy of a supernal intelligence" (*W,* 8:250).

Of course, some of Emerson's readers might find a poem praising Bacchus distasteful, even when the subject had undergone some "insistent spiritualising." The eminent temperance historian Daniel Dorchester, in a work published two years after Emerson died, expresses the temperance view of Bacchus when he labels him not the god of wine or of drinkers but of "drunkards," emphasizes the sensuality and sexual immorality associated with him, and praises negative depictions of Bacchus, such as Benjamin Parsons's tract, "Antibacchus" (Dorchester, 35, 257). Thus, even though the poem "Bacchus" eschews any confusion of symbolic and literal wine, its title evokes associations of passion and abandonment that would be unacceptable to a conventional temperance mentality.

An *unconventional* temperance mentality is something else again, particularly when found among members of Emerson's own intellectual circle. This is clear from the following anecdote about Henry David Thoreau and Bronson Alcott, where we see that Bacchus, as in Emerson's poem, is associated with loftier ecstasies than those provided by alcohol. At a chance meeting with Thoreau and Alcott outside a saloon at eleven o'clock one morning, Edwin Percy Whipple jokingly asked if the two men were about to have a drink. With a smugness that might understandably have driven his interlocutor straight to the bar of that very saloon, Alcott replied, "No, vulgar and ordinary stimulants are not for us. But if you can show us a place where we can drink Bacchus himself, the soul of the inspiration of the poet and the seer, we shall be your debtors forever" (Whipple, 243). The title of "Bacchus," then, speaks to an important part of Emerson, a part that includes but is not reducible to the more sensual, hedonistic qualities associated with the Roman god of wine. Like John Keats, who in "Ode to a Nightingale" calls for a beaker "full of the true, the blushful Hippocrene," Emerson says,

> Give me of the true,—
> Whose ample leaves and tendrils curled
> Among the silver hills of heaven
> Draw everlasting dew;
> Wine of wine,
> Blood of the world . . .
>
> (*W,* 9:125)

Yet unlike the British poet, who cries out that he will come to his visionary experience "not charioted by Bacchus and his pards" but rather "on the viewless wings of poesy," Emerson never actually rejects Bacchus, reclothe him though he does in transcendental garb. "Bacchus" retains a distinct echo of its namesake's associations with drinking and carousing.

The dual values of wine in "Bacchus" and "The Poet" may recall the Emersonian penchant for seeing the world in bipolar terms—the penchant that caused a frustrated Henry James, Sr., to exclaim "Oh, you man without a handle!" (quoted in Feidelson, 119). But Emerson's division between wines is not merely another instance of his famous inconsistencies or duality of vision, or of nineteenth-century America's profound ambivalence about intoxication. It is part of a whole tradition of distinctions between mundane and sublime forms of intoxication. As examples of this tradition we have already mentioned Keats's "Ode to a Nightingale" and Coleridge's striking notebook entry distinguishing between a Heavenly Bacchus and a Bastard Bacchus: "Man in the savage state as a water-drinker or rather Man before the Fall possessed of the Heavenly Bacchus (as Jac. Boehmen's Sophia or celestial Bride) his fall—forsaken by the savage state—and dreadful consequences of the interspersed vacancies left in his mind by the absence of Dionysos—the Bastard Bacchus comes to his Relief" (Coleridge, 3: entry 3263). Certainly the wine imagery of the Persian poets who influenced Emerson's verse, especially Hafiz, should be mentioned here. For, while Emerson resolutely refused to "make mystical divinity" out of the "erotic and bacchanalian songs of Hafiz," he notes that "the wine of Hafiz is not to be confounded with vulgar debauch." We should not "mistake him [Hafiz] for a low rioter" (*W*, 8:249–50). And, while the wine in Emerson's translation, "From the Persian of Hafiz," is unquestionably real, it rises above ordinary wine in its ability to "teach / Souls the ways of Paradise."[6]

Going back much further, we see the Emerson's distinction between kinds of wine deriving "from the Orphic and Pythagorean discipline of Temperance, and probably from Taylor's particular interpretations in *The Eleusinian and Bacchic Mysteries*" with its ultimate source in Plato's distinction among types of madness in the *Phaedrus* (Yoder, 97). Indeed, in the essay "Plato," after Emerson describes his subject as a "balanced soul" embodying a duality of qualities, he goes on to convey this duality partly through the image of an intoxicant: "Plato keeps the two vases, one of aether and one of pigment, at his side, and invariably uses both" (*W*, 1:49). In the same essay, Emerson describes Socrates, "the best example of that synthesis which constitutes Plato's extraordinary power," as a man who "can drink, too; has the strongest head in Athens; and, after leaving the whole party under the table, goes away, as if nothing had hap-

pened, to begin new dialogues with somebody that is sober"
(*W,* 1:64). Who but an American romantic would praise the most
venerable and legendary of Western philosophers for being able
to drink his fellows under the table![7] Socrates, "the sweetest
saint known to any history at that time" (*W,* 1:68), and Socrates,
the formidable tippler outdoing his fellow topers—the contrast
itself reflects Emerson's own ambivalence toward drinking, and
his various stances as Bacchic celebrant, as wine connoisseur, as
merry tippler, as serene temperance supporter, and as ecstatic,
water-drinking prophet of spiritual intoxication.

But apart from its relation to past tradition and to the basic
duality of Emerson's character and writing, the split between literal and metaphorical intoxication allowed Emerson the temperance man and Emerson the tippler to come together, with the
former side of Emerson expressing itself through the injunction
not to fall prey to "Devil's wine," and the latter singing hymns to
Bacchus—admittedly a Bacchus raised to a lofty spiritual plane.
Certainly the symbol of wine enabled Emerson to translate his
own fondness for wine to a transcendental, spiritual level; it also
allowed him to be bolder and more emphatic in some of his essays and poems than he otherwise might have been. The topics
of wine and drunkenness gave him a vigorous, striking set of images to use, while the metaphorical distance of such images from
literal drinking kept him free of the taint of immorality that
could so easily accrue to the sensuality of a Hafiz.[8]

It was this bold use of intoxication imagery, along with
Emerson's general emphasis on ecstatic states, that misled Yvor
Winters into seeing in Emerson a destructively hedonistic, demonic force: "Emerson believes that all good comes from surrender to instinct and emotion; all evil from the functioning of
the rational faculty. Emerson's ideal man would be . . . an au-
tomaton, a madman. . . . The doctrine of Emerson and Whitman,
if really put into practice, should naturally lead to suicide. . . . [I]f
the impulses are indulged systematically and passionately, they
can lead only to madness" (Winters, 477, 590).

But for all his emphasis on abandonment, Emerson retained

a profound suspicion of divorcing consciousness expansion from reason. "Passion is logical," wrote Emerson in the lecture version of "Poetry and the Imagination," and he went on to say, "I note that the vine, symbol of Bacchus, which intoxicates the world, is the most geometrical of all plants" (*W,* 8:365). The yoking of passion to logic here echoes William Hazlitt's "Nothing is so logical as passion" (Hazlitt, 4:180), which Emerson copied into his quotation book "Encyclopedia" (*JMN,* 6:185), where he also lists temperance itself as a passion. Far from willingly giving himself over to abandonment, Emerson feared losing the "keys of [his] mind" (*JMN,* 3:127), And in "May-Day" he expresses the need for a balance between ecstasy and self-control through a memorable rhyme; celebrating the excitement of Spring, he writes that the season will not

> . . . wanton skip with bacchic dance,
> But she has the temperance
> Of the gods, whereof she is one,—
> Masks her treasury of heat
> Under east winds crossed with sleet.
>                                   (*W,* 9:167)

"Bacchic dance"—"temperance": the rhyme, slant as it is, reinforces the contrast of the words themselves, a contrast that suggests the delicate equipoise necessary even in a state of spiritual intoxication, lest the keys of one's mind be lost to a despotic madness.

Emerson's pulling back from the inspired madness he so often seems to praise is apparent in a journal passage where Emerson writing on Thoreau sounds a good deal like Winters writing on Emerson. "Henry Thoreau is like the woodgod who solicits the wandering poet & draws him into . . . desarts idle, & bereaves him of his memory, & leaves him naked, plaiting vines & with twigs in his hand. Very seductive are the first steps from the town to the woods, but the End is want & madness" (*JMN,* 10:344). In another passage criticizing Emerson for a multitude of sins, Winters scornfully comments, "If we could find a truly consistent Emersonian, it is certain that he would understand nothing of pre-romantic poetry or of anything else; furthermore, he would have no particular rights in the matter. One might as well demand poetic rights for those who cannot read or speak, or poetic rights for idiots. Poetry is for the intelligent" (Winters, 479). Ironically, in "On Persian Poetry," Emerson himself anticipates Winters's last remark when he cites Pindar to the effect that all poetry "speaks to the intelligent" (*W*, 8:250).

In commenting on the journal passage in which Emerson speaks of Thoreau as seductive wood god, Porte has pointed out that Emerson's "excitement carries him to the brink of fear . . . and when his mood changes and the old inertia repossesses his soul, Emerson draws away from this corrupting Socrates, this Napoleonic egotist, this Spinoza of the jakes, this 'enchanter' who sings the siren-song of the 'NOT ME'" (Porte, *Representative Man*, 311). But so fascinated was Emerson by intoxication, so frightened and absorbed by it at the same time, that he repeatedly uses intoxicated states and intoxicants not only as literal topics or symbols but also as conceptual tools for explaining the world. In "Experience," our day-to-day life is analogous to an opium-induced lassitude: "Dream delivers us to dream, and there is no end to illusion" (*CW*, 3:30). At the same time, this lassitude of everyday experience, this dulling of the senses and the spirit, is remarkably suggestive of the depression following a "high" period of drug-produced euphoria—an experience that leaves the drug taker feeling cut off from the excitement of the drug but not yet really at home in the everyday world. The beginning lines of "Experience" could, in fact, be easily taken for the description of someone coming out of a drugged trance: "Where do we find ourselves? In a series, of which we do not know the extremes, and believe that it has none. We wake and find ourselves on a stair: there are stairs below us, which we seem to have ascended; there are stairs above us, many a one, which go upward and out of sight" (*CW*, 3:27).[9]

Yet this state of puzzled waking can itself be seen as one of intoxication, as Emerson does when he describes it as an intoxicated oblivion, with echoes of Plato's passage on the waters of Lethe at the end of *The Republic:* "But the Genius which, according to the old belief, stands at the door by which we enter, and gives us the lethe to drink, that we may tell no tales, mixed the cup too strongly, and we cannot shake off the lethargy now at noonday" (*CW,* 3:27). A similar image of life as a series of different kinds of intoxications informs a journal entry of 1865: "One drug needs another to expel it—if feasts, then wine; after wine, coffee; & after coffee, tobacco: if vanity, then pride; if anger, then war, sword & musket" (*JMN,* 15:69–70). In "Illusions," Emerson observes that "we live amid hallucinations" and asks, "Is not our faith in the impenetrability of matter more sedative than narcotics?" (*W,* 6:316, 318). These few statements represent only a fraction of Emerson's numerous instances of introducing intoxication imagery into contexts in which there is little, if any, reason to expect such imagery. Yet the very lack of overt links to intoxication in these instances only serves to highlight the importance of intoxication to Emerson, both as a phenomenon in and of itself and as a source of organizational metaphors for his own thinking on a wide range of issues.

When it comes to intoxication, then, we find Emerson's own soul to be balanced precariously between the competing tugs of reason and madness, control and abandonment, sobriety and drunkenness. Emerson's images of intoxicants and intoxication range across a wide diapason of significance from the most literal, mundane level to the most symbolic, with intoxication imagery even informing a number of passages completely unrelated to intoxication in any usual sense of the term. At times Emerson seems to love the very idea of intoxication, at times to fear it; and at times the desire and the fear blend into a complex feeling of attraction and repulsion, whether the intoxication be spiritual or not.

A similar tension between sobriety and intoxication is present in much American literature, not to mention its presence in American society as a whole, both in Emerson's time and our own. For all too many American writers, of course, the wine grown in the belly of the grape became the wine chanted in their lives as well as their art. The use of literal wine itself became a symbol of the free spirit's defiance of mindless convention and stifling sobriety. Hence the writer's often deliberate courting of intoxication as a form of rebellion and self-assertion in the face of what Emerson called the "taming of the imagination" (*W*, 8:372). And hence that legendary destructiveness in the lives of many American writers that Winters unjustly sought to lay at Emerson's door. But, with all this said, we need to remember that such a pursuit of intoxication is not reducible merely to Bohemian rebelliousness or antisocial individualism. In part this pursuit can reflect, to appropriate Thomas De Quincey's terms, a degrading bastardization of the "Heavenly Bacchus." Yet the intoxication theme also reflects an attempt to regain a freshness, spontaneity, and innocence of being and perception, to come closer to that exciting, nonrational quality of childhood that lies behind Baudelaire's description of the child as one who is "toujours ivre" [10] and behind Emerson's similar sense of the "continual pretty madness" of children (*CW*, 3:108).

Such an attempt or quest to discover the "milk of paradise" informs works as diverse as Coleridge's "Kubla Khan," De Quincey's *Confessions of an English Opium-Eater*, F. Scott Fitzgerald's *Tender Is the Night*, Malcolm Lowry's *Under the Volcano*, and John Berryman's *Recovery* and *Dream Songs*. We find it too in Emerson's constant search for visionary experience, as well as in the nostalgia for Eden that we meet on almost every page of his work. That nostalgia, wedded to a sublimely intoxicated vision of our possibilities for paradise, receives memorable expression in one of Emerson's most representative poems, "May-Day." In a passage celebrating the sympathetic harmony of nature, wine appears as part of the natural world, quickened by the rejuvenative force of the season; it also serves as a symbolic parallel to humanity's own earthbound yearning for Eden.

> When trellised grapes their flowers unmask,
> And the new-born tendrils twine,

The old wine darkling in the cask
Feels the bloom on the living vine,
And bursts the hoops at hint of Spring:
And so, perchance, in Adam's race,
Of Eden's bower some dream-like trace
Survived the Flight and swam the Flood,
And wakes the wish in youngest blood
To tread the forfeit Paradise,
And feed once more the exile's eyes.

(*W,* 9:166)

# Chapter 3

# The Little Tippler's Discerning Eye

## Dickinson and Visionary Drunkenness

Come slowly—Eden!
Lips unused to Thee—
Bashful—sip thy Jessamines—
As the fainting Bee—
Reaching late his flower,
Round her chamber hums—
Counts his nectars—
Enters—and is lost in Balms.
—Dickinson, poem 211

To see the little Tippler
Leaning against the—Sun—
—from Dickinson, poem 214

Much Madness is divinest Sense—
To a discerning Eye—
—from Dickinson, poem 435

The epigraphs to this chapter bespeak a persona for whom certain states of nonrational experience and perception are not to be feared or avoided but rather sought out, explored, and celebrated. A sensualist of the imagination, this persona seeks to delay "Eden's" arrival only to savor it more luxuriously—to hover for a moment, beelike, in the expectant contemplation of imminent bliss before yielding completely and irrevocably to its "Balms." Even a casual, seemingly insignificant detail can transport the speaker's willing imagination to another time or place, as Dickinson makes clear in one of her earlier poems.

> Many cross the Rhine
> In this cup of mine.
> Sip old Frankfort air
> From my brown Cigar.
>
> (poem 123)[1]

In light of the above passages and their many analogues in Dickinson, it is appropriate that alcohol—that potent agent of experiential and perceptual change—is among the main images in Dickinson's "poetic stock in trade" (Chase, 221).[2] Yet while I was writing this book, a number of people expressed their surprise at the inclusion of Emily Dickinson among writers dealing with intoxication. Such an "unladylike" topic hardly accords with the persistent popular notion of Dickinson as the shy, primly eccentric "Belle of Amherst," dressed in white and scribbling deathless poems on scraps of paper in her room. Nor is intoxication among Dickinson's most overt themes or among the topics most frequently analyzed by scholars of her work. But in light of her broad imaginative reach and links to the romantic tradition with its interest in altered states of consciousness,[3] Dickinson's use of intoxicant imagery is less surprising than it might at first appear. Indeed, hers is one of the most resonant and powerful voices to deal with intoxication in nineteenth-century American literature.

Unlike Emerson, Dickinson did not leave us a lifelong record of comments about drinking, drunkenness, temperance, opium, or intoxication in general. We know very little about intoxicant use in her private life, even with the enormous amount of information provided by Jay Leyda and Richard Sewall. Some isolated scraps of evidence about Emily's and her family's relations to intoxicants do exist. We know, for example, that her father was a prominent temperance leader in Amherst, though not a teetotaler: alcoholic beverages were served in the Dickinson household.[4] The fatal properties that some drugs can have would be known to Dickinson from her father's death, caused by a combination of a stroke and a low tolerance for morphine (Leyda, 2:224). In later years, Dickinson's intimate friend and sister-in-law, Susan Gilbert Dickinson, was rumored to be an alcoholic, as was her father before her (Sewall, 1:231). A playful awareness of, and interest in, intoxication imagery occasionally surfaces in Dickinson's letters, as in one of her replies to her "preceptor," T. W. Higginson, "Your letter gave no Drunkenness, because I tasted Rum before—Domingo comes but once," or in her praise of neighbor Nellie Sweetser's homemade wine, "Dear Nellie, To have woven Wine so delightfully, one must almost have been a Drunkard one's self—but that is the stealthy franchise of the demurest Lips. Drunkards of Summer are quite as frequent as Drunkards of Wine, and the Bee that comes Home sober is the Butt of the Clover" (2:408, 784–85).

That such snippets of information might be part of a larger, coherent mosaic of experiences, attitudes, and influences is entirely possible, but we simply do not know enough to tell. Where a coherent mosaic of meaning does emerge, however, is in the numerous references to intoxication and intoxicants in Dickinson's poetry.

The central fact about intoxication in Dickinson's work is its almost entirely metaphorical significance. As Dickinson says in her best-known poem on this topic, she tastes "a liquor never brewed" and gets drunk on such innocuous vintages as air and dew. But whether as metaphor or as literal subject, intoxication in Dickinson serves as a tool with which to mediate between the perils and promises of imaginative exploration, on the one hand, and the demands of a narrowly pragmatic, rationalistic society, on the other.

In about 1862, some two years after writing "I taste a liquor never brewed," Dickinson reaffirmed that poem's implicit distinction between inner and outer wine, while also revealing her affinity with other romantic writers in viewing alcohol as only one kind of intoxicant.

> Exhilaration—is within—
> There can no Outer Wine
> So royally intoxicate
> As that diviner Brand
>
> The Soul achieves—Herself—
> To drink—or set away
> For Visitor—or Sacrament—
> 'Tis not of Holiday
>
> To stimulate a Man
> Who hath the Ample Rhine
> Within his Closet—Best you can
> Exhale in offering.
>
> (poem 383)

Paralleling Emerson in "Bacchus" and in his essay "The Poet," as well as Keats in "Ode to a Nightingale" and "Hence Burgundy, Claret and Port," Dickinson lauds the intoxication of the spirit over that of the senses. And, as Baudelaire does in his exhortation "Enivrez-vous," she recognizes different levels and sources of intoxicated experience, although the "Best" is that achieved by "The Soul . . . Herself," rather than by the "Ample Rhine."

The obvious similarity between "Bacchus" and "I taste a liquor never brewed" raises the issue of how much Dickinson's intoxication motifs owe to Emerson, itself a subset of the larger topic of how much, in general, Dickinson borrowed from her older, celebrated contemporary. That Dickinson had in mind not only "Bacchus" but also parts of "The Poet" while writing "I taste a liquor never brewed" seems undeniable.[5] (Dickinson's lines, "Inebriate of Air—am I— / And Debauchee of Dew," may also owe an apparently unnoticed debt to Coleridge's phrase, "inebriate with dew," from his poem "The Rose.") But as always when comparing Dickinson and Emerson, we need to remember Michael G. Yetman's pithy warning that "Emily Dickinson did not spring full-grown from the head of Emerson, carrying a volume of

Shakespeare in one hand and the King James Bible in the other, no matter how major these three sources of inspiration are to be judged in her work" (Yetman, 130). In relation to our present topic, we need equally to guard against the oversimplification of imagining Emily Dickinson springing full-grown from the head of the critic, carrying a copy of "Bacchus" in one hand and a wine glass in the other. To be sure, Dickinson shares Emerson's preference for spiritual over physical forms of intoxication and a sense of paradisiacal joy in all life as an intoxication (a sense found also in Keats, who in "Hence Burgundy, Claret and Port" speaks of drinking from the sky as from a wine bowl); like Emerson, Dickinson believes that nature is a stimulant with the power to alter one's consciousness far beyond the capacities of any drug. But there are important differences in their treatment of intoxication as well.

Temperance, whether as historical movement or as mode of conduct, has not nearly the intensity for Dickinson that it does for Emerson, although the topic makes discreet appearances at various points in her poetry. To the extent that Dickinson does discuss temperance, she generally stands on the side of the wets, if only by implication and tone; condemning the fainthearted in "Who never wanted—maddest Joy," Dickinson proclaims, "the Banquet of Abstemiousness / Defaces that of Wine." Paying less attention to physical forms of intoxication than Emerson, Dickinson seems less fearful of such forms. Her few references to literal drinking or drunkenness lack the bitter condemnation of intemperance in Emerson. Ambiguous as they often are, Dickinson's depictions of intoxication are relatively free of the tortured wavering between the demands of sobriety and the desire for tippling present in Emerson and, as we shall see in the next chapter, Poe. Although Dickinson makes it clear that spiritual or imaginative intoxication is "diviner" than that proceeding from wine, she expends none of the energy that Emerson does on delineating the repulsive features of drunkenness. Obviously preferring what Emerson calls "God's Wine," Dickinson never consigns physical liquor to the province of the Devil; the superiority of the one does not necessarily imply the evil of the other. Consistent with this attitude is Dickinson's greater boldness in using intoxication imagery, as well as her less qualified drawing of parallels between herself and the drunkard. In describing this boldness, Karl Keller points out that in "I taste a liquor never brewed," the traditional romantic image of poetic inebriation becomes "quite a bit more humorous, personal, extreme, specific, daring; she pushes it until it describes *her*, until, in her reckless style, she becomes *it*" (Keller, 155). At least rhetorically, then, Dickinson goes beyond the Emerson who worries about losing the keys of his mind or who self-consciously defends himself to his journal, saying that he tipples on shipboard "with all my heart. . . . May I not?" (*JMN*, 4:239).

Nor does Dickinson share Emerson's association of intoxication with creativity. True, Dickinson's verse celebrates altered states of consciousness, and her famous test of poetry, as recounted by Higginson, implies a Dionysian perspective: "If I feel physically as if the top of my head were taken off, I know *that* is poetry" (*Letters*, 2:566). But Dickinson does not treat poetic creation as a process of inspired madness or intoxication. As Albert Gelpi has argued, whatever "Dickinson might say about the poet's vatic function," she stands more firmly in the Apollonian tradition of American poetic craftsmanship, the tradition including Edward Taylor, T. S. Eliot, Wallace Stevens, Robert Frost, Robert Lowell, and Elizabeth Bishop, than in the Dionysian tradition extending from Emerson and Walt Whitman to writers such as Carl Sandburg and Jack Kerouac (Gelpi, 146).

Nevertheless, this Apollonian poet in terms of craft is often distinctly Dionysian when it comes to subject matter. "I taste a liquor never brewed," for example, reveals a "genuinely Dionysian commitment," paralleling the praise of Dionysos in Nietzsche (Eddins, 107). Even when "the more traditional wine" is Dickinson's subject, "the word 'sacrament,'" Northrop Frye reminds us, "is seldom far away, for such imaginative drunkenness is a genuine communion" (Frye, 212). These comments point to the unusual intensity of Dickinson's concern with the theme of intoxication. This concern is divided between poems that cluster around two related issues: the ecstatic transcendence of the mundane and the alteration of perception, usually through some numbing of the perceptual powers that leads to spiritual lassitude or oblivion to pain.

At times, to be sure, Dickinson's references to intoxication function merely as figures of speech free from any larger significance. Even so, her repeated references to wine, drinking, intoxication, anodynes, and mood-altering balms and nectars produce a powerful cumulative impression of personae courting intoxication and of fascination with the nonrational and impulsive. Many of Dickinson's more than fifty poems using intoxication or intoxicant imagery imply that true joy is somehow incompatible with sobriety and contain images that impart a daring coloring even to Dickinson's affirmations of spiritual transcendence.[6] There are elements of sophistication and rebellious abandon that verge on radical chic in her pervasive, insistent use of intoxication metaphors in a temperance-dominated culture.[7] Writing of Dickinson's rebellious quality, Gelpi observes, "It was a reeling triumph to be a secret drinker while in the name of orthodox religion her father labored tirelessly for the Temperance League. He could close the bars of Amherst, but not the 'inns of Molten Blue' where she drank with saints and was served by angels" (Gelpi, 133–34).

The celestial connotations of saints and angels tie in with Dickinson's tendency to associate intoxication imagery with sublime, spiritually exhilarating experience and with religious terminology. In "Exultation is the going," the poet speaks of the "divine intoxication / Of the first league out from land"; in "Exhilaration—is within—," she describes that "diviner Brand" of wine that "the Soul achieves—Herself"; and in "Come slowly— Eden!" she connects Eden itself, however obliquely, to a bliss figured in terms of intoxicating balms and nectars.

On the most general level, in fact, intoxication in Dickinson is repeatedly associated with bliss, especially bliss in the natural world. The link between this delight and drinking or wine images in particular extends throughout Dickinson's work, from the late 1850s to the mid-1880s. In "Bring me the sunset in a cup," Dickinson asks, "How many cups the Bee partakes, / The Debauchee of Dews!" In another poem from the same period (ca. 1859), "These are the days when Birds come back," the poet longs to partake of summer's "sacred emblems" and its "immortal wine." The most famous poem linking intoxication to joy in nature is, of course, "I taste a liquor never brewed," a poem that has generated so much attention and criticism that there is no point in rehashing its myriad interpretations once again, although obviously it deserves a place in any discussion of intoxication in Dickinson.

It is important not to dismiss this poem as a mere conceit, however elegant or witty. Richard Chase, for instance, has condemned the poem as an unpleasantly coy, rococo exercise, and Charles R. Anderson, though more sympathetic, sees Dickinson's "beery spree" as a parody of Emerson's "Bacchus," or "simply a humorous fable of the poet's inspiration" (Chase, 228–29; Anderson, 75).

To be sure, Dickinson's poem betrays a certain coyness of tone and a self-consciously naughty flirtation with images of wine guzzled from tankards. One finds obvious whimsy as well, and quite possibly some parody of Emerson's "Bacchus." If so, there is probably also a touch of self-parody in the poem, or self-irony at least: the speaker is aware of being a "little tippler," aware of the game she is playing with the imagery of intoxication. But games can be serious and playful at the same time, and there is seriousness in Dickinson's almost obsessively repeated images and tropes deriving from intoxication. The little tippler who staggers, dew-drunk, into the sun, while apparently sober seraphs and saints stare at her (in wonder? in disapproval?), conveys in whimsical terms the more passionate yearning for ecstatic experience and expansion of consciousness found throughout Dickinson's work.

A clear example of the more serious, passionate side of Dickinson's "tippler" is the speaker of "A Drunkard cannot meet a Cork," another poem celebrating delight in nature. The poem's first line, with its image of an actual drunkard, is a surprising one for a nineteenth-century poem, especially one written by a respectable New England spinster. But this poem is yet another of Dickinson's many ways of surprising her readers, of breaking out of the narrow confines that conventional expectations and stereotypes (even after decades of sophisticated Dickinson criticism) still create. The first two lines of the poem suggest an attitude of understanding, if not exactly of sympathy, for the drunkard's point of view: "A Drunkard cannot meet a Cork / Without a Revery—." Through the image of a cork, rather than the more predictable bottle or glass—not to mention the fluid contained therein—Dickinson achieves a synecdoche that is at once lucid and densely suggestive. Thus the poem's opening lines vividly exemplify Dickinson's dictum, "Tell all the Truth but tell it slant—/Success in Circuit lies" (poem 1129). The very obliqueness of a cork's connection to drink aptly conveys alcoholism's insidious power. After all, bottles and glasses are far more familiar and direct stand-ins for drink and its fatal attractions than are corks: those vessels hold the intoxicating liquid and thus are the vehicles by which that liquid enters the body. But in this poem Dickinson conveys liquor's power over the alcoholic all the more compellingly by using the image of a relatively ancillary, casually discarded bit of drinking paraphernalia. So pervasive is addiction's impact that even through a cork it exerts its irresistible influence, rendering the "Drunkard" helpless before it, as the word "cannot," in the first line, suggests. Drink's power emerges also in the virtual personification of the cork, which the drunkard *meets* as if it were a living thing. Instead of condemning the alcoholic, Dickinson makes a factual observation about the way that apparently trivial details can ignite the supersensitized cravings resulting from addiction. Implicit in that observation is yet another one, linking drunkenness and dreaming, or "revery." And, thanks to the Reverend Lyman Beecher (as noted in the introduction), we all know how bad *that* is. But in Dickinson, the implicit link between revery and intoxication immediately leads to more familiar Dickinsonian topics: delight in memory's power, in the beauties of spring and summer, in the nearly hallucinatory pleasures of experiencing nature directly. Yet all of these statements stem from, and continue, the original analogy between the speaker and a drunkard; as a cork is to the drunk, so a "fly" is to her. Neither is a "moderate drinker," for moderate drinkers do "not deserve the spring"; both speaker and drunk revel in revery; both are dreamers.

The *speaker's* reveries, however, are sparked not by the whiff of a cork but by a "fly" (probably meaning a butterfly or moth, when appearing in a nineteenth-century poem); still, the parallel between the drunkard and the speaker is extended by the intoxication imagery dominating the entire poem. What is the result of meeting the "fly"? "Jamaicas of Remembrance," whole islands-full of rum, flooding the speaker's consciousness. The poem goes on to describe the speaker as "reeling," to condemn the paltry, "moderate drinker," and to assert "Of juleps, part are in the Jug / And more are in the joy," an echo of the earlier poem, "Between the form of Life and Life":

> Between the form of Life and Life
> The difference is as big
> As Liquor at the Lip between
> And Liquor in the Jug.

"A Drunkard cannot meet a Cork" then concludes with the favorite Dickinson image of the drinking bee: "Your connoisseur in Liquors / Consults the Bumble Bee," thus reinforcing the link between the poem's imagery of intoxication and the theme of joy in nature.

In poems like "Come slowly—Eden!" "I taste a liquor never brewed," and "A Drunkard cannot meet a Cork," the pleasure experienced is so intense that it sends the speaker reeling, lifted up into a special world of giddy delight. In "A Drunkard cannot meet a Cork," it is actually a Wordsworthian recollection of delight in the natural world, rather than the direct experience of it, that kindles the poet's joy. Memory as a source of transcendent experience appears also in the following poem that, like the others discussed here, draws on intoxication imagery. The poem "Through those old Grounds of memory" begins by asserting that "the sauntering alone" through those grounds is "a divine intemperance." It is also something that a "prudent man would shun," he being, presumably, kin to that "moderate drinker of delight" who "does not deserve the spring" in the earlier poem, "A Drunkard cannot meet a Cork." The prudential, moreover, might miss the importance of the adjective in the phrase "divine intemperance." Here, as in the poem "Exhilaration—is within—," where Dickinson refers to the "diviner Brand" of spiritual wine, the intoxication is of an intensely metaphysical, internal nature.

Continuing the distinction between inner and outer wine evident in her other poems, "Through those old Grounds of memory" goes on to state,

> Of liquors that are vended
> 'Tis easy to beware
> But statutes do not meddle
> With the internal bar.

The emphasis in these four lines is not, as it might be in Emerson, on the actual dangers of literal drinking but rather on the freedom of visionary intoxication from the constraints attendant on the use of alcohol. Why should one beware of vended liquors? The implied answer is, because of legal penalties: the contrast between vended and internal liquors is not that one is morally superior to the other but that one form of inebriation is easier to prosecute. Thus the focus of the distinction is the inefficacy of "statutes" vis-à-vis internal intoxication. In the line, "With the eternal bar," Dickinson is surely punning (outrageously) on the line's final word. In light of the references to *vended* liquors and *statutes,* can we ignore the sense of "bar" as a drinking counter or establishment for drinking? Both of these meanings of the word were current long before Dickinson's time and continued to be so in her day. Such punning also makes perfect sense in terms of Gelpi's observation, noted earlier, that Dickinson's temperance-supporting father "could close the bars of Amherst" but not her own internal "inns of Molten Blue."[8]

The poems just discussed constitute Dickinson's most obvious and familiar uses of intoxication as a metaphor for joy. But the internality of the drunkenness she praises reminds us also of the internality of perception for Dickinson, and of her tendency to depict that internality through alcohol and drug imagery. This depiction is itself closely related to the relations between perception and madness in Dickinson's work, where the madman, like the drunk, often perceives a truth beyond the reach of the rational.

In writing of perception and madness, Dickinson reveals a rich awareness of what Lillian Feder has called "the remarkable insight that can emerge in conjunction with the symptoms of insanity" and that can help to illuminate "the bases of organized hypocrisies" (Feder, 98). Dickinson's most explicit statement on insanity and perception is the famous poem that follows:

> Much Madness is divinest sense—
> To a discerning Eye—
> Much Sense—the starkest Madness—
> 'Tis the Majority
> In this, as All, prevail—
> Assent—and you are sane—
> Demur—you're straightway dangerous—
> And handled with a Chain.

A similar reversal of sanity and madness occurs in "I think I was enchanted," with its hallucinatory imagery and bizarre metamorphoses.

> And whether it was noon at night—
> Or only Heaven—at Noon—
> For very Lunacy of Light
> I had not power to tell—
>
> The Bees—became as Butterflies—
> The Butterflies—as Swans—

> Approached—and spurned the narrow Grass—
> And just the meanest Tunes
>
> That Nature murmured to herself
> To keep herself in Cheer—
> I took for Giants—practising—
> Titanic Opera—

The poet's evaluation of these perceptions and experiences is that they constitute "a Divine Insanity—/ The Danger to be sane," a statement recalling the "divine intoxication" and "divine intemperance" mentioned in other poems stressing the alteration of normal consciousness.

As "I think I was enchanted" shows, Dickinson was well aware of the different realities that different perceptions create. She was also intrigued by the imaging of altered states of perception in terms of intoxication—especially a kind of drugged condition. In her poems of rapture, Dickinson emphasizes not so much change of perception as change of emotional state, delirious joy conveyed by images of drinking, sacrament, or drunken stumbling. Poems of changed perception, in contrast, tend to use references to numbed oblivion or to druglike intoxicants, as in "A Drowsiness diffuses" or "A Doubt if it be us." More explicit references include "those little Anodynes / That deaden suffering" in "The Heart asks Pleasure—first" and the "Cups of artificial Drowse" in the poem "Bereaved of all, I went abroad," where the attempt to "steep . . . away" the shape of the "Grave" through various means, including drugs, proves vain: the "spade" used to dig the grave remains as an all too palpable reminder of death at the poem's end. Dickinson's point here receives even pithier formulation in "This World is not Conclusion," where she says, "Narcotics cannot still the Tooth / That nibbles at the soul," and receives a kind of follow-up in "Severer Service of myself." Here the poet concludes a list of attempts to fill the void left by emotional pain with the lines,

> No Drug for Consciousness—can be—
> Alternative to die

Is Nature's only Pharmacy
For Being's Malady—

Death itself emerges as a far more effective solution for "the awful Vacuum" described in "Severer Service of myself" than any "Cups of artificial Drowse" or "Drug for Consciousness." There is, after all, no narcotic that can still the tooth that nibbles at the soul.[9]

Although drug imagery is prevalent among the poems of altered perception, it is a poem about drinking, "The Ditch is dear to the Drunken man," in which Dickinson gives us her most extensive treatment of perception linked to intoxication imagery.

> The Ditch is dear to the Drunken man
> For is it not his Bed—
> His Advocate—his Edifice?
> How safe his fallen Head
> In her disheveled Sanctity—
> Above him is the sky—
> Oblivion bending over him
> And Honor leagues away

The poem begins with the first three of four accented words alliterating: "Ditch," "dear," "Drunken." And in that simple, straightforward line there is, as in "A Drunkard cannot meet a Cork," no pious judgment of the drunkard, only an observation that, if anything, suggests sympathy. These qualities expand, in line two, into a fuller, more empathic rendition and sharing of the drunkard's perspective that receive force from the rhetorical nature of Dickinson's questions: "For is it not his Bed— / His Advocate— his Edifice?" The ditch is transformed in meaning from a literal ditch to a bed because the drunk perceives it as such. From this point on, the metaphorical significance of the ditch grows, but without Dickinson ever losing touch with the literal reality of a drunkard's lot (and in this case, not a drunkard who would be tempted by air, dew, nectar, or any other such transcendental intoxicants!). The ditch, then, shifts in meaning as the perceptions of it shift. On one level, the word "ditch" is merely the proper verbal sign for the trough in the ground where the drunkard lies. Yet Dickinson shows us that it is not just a "ditch" but a "Bed," "Advocate," "Edifice," place of "Sanctity" and "Oblivion." This buildup from the concreteness of "ditch" to the last abstract terms helps to prepare the poem's concluding irony, where the final abstract, lofty word—"Honor"—appears and where honor, unlike "Oblivion," is shown to be "leagues away" from the drunkard's perception. At poem's end, the ditch emerges as a very particular kind of advocate and edifice—as a haven from the shame that awareness of honor would inevitably produce. The poem's conclusion, like its beginning, refuses to gloss over the ugliness of drunken behavior. This in turn makes the poem's sympathy an open-eyed one, and hence one that is all the more credible and moving. In contrast, an earlier poem (ca. 1872), obliquely referring to drunkenness, does not share a drunkard's perspective but coolly and rather amusedly regards the foolish brawling of "The Popular Heart."

> The Popular Heart is a Cannon first—
> And subsequent a Drum—
> Bells for an Auxiliary
> And an Afterward of Rum—
>
> Not a Tomorrow to know its name
> Nor a Past to stare—
> Ditches for Realms and a Trip to Jail
> For a Souvenir—

The sarcasm of a phrase like "Ditches for Realms" gives way to the more pathetic irony of "The Ditch is dear to the Drunken man," but in both poems Dickinson sees quite clearly the negative side of intoxication. In the later poem, however, she can simultaneously appreciate both the drunkard's wretchedness and his angle of vision that inverts conventional meanings, just as "the little tippler" inverted such meanings and perspectives in her own poetry.

Crucial to Dickinson's inversion of conventional points of

view is her use of intoxication imagery, which also contributes to the atmosphere of daring rebellion that characterizes many of her poems. Of course, Dickinson's emphasis on inner intoxication is not sui generis, as it links her to the transcendentalist tradition of her time that sought spiritual, not physical, drunkenness and that was in turn related to the long-established metaphorical connections between intoxication and visionary experience discussed in chapter 1. This background helps to explain how "I taste a liquor never brewed" could appear, under the title "The May-Wine" (a title *not* supplied by Dickinson) in the eminently respectable *Springfield Republican*. But images of intoxication occur so frequently in her work, and with so consistent a paralleling of drunkenness or of a drug-induced haze with the poet's own condition, that in tone and implication Dickinson goes far beyond even Emerson in challenging the sober pieties of temperate New England. At the same time, she avoids the self-conscious decadence and sensationalism of Poe's writings on intoxication. Yet more than any other major nineteenth-century American writer, Dickinson shares with these two figures a concern with intoxication as a serious theme. And with them, too, as with romantic writers generally, Dickinson "adopts an outsider's stance, a mood of continual desire, a mode of continual quest" (Weisbuch, 7). For Dickinson this stance involves a cultivation of parallels with other outsider figures: the mad, the ill, the drugged, the drunken.

In developing these parallels, Dickinson joins Emerson, Poe, Hawthorne, and Melville in anticipating many twentieth-century American writers who use similar parallels to distinguish themselves or their fictional characters from mainstream American society. The list of such modern American authors could go on indefinitely: Ernest Hemingway, Djuna Barnes, Eugene O'Neill, Tennessee Williams, Carson McCullers, William Styron, Norman Mailer, William Kennedy, the Beats. But the greatest importance of intoxication in Dickinson's work is that it provided her with a set of highly original, adaptable images with which to explore various levels of consciousness, perception, and transcendent experience. The imagery of intoxication helped her to show how different imaginative states and perceptions create different realities—how the infinitely hopeful human mind can pathetically turn a ditch into an "Edifice," or triumphantly transform a New England summertime garden into Eden.

# Chapter 4

# Beyond the Sober Eye of Reason

## Poe and the Paradoxes of Intoxication

There are moments when, even to the sober eye of Reason, the world of our sad Humanity may assume the semblance of a Hell.

—Poe, "The Premature Burial"

Man, being reasonable, must get drunk;
The best of life is but intoxication.

—Byron, *Don Juan*

We shall get drunk when we please.

—Poe, *Broadway Journal* (1845)

I am done forever with drink.

—Poe letter, July 22, 1846

And when they dragged your retching flesh,
Your trembling hands that night through Baltimore—
That last night on the ballot rounds, did you
Shaking, did you deny the ticket, Poe?

—Hart Crane, "The Bridge"

No American writer has been as consistently or notoriously linked with intoxication as Edgar Allan Poe. Despite evidence suggesting that he was neither a habitual heavy drinker nor a drug addict, his genuine problems with drink and the legends surrounding his life and strange death have perpetuated a mythic image of Poe as the ultimate inebriate-seer-junkie-genius of American literature. An amusing parody of this myth may be found in Stuart Levine's rendering of the "old image of Poe"—a wild-eyed, cackling pervert in a gloomy garret, scribbling away between swigs of liquor and shots of "opium, morphine, laudanum, hashish, who-knows-what" (Levine, "Introduction," xv).[1]

Old though it may be, however, such an image still persists today, despite dents left in it by responsible scholarly studies of Poe's life, and despite even the earnest attempts of those critics who, in the words of Alethea Hayter, "have made Poe into such a sober responsible citizen that one feels one is reading about Addison." (Hayter, 146). Hayter's point is well taken, and there is no point in burying one's head in the sand and ignoring Poe's susceptibility to even small amounts of liquor, or the professional and personal difficulties that drink brought him.[2] As Edward Wagenknecht has written, drinking remains "in a sense the greatest of all problems in Poe's biography" (Wagenknecht, 30)—as well it might for a man whose own attitudes toward and experiences with intoxication are so fraught with puzzles, paradoxes, and contradictions. There are, for example, the conflicting reports of his drinking habits (sensibly analyzed by Wagenknecht and, more recently, by Kenneth Silverman), as well as the pathetic tone of many of his letters, rationalizing or apologizing for his intemperance. There is also Poe's curious relationship to the temperance movement. Poe disagreed with the proposal to close the "Rum Palaces, and Rum Hovels, on the Sabbath," only because of its violation of "the entire separation of Church and State"; otherwise, Poe seems to have found the idea of closing down rum shops laudable (*Doings,* 39). Yet he satirizes temperance ideals or methods several times in both his fiction and nonfiction, and in 1845 he was attacked in the temperance press for supposedly being intoxicated at a poetry reading in Boston. Poe reciprocated with an acerbic riposte that led only to more attacks on his character and to continued skirmishing between Poe and temperance publications.[3] Finally, in the last year of his life, the notorious Poe himself joined the ranks of virtue, becoming a member of the Sons of Temperance. Yet less than two months later, this prize fish caught from the sea of alcohol was found semiconscious at a Baltimore polling booth, dying in an apparent attack of delirium tremens.[4]

The complexity and contradictions of intoxication in Poe's life are fully matched by the complexity and contradictions of this issue in his art.[5] Although specific references to intoxication in Poe's poetry and essays are scant, his fiction, particularly the tales and *The Narrative of Arthur Gordon Pym,* virtually overflows with diverse, often conflicting images of wine, hard liquor, and drunken or drug-using characters. Alcohol and opium both are important to many of Poe's plots, to his explorations of altered consciousness, to his evocation of the comic and tragic alike. There are even strong elements of the transcendent and of the yearning for Eden in Poe's intoxication imagery, though rendered in a tone, and fraught with implications, quite distinct from those found in Emerson or Dickinson. Thus intoxication in Poe is a challenging, even puzzling problem that calls for far more study than it has received. My purposes here will be to analyze the prevailing patterns of this problem and to clarify its significance in the work of a writer who is at once so anomalous and so influential a figure in American and European literary history.

The contradictoriness mentioned above undercuts critical attempts to pin Poe down to a single, consistent opinion regarding alcohol or intoxication. L. Moffitt Cecil, for instance, has argued that alcohol in Poe is almost always negatively described (Cecil, 42). But, as Wagenknecht observed of a similar point made much earlier by J. Appleton Morgan, "That last is something of an overstatement" (Wagenknecht, 37). Intemperance is a "fiend" in "The Black Cat" but a source of amusement and even illumination in "The Angel of the Odd"; opium in "Ligeia" is a form of delusion and bondage, but in the same tale, the lovely Ligeia's face is praised in terms of an "opium dream"; drink is associated with pathos and squalor in "The Man of the Crowd" but with elegant, albeit decadent pleasure in "The Masque of the Red Death": "there were musicians, there was Beauty, there was wine."[6]

Paradox, then, is a distinctive feature of many of Poe's images of intoxication. To be sure, drunkenness and addiction are familiar elements in Poe's paraphernalia of horror or grotesque humor, but beyond this, we will discover how strong a philosophical role intoxication plays in Poe's studies of psychic disintegration and altered states of perception. Poe, more than any other romantic, including De Quincey, and certainly more than transcendentalists like Emerson, deals with realistic depictions of actual drinking or drug taking. But it is much more with such issues as disintegration or perception, rather than temperance or intemperance, that Poe's deepest concerns lie. And of particular interest in his work is that vague area where the lines between sobriety and intoxication blur, where the imagination begins to create its own reality and gives birth to those fantasies that, in the words of Theseus from *A Midsummer Night's Dream,* "apprehend / More than cool reason ever comprehends."

The roots of Poe's interest in intoxication are not hard to find. Poe's own problems with drinking, as well as those of his brother, William Henry Poe, offer a partial explanation for his numerous references to intoxication. But there is also the influence of literary fashion. For a writer as sensitive as Poe to the interests of his audience, and as aware of trends in fashionable magazines like *Blackwood's,* it is natural that the style of easy banter about drunkenness, the wordplay and allusions to drink and opium in such sources as the "Noctes Ambrosianae" series that appeared in *Blackwood's* from 1822 to 1835, or the intoxication motifs in the works of writers like Thomas Love Peacock, De Quincey, and Byron, would be echoed in Poe. In fact, ever since "the publication of *The Confessions of an English Opium-Eater,* opium had become as much a standard accessory of the Romantic hero as a ruined castle in the Appenines had been a generation earlier" (Hayter, 135). On a more philosophical level, Poe's images of intoxication are rooted in his (and the romantic movement's) well-known fascination with the tension between the emotional/intuitive and dispassionate/ratiocinative aspects of the human psyche. Unlike Emerson, Poe shows little interest in intoxication as a social problem. His work contains a few examples of the social evils of drink, as in "The Black Cat" and "The Man of the Crowd." And he takes a satiric jab now and then at the temperance movement: in "Never Bet the Devil Your Head," for example, the eight-month-old Toby Dammit refuses to sign a temperance pledge, whereby Poe presumably mocks the tendency to extend pledges even to children. Social reform in general, including temperance, is the target of satire in "The Angel of the Odd" (Gerber, 88–93). Apart from this, Poe's concern is with private experiences and perceptions and with the relationship between intoxication and individual human behavior. Even when he paints intoxication in dark colors, Poe is far removed from the attitudes of the temperance movement, which were tinged by a strong sense of alcohol's negative effects on society as a whole. With intoxication, as with so much else in Poe, the center of gravity is not the outer social world but the inner universe of the individual mind.

Within this universe, Poe's images of intoxication encompass a wide variety of moral and tonal nuances. This is particularly true of Poe's references to alcohol. His images of opium or morphine are consistently serious, often somber. Such a tone, of course, accords with traditional literary descriptions of opium use. Although John Wilson's contributions to the "Noctes Ambrosianae" series in *Blackwood's* poke good-natured fun at De Quincey's opium habit,[7] the prevailing tone of references to opium in literature has been one of seriousness, mystery, sometimes of horror, often of adulation. About opium, too, there has always hovered an association with dreams and purportedly visionary experience conducive to solemnity. Alcohol, in contrast, has been associated with the comic as well as the serious from ancient times—fittingly so, when one remembers that it was the worship of Dionysos, god of wine, that gave rise to both tragedy and comedy. In Poe, too, drink serves the purposes of both the tragic and the comic muses.

In addition to possessing a seriousness of tone, Poe's references to opium tend to take place in aristocratic, refined settings. In this respect, Poe reflects the prevalent early to mid-nineteenth-century association of opium with gentility and wealth. Although opium was widely available in the United States, its price and control by prescription resulted in its being used mostly by the middle and upper classes, unlike the more socially promiscuous alcohol (Rorabaugh, 176–77). In other words, if in the nineteenth century religion (along with alcohol) was the opiate of the people, opium was the opiate of the elite. Some writers even explicitly linked opium to genteel or sophisticated behavior. Walter Colton, for instance, writing for *Knickerbocker* magazine in 1836, claimed that opium "allows a man to be a gentleman; it makes him a visionary." Later in the nineteenth century, various American periodicals, despite growing concern about opium use among the lower classes, explicitly compared opium favorably with alcohol, as did Stephen Crane in a newspaper article of 1896. In England, Francis Thompson was echoing De Quincey's praise of opium as a refined, noble substance compared to alcohol, while that paragon of exquisite taste and decadent pleasure, Oscar Wilde's Lord Henry Wotton, smokes an opium-tainted cigarette in the opening scene of *The Picture of Dorian Gray*.[8]

Moreover, unlike alcohol, opium in Poe generally appears in works involving what was for him the most poetically melancholy of subjects: the death of a beautiful woman. Opium figures prominently in "Ligeia," "The Fall of the House of Usher," and briefly but significantly in the original versions of "Berenice" and "The Oval Portrait." In fact, in "Ligeia," opium is used to express the feminine beauty of Ligeia's face, which had the "radiance of an opium-dream—an airy and spirit-lifting vision more wildly divine than the phantasies which hovered about the slumbering souls of the daughters of Delos" (*Works*, 2:311). (The morphine in "A Tale of the Ragged Mountains" is not related to the death-of-a-beautiful-woman theme, but the tale's protagonist, Bedloe, fits the upper-class connection with opium by being a rich southern gentleman.) Poe's drinkers are overwhelmingly male, his drug users exclusively so. But the presence of opium in stories in which a female character is important perhaps derives from the supposedly more "feminine" qualities of that drug—its conduciveness to passivity and lassitude, its association with refinement and introspection, its greater availability and acceptability, relative to drink, for "proper" women in nineteenth-century America (Morgan, *Drugs in America,* 90). Certainly Poe's drug-using characters diverge from conventional images of manliness and strength; we may mention here the enervated, overly sensitive natures of Roderick Usher, the narrator of "Ligeia," or of Augustus Bedloe.

As far as Poe's women drinkers are concerned, except for the sickly Rowena, who is prescribed some medicinal wine in "Ligeia," one will find little more than comic grotesques, such as the physically hideous, drunken women in "King Pest" or the madwomen in "The System of Dr. Tarr and Professor Fether." Like most other writers of his time, Poe could present women who drink more than an occasional sip only as comic or repulsive or both. In Charles Dickens, for instance, we may recall the vile Mrs. Blackpool of *Hard Times,* or the ludicrous Mrs. Gamp of *Martin Chuzzlewit.* And when George Eliot, in "Janet's Repentance," presented an honest but sympathetic portrayal of a female alcoholic, she had to exercise unusual firmness in getting the story published at all—not because of its literary quality but because of its supposedly unseemly topic.[9]

Apart from the distinctions noted here, however, Poe does not sharply divide opium from alcohol. Indeed, he draws an explicit parallel between the two substances in "The Fall of the House of Usher," when he writes that Usher's voice often sounded like that of "the lost drunkard, or the irreclaimable eater of opium, during the periods of his most intense excitement" (*Works,* 2:402). More important than the differences between alcohol and opium is the tendency of Poe's images of intoxication, from whatever source, to range from the positive to the negative to the ambiguous, from the comic to the horrifying to various combinations of the two.

Among Poe's intoxicants, as we have already noted, alcohol especially is often associated not only with tragedy but also with humor or lightheartedness, for example, the whimsy of "Bon-Bon," or the broadly comic escapades in "King Pest" and "The Angel of the Odd." There is also the comic relief, if one can call it that, of the hiccuping servant Ugo in Poe's little-known verse play, *Politian,* or the carefree tone of "Lines on Ale":

> Fill with mingled cream and amber,
> I will drain that glass again.
> Such hilarious visions clamber
> Through the chamber of my brain—
>
> Quaintest thoughts—queerest fancies
> Come to life and fade away;
> What care I how time advances?
> I am drinking ale today.
>
> (*Works,* 1:449)[10]

Again on the positive side of the question, Pollin reminds us that some of Poe's tales express "approval of intemperance" and that even the tales condemning drink do so with such "subversive pleasure in the means of depravity that no temperance worker could approve of them" (Pollin, 122). It is an overstatement in the opposite direction from Cecil and Morgan to assert, as does Marie Bonaparte, that Poe's "works never speak ill of" opium (Bonaparte, 85). True, Poe never overtly condemns opium, but the narrator of "Ligeia" is given the hardly positive description of being "habitually fettered in the shackles of the drug" (*Works,* 2:323), and acts of bizarre and horrific behavior are implicitly linked with opium in "Ligeia," "The Fall of the House of Usher," and the first version of "Berenice," in which the narrator, who yanks the teeth from Berenice's scarcely buried corpse, is an eater of opium.

As all this implies, Poe sets forth no single attitude toward intoxication. Its almost bewilderingly broad range of associations suggests an unresolved ambivalence that may well reflect a similar ambivalence in Poe's personal views, not to mention the ambiguous status of intoxication and intoxicants in American culture. The absence of a single unified vision of intoxication does not, however, mean that Poe's treatment of this theme dissolves into a shapeless mass of inconsistencies. For all their diversity, Poe's intoxication motifs tend to settle into one of two distinct but often intersecting areas—first, what D. H. Lawrence called the "disintegrative function" in Poe's works (Lawrence, 70), and second, the alteration of perception.[11] These two themes are most closely linked when disintegration actually leads to a more profound spiritual perception than that available in normal circumstances, when the "delirious eye" glimpses a truth unseen by the "sober eye of Reason." As Edward Davidson observes, much in Poe suggests that such things as delirium or horror "might be ways into farther and deeper understanding. Horror, madness and death are man's avenues into the ultimate rationale of existence of which our own mortal existence is but a crude fragment" (Davidson, 134). To this list of Poe's "avenues," one may appropriately add intoxication.

On the simplest level, the relationship of intoxication to the "disintegrative function" is evident when images of drink or drugs merely accompany or intensify a larger pattern of general chaos or destruction. The other, more complex level is that where intoxication images are closely tied to the disintegration of the individual psyche, often involving some significant change in a character's personal identity.

It is on the first of these levels that intoxication operates in tales like "King Pest" and "The System of Dr. Tarr and Professor Fether," both of which serve as antidotes to the view that intoxication in Poe necessarily plays a villainous role, although in neither work is the use of intoxicants seen as positive. "King Pest" perfectly exemplifies that frequent blend in Poe that Benjamin Franklin Fisher IV has described as "horror and humor framed by intoxication" (Fisher, 11).[12] Fusing images of extravagant drinking with violence, chaos, death, disease, and raucous humor, the story shows how two drunken sailors, Legs and Hugh Tarpaulin, outdrink and outfight the pestilential crew of drunkards whom they find in an undertaker's shop. Appropriately for such an environment, the drunkards, including his majesty King Pest the First, and the Arch Duchess Ana-Pest, are surrounded by rather obvious emblems of death: skulls serve as cups, the carousers sit on coffin-trestles, one of the drunken company sports "sable hearse-plumes," skeletons dangle about, and coffins line the walls. But the tale's rampant images of death and destruction are modified by the occasional mock dignity of the narration, and by such farcical incidents as Hugh's near-drowning in a puncheon of ale. And at the end, the two sailors emerge, even drunker than before but victorious, having dispersed the male members of the company and hauled off as a dubious prize the two monstrous females. The entire story embodies a kind of macabre Rabelaisianism, with Poe's gruesome evocations of death inverting the cruder and unquestionably more life-affirming qualities of Gargantua and Pantagruel. In "King Pest," the destructive, fatal consequences and associations of alcohol veer into grotesque comedy, while the madcap festivities and raucous boozing of the characters are persistently tinged with reminders of chaos and death. Thus "King Pest" refuses to give itself up to either a positive, convivially festive or negative, drink-as-doom interpretation.

Though less thoroughly permeated with the fumes of liquor, "The System of Dr. Tarr and Professor Fether" resembles "King Pest" in linking drink to the chaotic disintegration of the rational, normal order of things. In a lunatic asylum, a band of drunken inmates who have overcome and jailed their keepers plays host to the naive narrator, leading him to believe they are the relatives and guests of the asylum's director. Their sumptuous feast is marked by bizarre antics, fomented by the great quantities of wine consumed, until the keepers break free and reclaim their wine-bibbing, insane charges.

The obvious associations of drinking and death in "King Pest," as well as the disintegration of rational control in "The System of Dr. Tarr and Professor Fether," reappear, albeit in substantially different form, in "The Assignation." Their treatment here is more serious, although the tale reflects what Poe himself called a quality of "half banter, half satire" (*Letters*, 1:84) characteristic of his projected *Tales of the Folio Club*, which were to include "The Assignation." Like many of the Folio Club tales, "The Assignation," constituting a supposedly drunken reworking of events from Byron's Italian adventures, may "yield simultaneous compatible comic and serious readings" (Fisher, 3).

As far as drinking is concerned, the mingling of the comic and the serious appears toward the end of "The Assignation," when the quasi-Byronic protagonist receives the narrator in his Venetian palace. This being Poe, the "palazzo" in question is, of course, a building of "gloomy yet fantastic pomp" and "unparalleled splendor" (*Works*, 2:156–57). The narrator's bibulously loquacious host, known as "the stranger," chatters away in a "mingled tone of levity and solemnity" (*Works*, 2:161). He finally presses drink on his guest in a manner that cannot help suggesting a possible satiric slap at what Poe once called the "temptation held out on all sides by the spirit of Southern conviviality," and which he himself blamed for some of his difficulties with drink (*Letters*, 1:156–57). (The motif of forcing another to drink occurs also in "Hop-Frog" and in *The Narrative of Arthur Gordon Pym*, where the mate twice forces Augustus to drink rum.) The stranger insistently repeats the command-invitation "let us drink," and proceeds to gulp down his wine with a haste that is laughable considering his pretensions to sophistication and refinement: "And having made me pledge him in a bumper" (note here the narrator's hint at the drink being forced on him), the host performs the impressive feat of swallowing "in rapid succession several goblets of the wine" (*Works*, 2:165).

Obviously seeking oblivion through drink, the host rambles on, asserting that "to dream has been the business of my life" (*Works*, 2:165), a lilting line that could have come straight out of one of Poe's lyrical tributes to dreams, such as "A Dream Within a Dream," "Dream-Land," "A Dream," or "Dreams." Here we have a good example of Poe's elusiveness when it comes to categorizing some of his works by tone or attitude; a startling irreverence may intrude onto a seemingly somber mood, or a passage of "half banter, half satire" may be invaded by a sentiment that could be uttered with complete sincerity by Poe in another context. With the reference to dreams and the yearning for the "land of real dreams" (*Works*, 2:166), the humor of "The Assignation" takes on an admixture of greater seriousness, far-fetched as its denouement of psychic blending may be. (It is certainly not much more far-fetched than the blending of identities in "The Fall of the House of Usher," which involves not just two people but a house, no less!)

In this concluding part of "The Assignation," the ancient symbolic association between intoxication and death becomes crucial. Indeed, we learn that after having recited or, rather, "ejaculated" Henry King's famous lines about meeting "in that hollow vale," the stranger sprawls on an ottoman, "confessing the power of the wine" (*Works*, 2:166). At just this moment, news comes of the mistress Aphrodite's death by poison. The narrator flies to wake his host only to find him dead, with "a cracked and blackened goblet" (*Works*, 2:166), the instrument of drunkenness and death, beside him. In dying drunk, the stranger becomes a nineteenth-century version of an ancient notion, linked with Dionysos and described by the distinguished alcohol researcher E. M. Jellinek: "the deceased [is] carried to his grave in a drunken condition. . . . [I]nconsistent as it may seem, the dead can be brought in a drunken condition to the hereafter." Regarding this concept, Jellinek writes that "drunkenness can be a kind of shortcut to the higher life, the achievement of a higher state without an emotional and intellectual effort. The alcoholic 'dies' hundreds of times, and, if one takes a psychoanalytic view, his drinking may be seen to symbolize an unconscious wish for self-destruction" ("Symbolism," 857–58).

Intoxication in "The Assignation," if perhaps not definitely used to attain "a higher state," certainly appears as a key accompaniment to the stranger's longing for such a state, for the "land of real dreams." The metaphorical link between alcohol and self-destruction noted by Jellinek turns literal at the story's end, where intoxication actually becomes the ingestion of some lethal—that is, toxic—substance. "The power of the wine" is the power of poison. The only difference between the stranger's case and Jellinek's description of symbolic suicide is that the former's self-destructive tendencies seem not at all "unconscious."

Within this tale that mingles satire, melodramatic posturing, gloomy Gothic decor, and occult mystery, drink originally appears as a source of humor, as in the tipsy eloquence of the narrator and his multigoblet-draining host. But, like the stranger's own speech, which combines a "tone of levity and solemnity," drink in the tale has its more somber, thoughtful ramifications. Intoxication is a stimulus to imagining the "land of real dreams," a phrase reminiscent of Poe's most lyrical, ardent poems on transcendent experience. The stranger's drinking is linked to the deliberate courting of disaster and death that marks his final moments. And it reflects, in an oblique and quite possibly unintended way, the Dionysian association of drinking with death and the passage to a higher state or afterlife.

The exaggerated, half-serious, half-mocking framework of "The Assignation" suggests an important theme present in less patently ludicrous tales: the mysterious fusion of separate identities, often involving a character's relations with an alter ego. "The Assignation" is a kind of borderline tale, standing between those tales using intoxication as part of a general pattern of disintegration and those in which intoxication figures prominently in the disintegration or transformation of individual identity. In many of the more serious tales the intoxication motif of "The Assignation" reappears, particularly where the issue of personal identity involves some change or disintegration of the self, usually in a horrific way.

In tales like "Ligeia" and "William Wilson," the narrators' obsessions with an alter ego are colored by frequent references to intoxication or intoxicants: in "Ligeia," to opium and wine; in "William Wilson," to intemperate drinking. In "The Fall of the House of Usher," the gradual merging of the house's identity with those of the already partly merged identities of Roderick and his sister takes place in a foglike, hallucinatory atmosphere that Poe explicitly connects to opium in the story's famous first paragraph. But the link between intoxication and the permutations of individual identity, especially with the destruction of identity, is at its most explicit in "The Black Cat."

Unlike "Usher," where Roderick is already caught in the coils of opium and, possibly, alcohol, or "The Man of the Crowd," in which a pathetic drunk's identity has disintegrated long ago, "The Black Cat" shows us the very process of disintegration, which Poe specifically blames on alcohol. Poe begins by setting up a situation in which a basically likable personality degenerates into a seething mass of malevolence. The narrator is, at first, known for "docility and humanity," "tenderness of heart," and especially his fondness for animals (*Works,* 3:850). But then, over a period of "several years," these benign qualities disappear "through the instrumentality of the Fiend Intemperance" (*Works,* 3:851). Some shreds of the narrator's original affection for his cat, Pluto, remain, but "my disease," he explains, "grew upon me—for what disease is like Alcohol!" The narrator's "original soul seemed, at once, to take its flight from my body," and his new, sadistic identity vents itself in the horrible mutilation and, finally, hanging of Pluto (*Works,* 3:851).

Despite the rather florid terms in which he speaks of the protagonist's drunken violence, Poe's reference to alcohol as a disease aligns him with more advanced, sympathetic views of the alcoholic. The "disease concept of alcoholism," as it is often called, gained wide currency only in the twentieth century, but it is a common mistake to assume that it did not even exist in earlier eras. The notion of alcoholism as a disease might well have been known to Poe from the work of such famous scholars of intemperance as Benjamin Rush or Thomas Trotter. Rush was particularly well known, and his famous "moral and physical thermometer," correlating various drinks with their supposed effects, was reprinted frequently in the nineteenth century. While we cannot be sure that Poe knew Rush's work, it seems likely that he would be familiar with the disease concept of alcoholism in light of Rush's fame and of his own apparent familiarity with contemporary medical studies of alcohol.[13]

"The Black Cat" also exhibits some parallels to the structure of much temperance fiction of Poe's time. A normal human being starts to drink; usually the first victims of his inebriation are his wife and children (in the childless household of Poe's tale it is the pets who suffer in lieu of children). In compressed form, Poe's story suggests the common temperance theme of the *progressive* nature of alcoholism, as the narrator stoops to coarse behavior, to physical violence and crime, and ends in near-madness. It even suggests the standard temperance motif of socioeconomic deprivation, although in Poe's tale the narrator's poverty is not directly blamed on his drinking.

An important distinction needs to be made, at this point, between temperance fiction and "The Black Cat."[14] It lies in the latter's freedom from the single-minded, one-dimensional perspective of that fiction. Without question, Poe damns drinking here with all the ferocity of a temperance warrior or of a man who, like Poe himself, had bitterly suffered because of drink. But for all that, alcohol in "The Black Cat" is part of an even larger pattern of concerns with the nature of evil and with moral and intellectual decay. On the most superficial level, liquor in "The Black Cat" spawns cruel, ugly actions and impulses. But as the tale progresses, the protagonist's alcoholism becomes the key that unlocks the door to something more chilling and (to Poe) more deeply ingrained in human nature than "the Fiend Intemperance." This is the "spirit of PERVERSENESS," the deliberate seeking out of that which the narrator knows to be "vile" (*Works*, 3:852). Imbued with such a spirit, the narrator of "The Black Cat" shares an affinity less with the temperance tale's stereotypical besotted lout than with the character of Dostoevsky's Marmeladov, who in *Crime and Punishment* willfully (perversely, we might say) drinks himself and his family into penury and disgrace.

For neither Marmeladov nor Poe's narrator does alcoholism explain everything away. Marmeladov reveals that drink is but the tool of a larger compulsion to know guilt and to suffer: "Do you think," he asks, "you who sold it, that this bottle of yours has been sweet to me? Affliction, I sought affliction at the bottom of it, tears and affliction, and I found them, I tasted them" (Dostoevsky, 19). The narrator of "The Black Cat," after expatiating on his "gin-nurtured" vices, describes "perverseness" as fundamental to human nature. Perverseness, he claims, "is one of the primitive impulses of the human heart—one of the indivisible primary faculties, or sentiments, which give direction to the character of Man" (*Works,* 3:852). As such, the spirit of perverseness, like Marmeladov's will-to-suffer, is antecedent to more immediate evils, like alcoholism. The roots of perverseness lie deeper than those of intemperance—perhaps they even *are* the roots of intemperance.

Thus in "The Black Cat" drink operates on two levels. On the most obvious one, it is a destructive instrument, ravaging heart and intellect and leading to complete moral and psychological ruin; on the other, drink is equally ravaging, but it appears more as an effect than a cause, just as it does in Poe's letter to George Eveleth, dated January 4, 1848. Describing his anguish over his wife Virginia's ill health, Poe asserts that his sufferings drove him "insane, with long intervals of horrible sanity. During these fits of absolute unconsciousness I drank, God only knows how often or how much. As a matter of course, my enemies referred the insanity to the drink rather than the drink to the insanity" (*Letters,* 2:356). Like Poe's letter, "The Black Cat" confronts us with the choice of referring the insanity to the drink or the drink to the insanity. It is a choice with which researchers and students of alcoholism still wrestle today.[15]

Whether as cause or as symptom, intoxication also figures prominently elsewhere in Poe's tales of personal disintegration and identity change. There is the splitting of identity in the

heavy-drinking William Wilson, the frequently maddening effects of drink in *The Narrative of Arthur Gordon Pym,* the opium-
addicted narrator's merging with Ligeia in the tale that bears her
name, not to mention Ligeia's own seeming merger with Rowena
after the latter consumes some mysterious, possibly drugged
wine. But in addition to linking disintegration to images of drugs
or alcohol, these tales all contain hints of the second major function of intoxication in Poe—its use as a cause and image of altered perception.

Examples of distorted or heightened perception in these tales
are numerous. In "The Black Cat," the drunken narrator sits "half
stupified, in a den of more than infamy" (*Works,* 3:854), when
he perceives in a kind of hallucinatory trance the huge cat that
reminds him of Pluto. The narrator of "Ligeia" is beset by uncer-
tainties about what he really sees, or merely dreams or imagines, as various "opium-engendered" visions float before his
"unquiet eye" (*Works,* 2:326). Two of William Wilson's most dramatic moments of confrontation with his alter ego occur when
Wilson is drinking; it is almost as if Wilson becomes more sensitive to the promptings of his neglected moral self when he is
intoxicated. The beginning of "The Fall of the House of Usher"
gives us an opium-laden atmosphere, where the very windows
of the house are like vacant eyes—perhaps the eyes of the "rev-
eller upon opium" during his "after-dream" (*Works,* 2:397),
which is what the narrator thinks of while gazing at the house
and its depressing domain. Throughout this story, the perceptions of Roderick Usher, opium eater and possible drunkard, are
colored by "phantasmagoric conceptions" and "wild fantasias"
(*Works,* 2:405–06). There is also Usher's "morbid acuteness of
the senses" (*Works,* 2:403), probably brought on by opium, just
as morphine brings on the hyperaesthesia experienced by Bedloe in "A Tale of the Ragged Mountains."[16]

These examples are all part of Poe's larger interest in perception. Everywhere one looks in Poe one finds evidence of the
characteristic romantic concern with the ways we perceive or
misperceive things, whether physical or spiritual, whether "real"

or imaginary or a combination of both. And often this concern reveals itself in an examination of perceiving obliquely, or from some unusual or even abnormal perspective, as in the following passage from Poe's "A Chapter of Suggestions": "That intuitive and seemingly casual perception by which we often attain knowledge, when reason herself falters and abandons the effort, appears to resemble the sudden glancing at a star, by which we see it more clearly than by a direct gaze; or the half-closing the eyes in looking at a plot of grass the more fully to appreciate the intensity of its green" (*Writings*, 2:471).

The relationship between perception and one's psychic state, the effect of imagination on what we perceive, the boundaries between appearance and truth, sanity and madness, sobriety and intoxication—all of these issues are interwoven in Poe's work. Fascinated with transitional and borderline states in the human psyche, Poe is no less interested in probing the ways that perception changes in the passage from one state to another, as well as the ways that various states of mind enhance or distort perception. The narrator of "Eleonora," for instance, reflects many of his creator's preoccupations when he says that

> the question is not yet settled, whether madness is or is not the loftiest intelligence—whether much that is glorious—whether all that is profound—does not spring from disease of thought— from moods of mind exalted at the expense of the general intellect. They who dream by day are cognizant of many things which escape those who dream only by night. In their grey visions they obtain glimpses of eternity, and thrill, in awaking, to find that they have been upon the verge of the great secret. (Works, 2:638)

Similarly, the narrator of "The Tell-Tale Heart" demands, "Why *will* you say that I am mad? The disease had sharpened my senses—not destroyed—not dulled them" (*Works*, 3:792); and in "A Chapter of Suggestions," Poe proclaims, "There are moments, indeed, in which he [the imaginative man] perceives the faint perfumes, and hears the melodies of a happier world. Some of the most profound knowledge—perhaps all *very* profound knowledge—has originated from a highly stimulated imagination." Later in the same "Chapter," Poe writes that the "earnest longing for artificial excitement, which, unhappily, has characterized too many eminent men" (can Poe be thinking of himself here?) "may thus be regarded as a psychal want, or necessity" (*Writings,* 2:472). In a similar vein, the narrator of "Bon-Bon" declares that "there are few men of extraordinary profundity who are found wanting in an inclination for the bottle. Whether this inclination be an exciting cause, or rather a valid proof, of such profundity, it is a nice thing to say" (*Works,* 2:98).

It is hard to read such statements and not think of Poe's own experiences of intoxication, or of the numerous instances of drunken, drugged, or seemingly intoxicated perception in his work. How does one see? How does one know what one sees to be true? Is much madness truly divinest sense to a discerning eye? Does Philip drunk see a truth forever closed to Philip sober? Is there some truth the dead know? Some truth the dead drunk know? Such questions speak to that part of Poe that attributes other than purely negative qualities to the illogical, the mad, or the intoxicated.

In Poe, perception is not necessarily destroyed by intoxication or conditions analogous to it. True, the narrator of "The Black Cat" drowns his guilt in alcohol and becomes incapable of perceiving his own moral decay when drunk. Yet in "Hop-Frog," although the title character is driven half-mad by liquor, it is when he is drunk that he is inspired by the grotesquely brilliant plan that simultaneously avenges himself and Tripetta and liberates them from their liquor-swilling, liquor-pushing king. In "Shadow—A Parable," the revelers, though drunk and singing the songs of Anacreon, "which are madness" (*Works,* 2:190), seem to possess unusual insight into the nature of death and melancholy, with which their drinking is associated. For Augustus Bedloe, in "A Tale of the Ragged Mountains," morphine endows "all the external world with an intensity of interest" (*Works,* 3:943). In "William Wilson," as we have already noted, twice Wilson's conscience appears forcefully just when Wilson has been drinking. It is as if intoxication, ironically, has given Wilson a certain sensitivity or spiritual acuteness that enables him to hear his sober alter ego more clearly. Of course, Wilson's drinking is clearly a vice in this tale, and the spiritual acuteness attendant on it is no more an amelioration of Wilson's intemperance than Lady Macbeth's heightened sensitivity to blood is an amelioration of her murderous acts. With regard to the whole question of the morality or immorality of intoxication, we need to remember that Poe's explorations of intoxicated perception are just that—explorations—some of them suggesting negative, others positive qualities, rather than being out-and-out condemnations or celebrations of such perception.

Poe's most sustained treatments of intoxication and perception are to be found in *The Narrative of Arthur Gordon Pym,* "Ligeia," and "The Angel of the Odd." The first of these provides numerous scattered references to intoxicated perception, while the second deals more specifically with the role of the imagination in such perception. In the third, Poe gives us his most concentrated, sharply focused use of intoxication imagery to explore the relations among perception, rationality, and the imagination.

In a sense, the entire *Narrative of Arthur Gordon Pym* is the spinoff of a drunken spree: all that befalls Pym stems from that night at the beginning, when he and Augustus drunkenly set forth in the *Ariel*. From that point on, much of the narrative can be seen as a kind of dialogue within Pym (and possibly Poe) on the nature and effects of intoxication. And within this dialogue, many of Pym's comments deal directly or indirectly with intoxicated perception. The very first chapter includes Pym's intoxicated, uncertain perceptions of Augustus's condition. Augustus first seems drunk to Pym, but the former's skill at counterfeiting sobriety coupled, no doubt, with Pym's own drunkenness convince him that Augustus is the soul of rationality and that his "mad idea" of going out in a boat at night is "one of the most delightful and reasonable things in the world" (*Writings,* 1:58).

Early in the text, Pym undergoes experiences suggestive of an alcoholic blackout: his unconsciousness upon the collision of the *Penguin* with the *Ariel* and his incarceration in the hold of the *Grampus,* where he loses his sense of time (no doubt exacerbated by the "half a dozen bottles of cordials and liqueurs" [*Writings,* 1:69] that Augustus rather generously provides for him). There, in the hold, Pym compares his mental state to that caused by opium: "I revolved in my brain a multitude of absurd expedients for procuring light—such expedients precisely as a man in the perturbed sleep occasioned by opium would be apt to fall upon for a similar purpose—each and all of which appear by turns to the dreamer the most reasonable and the most preposterous of conceptions, just as the reasoning or imaginative faculties flicker, alternately, one above the other" (*Writings,* 1:78). In the unwholesome air of the hold, he falls "into a state of profound sleep, or rather stupor" (*Writings,* 1:72), in which his dreams resemble the horrors of delirium tremens: immense serpents entwine Pym; strange, animated trees scream in agony; a terrifying lion threatens him. The theme of delirium is picked up several times later in the text, for example, when Pym's companions, having had nothing to eat or drink but port wine for six days, sink into "extravagances and imbecilities" (*Writings,* 1:130). By this point, Pym's own perceptual powers have been so affected that he is not sure whether or not he too may have been guilty of such things. He has been too often drunk, too long surrounded by those who are drunk, too immersed in the generally hallucinatory atmosphere of that drunken boat, the *Grampus,* to distinguish clearly between what he calls "sober and naked reality" and "a frightful dream" (*Writings,* 1:148).

Beginning with a drunken lark, the adventures of Pym proceed further and further into mysterious regions of consciousness and fantasy, so that near the narrative's end Pym finds his "fancies creating their own realities"; he has reached the point where he hallucinates without drink (*Writings,* 1:197). Although, in fact, drink disappears in the last pages of *Pym,* an echo of earlier descriptions of intoxication persists as Pym, Peters, and Nu-Nu head, in a bizarre dream landscape, toward the cataract wherein dwells the huge white figure. Peters sits in a state of apathy, while Nu-Nu, overcome by the accidental flash of Pym's white handkerchief in his face, sinks into "drowsiness and stupor." Pym himself, the most alert of this lethargic trio, feels a "numbness of body and mind" and "a dreaminess of sensation" (*Writings,* 1:204). All three of these characters show symptoms that Poe elsewhere has used to indicate various stages of intoxication.

As Pym progresses from the opening account of his alcohol-inspired excursion with Augustus to his final, opium-dreamlike voyage into the heart of whiteness, he moves from a world of ostensible rationality into ever-deepening vortices of experience and perception that are best characterized by such terms as "madness," "illusion," "intoxication." In tracing this movement, Poe uses both specific references to intoxication and images suggestive of it as a leitmotiv that binds the work together aesthetically. Simultaneously, intoxication in *Pym* intensifies the sense of fragmentation and strangeness attendant on altered perception and on the mind's part in forming the reality it beholds.

When Pym, clinging to the cliff with Peters, speaks of his fancies creating their own realities, he is but a step away from giving us the romantic concept of the imagination's power to create its own reality. This concept appears not only in Emerson and Dickinson but also, across the Atlantic, in such romantics as Coleridge and Wordsworth and, most famously (at least as far as the English-speaking tradition is concerned), in Shakespeare's lines on the imagination bodying forth the "the forms of things unknown" in *A Midsummer Night's Dream*. But Poe's interest in the powers of the imagination is ambivalent, qualified by his fascination with the powers and limits of ratiocination and his distrust of romantic bombast, however guilty he himself may sometimes be of the latter. Thus in discussing the imagination's links to its own creations in "The Philosophy of Composition," Poe takes pains to distance himself from a Shakespearean "fine frenzy," from what he sees as the specious emphasis on "ecstatic intuition" (*Essays,* 14). But in some of his tales, at least, Poe seems more willing to entertain the notion of imagination impelled by something other than reason or calculation; and that something he often expresses by figures of intoxication, under whose influence the imagination's creations are perceived as real.

A fairly simple correspondence between the stimulated imagination and an intoxicant is mentioned in Poe's description of Bedloe in "A Tale of the Ragged Mountains": "His imagination was singularly vigorous and creative; and no doubt it derived additional force from the habitual use of morphine, which he swallowed in great quantity" (*Works*, 3:942). In the more famous "Ligeia," the importance of an opium-influenced imagination to perception or misperception far exceeds that in the tale of Mr. Bedloe. The narrator of "Ligeia," "a bounden slave in the trammels of opium" (*Works*, 2:320), is dominated by his opium dreams to the point that neither he nor his reader is sure just how far to trust his perceptions. The narrator repeatedly tells us of his uncertainty about what he perceives. At one point, three or four ruby-colored drops mysteriously fall into the goblet of wine given by the narrator to his second wife, Rowena. What are they? Perhaps laudanum, or the elixir vitae, or a corporeal distillation of Ligeia herself, or, as is possible in Poe, a combination of all three.[17] When these drops fall into Rowena's goblet, the narrator is not even sure how they got there, or if in fact he simply imagined them. After all, his imagination had been "rendered morbidly active by the terror of the lady, by the opium, and by the hour" (*Works*, 2:325). (The hour is, of course, a late one.)

Influential as opium is on the narrator's imagination and perceptions, we should not be too quick to reduce the entire tale to an opium-induced hallucination. Opium here is a device for enriching the tale's sense of delirium, for intensifying and *partially* explaining the warped world of the narrator. As T. O. Mabbott has wittily noted, the use of opium lets the "matter-of-fact reader" interpret "Ligeia" as a mere hallucination (*Works*, 2:308).

But such a superficial reading ignores the more suggestive functions of opium here, with its implications of a reality beyond that of everyday reason, its suggestions of a state of mind in which fantasy and sense experience meet in a hallucinatory, potentially dangerous blend. Opium is a key element in achieving this blend, not a broom with which to sweep aside the metaphysical, supernatural, or occult issues that, for all his well-known satirical treatments of such subjects, remained important to Poe. Though in "Ligeia," as elsewhere, Poe is quite literal about intoxication—the drug is really opium, not something for which opium is an allegorical stand-in—not one of his works is "about" opium, or wine, or alcoholism, in the sense that temperance tales or, on a higher artistic level, Stephen Crane's *George's Mother* or Charles Jackson's *The Lost Weekend* are about such issues.

Intoxicants in Poe are not symbols in any simplistic sense, but they are symbolically suggestive of that which lies beyond reason, and they are important to Poe in helping to convey a sense of the mysterious intersection of the natural and the supernatural. Opium in a tale like "Ligeia" is significant precisely because, in addition to providing Poe's much-loved overtones of decadence and derangement, it suggests an ambiguity about the nature of the experiences described. As so often in Poe, "Ligeia" pivots on the uncertainty of the narrator and characters as to the extent that events are affected by the supernatural or the merely natural.[18] "My dream, then, was not all a dream" (*Writings,* 1:72) says Pym after he awakes from his nightmare about the fearsome lion to find his dog, Tiger, pressing his paws upon his bosom.

Opium (or wine, or liquor—the specific intoxicant is not important) provides images that enable Poe to express this sense of the interpretation of different realms of reality.

Thus alcohol and drugs in Poe generally differ sharply in significance from, say, the use of drugs in a story like Arthur Conan Doyle's "The Adventure of the Creeping Man." In this tale, Sherlock Holmes cracks the secret of a professor whose use of drugs profoundly and degradingly alters his personality. But the issue of drugs in the Doyle story is a medical, purely physiological affair, quite free of the metaphysical ramifications of Poe's studies of identity or perception. (Holmes's own use of cocaine, of course, is a more complex issue, involving important elements of characterization and of Holmes's relation to Victorian society.) Thus just as Poe wrote that the terror in his works was "not of Germany, but of the soul" (*Works*, 2:473), so too we may say that the intoxication in his works is not of opium, but of the soul.

This spiritual dimension becomes evident even in so farcical a story as "The Angel of the Odd," in which accurate perception is paradoxically more akin to intoxication than to sobriety. The narrator, though drinking heavily in the opening scene, clings stubbornly to a worldview that rejects the fantastic, the "odd." Saturated with images of alcohol (down to the crow that, drunk on brandy-soaked corn, flies off with the narrator's trousers), the tale proceeds to debunk the unimaginativeness and "narrow rationalism of the speaker" (Gargano, 27). In "The Angel of the Odd," intoxication serves two basic functions: it shows the befuddlement of the pompous narrator, and it appears as an agent of the odd, the nonrational, the inexplicable. The tale is built up of paradoxical incidents involving playful reversals of expectations, including those about drunkenness and sobriety. The angel of the odd himself serves as a kind of comic cosmic bartender, constantly plying the poor narrator with liquor. Moreover, the angel consistently links a true perception of things, which requires the acknowledgment of the "odd," to intoxication. Yet the angel paradoxically characterizes the narrator's belated recognition of the power of the "odd" in life as an instance of particularly sober ("zober") perception.

In Poe's depictions of intoxication we can take nothing for granted. The conventional association of drink with muddled perception in a tale like "The Black Cat" gives way in "The Angel of the Odd" to the association of drunkenness with a higher sobriety, a humorous version of Philo's concept of "sobria ebrietas" (Philo, "On Drunkenness," 3:395–99). The maddening effect of liquor in *Pym* is balanced by more beneficent, nourishing effects in the same work; in "The Cask of Amontillado," the same drink that befuddles and weakens Fortunato only adds vigor to Montresor's diabolical fancies and strengthens his purpose; we have already noted similar complexities in "William Wilson" and "Hop-Frog."

Whatever Poe's feelings in everyday life about intoxication,

in his works we may detect a complex mingling of fear, amusement, repulsion, desire, and, above all, fascination. We may also
detect yet a deeper fascination with intoxication as an emblem
or paradigm of the transition from the world of mundane rationality (the "cool reason" of Shakespeare's Theseus) to a world
beyond—be it a hellish madness or a sublime, Edenic dream. In
his early poem "Al Aaraaf," the intersection with a heavenly
world can be "torturing" (the word is Poe's); the nectar-maddened
bee, counterpart of and contrast to the humble and drunken
bees of Emerson and Dickinson, respectively, is tortured "with
madness, and unwonted reverie" by the "honied dew" from
heaven (*Works,* 1:101). Nowhere in Poe is intoxication more
paradoxical or double-edged than it is here. And the price of the
"buoyancy of spirit attendant upon intoxication" in "Al Aaraaf,"
as Poe explains in one of his notes to the poem, is "final death
and annihilation" (*Works,* 1:112). Yet though it is associated with
death, intoxication in this poem (which Poe in his note ex-
pressly parallels with the state of passionate love) also gives a
taste, however torturing and maddening, of heaven, as the poor
bee knows all too well.

And perhaps herein lies the source for some of Poe's fascination with the imagery of drugs and drink: intoxication's traditional link with the imagination's power to transcend earthly
limits, whether for good or ill. In this regard, Poe's roots extend
back to the drunkenness offered by Dionysos. In Euripides' *Bacchae,* Dionysos's *pharmakon* means both "poison" and "cure"; in
so doing, the word unites the "destructive and beneficent poles
of the god's [Dionysos's] nature. Connected with medicine and
disease, *pharmakon* also links the theme of the Dionysiac joy to
the questions of sanity and madness" (Segal, *Dionysiac Poetics,*
309–10).[19]

As in the *Bacchae,* intoxication in Poe has many powers,
many meanings. It can poison or cure, distort or illuminate, provide the artificial stimulus to the imagination that Poe links with
profound knowledge in "A Chapter of Suggestions." And in the
tangled web of Poe's fictional intoxications, perhaps we may

also see something of the interplay of desire, fear, self-destruction, despair, and hope that we find in the following lines from Poe's "The Lake." The poem is not "about" intoxication as such, but it expresses something of the apocalyptic impulse that often lies behind intoxication in Poe's art and, perhaps, in his life.

> Death was in that poisonous wave,
> And in its gulf a fitting grave
> For him who thence could solace bring
> To his lone imagining—
> Whose solitary soul could make
> An Eden of that dim lake.
>
> (*Works*, 1:86)

# Chapter 5

# The Gentleman's Part

## Drinking and Moral Style in Cooper

There is a familiar and too much despised branch of
civilization, of which the population of this country
is singularly and unhappily ignorant; that of cook-
ery. The art of eating and drinking, is one of those on
which more depends perhaps than on any other,
since health, activity of mind, constitutional enjoyment, even learning, refinement, and to a certain degree, morals, are all, more or less, connected with
our diet.

—Cooper, *The American Democrat*

Drunkenness . . . is a practice of no slight importance,
and it requires no mean legislator to understand it.
—Plato, *Laws*

Now there can be too much of bodily goods, and the
bad man is bad by virtue of pursuing the excess, not
by virtue of pursuing the necessary pleasures (for *all*
men enjoy in some way or other both dainty foods
and wines and sexual intercourse, but not all men do
so as they ought).
—Aristotle, *Nichomachean Ethics*, bk. 7

Despite their many differences, Emerson, Dickinson, and Poe share certain basic perspectives on intoxication that coalesce into a major dimension of antebellum literature. Each of these writers emphasizes intoxication's links to heightened or distorted perception and consciousness, to the imagination, and to a pursuit of transcendent experience in which the boundaries between the divine and the demonic easily blur. Such concerns establish the kinship of these American writers not only to each other but also to European authors expressing a similar Dionysian awareness through the imagery of intoxicants, most notably Coleridge, De Quincey, Byron, Keats, Hoffmann, Novalis, Dostoevsky, Baudelaire, and Rimbaud.

For the major antebellum author to whom we now turn, however, intoxicant use is not as immediately obvious an issue as it is for the subjects of earlier chapters. Nevertheless, the varied cultural roles of intoxicants—in this case meaning exclusively alcohol—constitute a surprisingly substantial element in the work of James Fenimore Cooper. In contrast to both the temperance movement and the romantic Dionysianism we have already explored, Cooper espouses an ideal of vinous conviviality, connoisseurship, and what might be called "Pickwickian" or, in its rowdier variants, "Falstaffian" carousing and male camaraderie. Throughout his long career, Cooper engaged in a vigorous dialogue with attitudes toward temperance and drinking that were prevalent in his society. This dialogue centered on two basic areas of concern: the increasingly powerful American temperance movement and the distinction between various forms of "good" and "bad" drinking.

Upon temperance, especially in its more militantly ideological aspect, Cooper poured his disdain, condemning what he saw as hypocrisy and pietistic meddling. At the same time, Cooper produced fictional treatments of intoxication that can best be described as neither wet nor dry: work suggestive of a fellow traveler's uneasy ambivalence regarding temperance. As for the second concern, we find that "good" alcohol use primarily involves hearty (usually male) conviviality; enjoyment of liquor as an extension of nature's bounty; observance of festive traditions; and the skillful, moderate use of alcohol in a manner that represents a fusion of moral probity with gentlemanly epicureanism and good taste. On the negative side, as we might expect, we find alcoholism and drunkenness—problems that Cooper associates with a failure of skill, character, or taste, but also occasionally with external social pressure or circumstances. (Although Cooper is sensitive to the question of whether the drunkard is villain or victim, the notion of alcoholism as a disease is virtually invisible here.) Again on the negative side of drinking we see false conviviality (falseness here being determined by vulgarity or hypocritical, manipulative overtures) and escapism from life's challenges through liquor.

Writing in 1931, the Cooper biographer Henry Boynton claimed that his subject was "one of the few famous men of his century whom no contemporary ever saw drunk, or dreamed that he saw drunk, or even said that he saw drunk, in any place or on any occasion" (Boynton, 106). Boynton may well be exaggerating, but he aptly captures the essential sobriety—the stolidity, even—that characterizes so many of Cooper's heroes and narrative personae. Yet, as the Cooper epigraph to this chapter suggests, Cooper's interest in drinking was by no means reducible to that of a sobersides clucking disapprovingly over the divagations of the dissipated. From his very first, deservedly neglected novel, the pseudo-Jane Austenish *Precaution* (1820), through such superior works as *The Pioneers* (1823), *The Last of the Mohicans* (1826), and *Satanstoe* (1845), to his last, mordantly satirical novel, *The Ways of the Hour* (1850), drinkers, drunkenness, and the competing claims of temperance and conviviality play a prominent role in Cooper's fiction.

Cooper's attitudes to drink were formed early and retained their essential shape over time. In his later works, Cooper does tend toward a slightly darker view of drinking and becomes more responsive to the concerns of temperance, despite his continuing attacks on teetotalism. But an awareness of alcohol's potentially tragic effects was always present in Cooper; his later seriousness about the topic (relieved by occasional flashes of humor) indicates not the introduction of a new element but rather the intensification of a long-standing concern.

Blending morals with manners, Cooper's fiction consistently promulgates an ethicoaesthetic standard for drinking that may be termed a "moral style," whereby both the temperance movement (particularly in its more strident incarnations) and the evils of drunkenness are condemned as deviations from the middle path of true temperance, right measure, and gentlemanly good taste. Throughout his three-decade-long career, Cooper uses drinking style as an index to the moral and cultural evaluation of character and as a prism through which he can examine, analyze, and (as on so many other occasions) excoriate the contemporary American scene.

In general, Cooper describes drink, whether positively or negatively, in definite, unequivocal terms, often inserting pointed asides to his reader. But beneath the assured tone (which so often turns into pontification) one senses a sneaking ambivalence toward the topic of intoxication. It is as if Cooper is torn between two sets of oppositions: between the distastefulness of drunkenness and his fascination with it, on the one hand, and between his disapproval of alcohol's tragic consequences and his awareness of its comic potential, on the other. Although not always evident, this ambivalence emerges both in specific, individual instances and in a broader overview of intoxication in Cooper.

In examining drink in Cooper, I begin with drunkenness and alcoholism, then turn to the temperance movement and to drinking style, under which rubric I include the related issues of festivity, conviviality, and connoisseurship. Of these, the issue of alcoholic or heavy drinking is the most obvious. Indeed, the sheer number of heavy or problem drinkers in Cooper surpasses such characters in the work of any other writer dealt with in this book. Nor are all such characters negative or malign. In fact, Cooper often drew the comic, harmless drunk with a relish equaled only by Dickens or Twain. Already in his second novel, *The Spy* (set in the American revolutionary war), Cooper sympathetically presents the raucously comic drinking sponsored by Betty Flanagan, the Irish camp follower who sets up her "hotel" within easy access of the revolutionary troops, and whose delineation by Cooper received high praise as an example of Irish type drawing from Maria Edgeworth.[1]

Acting as a kind of American colonial Mistress Quickly, Betty Flanagan presides over an atmosphere of Falstaffian carousing indulgently described by Cooper.[2] Similar in spirit but slightly more refined and domestic in tone are the wonderfully comic potations in *The Pioneers* of that devotee of all things alcoholic, the aptly named Benjamin Pump. Benjamin's scene with the housemaid, Remarkable Pettibone, illustrates Cooper's talent for a kind of pre-Dickensian lowlife comedy, in which Benjamin and Remarkable spend a pleasant hour of drinking and flirting late on Christmas Eve. All begins well, with much amity and talk of drink's beneficent influences, until, well along in their cups, the two quarrel inanely, with Remarkable leaving in a huff and Benjamin falling sullenly but soundly asleep. Recalling Shakespeare's use of bibulous rustics for humorous effect (e.g., in *Twelfth Night* and *A Midsummer Night's Dream* as well as in the Falstaff plays), Cooper provides, in comic guise, a vivid exploration of the alcohol-influenced psyche, as the verboseness, camaraderie, exaggerated sociability, and equally exaggerated self-dignity apparent in Benjamin and Remarkable's tête-à-tête inevitably result in a ludicrous squabble.

Rarely has the notion of drink as a "*good* man's failing" been more obvious than in Cooper's treatment of Benjamin Pump. His drinking is clearly a flaw: Judge Temple, for example, must go about locking up his own house in the wee hours while his retainers and relatives, most noticeably Pump, snore away in a drunken stupor. But Pump's drinking becomes an almost endearing foible rather than a vice because of Cooper's humorous presentation and Pump's own irrepressible joie de vivre and more positive qualities of loyalty, gratitude, and generosity. These characteristics are especially apparent in Pump's offer to help reduce Natty's hundred-dollar fine after Natty has saved

Pump from drowning, and in his spontaneous gesture of getting into the stocks next to Natty to keep him company. "Comique sans être bouffon," as the great French Cooper scholar, Marcel Clavel has put it, Pump never degenerates into the trivial "lovable sot" stereotype popular in nineteenth-century drama but deserves inclusion with such richly drawn wine-loving worthies as Dickens's Mr. Micawber, whose amusing failings in no wise detract from their full humanity (Clavel, 376).

Continuing the comic-drunk motif begun in *The Pioneers,* in 1824 Cooper published *The Pilot,* considerable portions of which recount the drink-related misadventures of the veteran seamen Manual and Boroughcliffe. Comrades—and topers—in arms, these convivially drinking bachelors receive almost invariably light treatment from Cooper, although his humor takes on a darker coloring from the drink-related deaths of both men. The first to go is Manual, shot to death by a guard because he drunkenly forgets to give the correct military password. But just as we suspect that Cooper is about to deliver a quasi-temperance homily on the follies of drink, the text shifts to a tongue-in-cheek account of Manual's bereaved friend, Boroughcliffe, as he sets out to find a lost cask of Madeira wine ordered by Manual but now lost. The strains of Boroughcliffe's journey, his contraction of a fever, his stubborn refusal to obey his doctor's injunctions against drinking, and his resultant death are the perfect ingredients for a classic temperance tale. But Cooper treats the entire situation with a lightness of tone and comic absurdity that keep us from either lamenting the death or questioning too seriously the dangers of drink.

Even in later novels, where Cooper generally becomes more somber about drinking, his old fondness for the light touch regarding liquor shines through. Examples include the harmless inebriety of Harris, the young man in *Satanstoe* who drunkenly plays the role of Martha in Addison's *Cato;* the comic stereotype of the eloquent drunken Irishman Mike in *Wyandotté;* and the labored joke about some gullible, liquor-loving Indians being led to believe that a brook into which whiskey has been spilled is actually a natural alcohol spring in the late novel, *The Oak-Openings.*

Interspersed with these comic figures are a great number of more serious, though undeveloped, examples of alcoholic or drunken characters. Some of these Cooper views with complete disgust, like the virtually subhuman alcoholic informer in *The Prairie,* who literally dies in the gutter. But more often Cooper views the drunkard not as villain but as weak-willed victim of his own appetites. Thomas Davis, for instance, the hapless alcoholic gardener in Cooper's first novel, *Precaution,* receives the stern but sympathetic attention of John Denbigh (Cooper's apparent spokesman in the novel). Although disapproving of his drinking, the virtuous, upper-class Denbigh aids Davis and delivers the first in that long line of somber, unintentionally pompous speeches that Cooper's gentlemen read to their inferiors. In his self-congratulatory condescension, Denbigh ends up sounding like an unintentional male parody of Austen's Lady Catherine de Bourgh.

But in spite of this, Denbigh's (and Cooper's) censure is considerably tempered by sympathy, an attitude that is even more apparent in the cases of the drunkard known as Baiting Joe in *The Sea Lions* and the pathetic Mr. Monday in *Homeward Bound.* Baiting Joe is a character of unrelieved wretchedness, whose poverty and suffering make any reaction other than pity impossible. In contrast, the alcoholic Mr. Monday begins as a vaguely comic drunk, as seen in his inconsistency, fecklessness, and stout denial of the obvious, namely, that he drinks too much and gets drunk easily. But Monday gains a measure of tragic dignity as he lies dying, tearfully remembering his mother in a sentimental but credible situation, regretting his "weakness," and summoning up what is left of his depleted psychic reserves to face death calmly if fearfully. Much more focused and substantive than these instances, however, are Cooper's depictions of North American Indian drinking in three important novels—*The Pioneers, Wyandotté,* and *The Last of the Mohicans*—and his extended treatment of Gershom Waring's alcoholism in *The Oak-Openings.*

Of Cooper's Indians, Kay S. House has written, "almost everyone knew, in the first half of the nineteenth century, that small-pox and whiskey were lethal to the Indian; hence both became for Cooper convenient symbols of civilization's silent and corroding destruction of native beauty" (House, 251–52). This notion has, of course, informed many a statement on Indian-white relations. In 1673, Increase Mather inveighed against those who corrupted Indians with liquor. Later, and with characteristically eloquent indignation, Margaret Fuller made the following complaint about white traders and trappers: "Worst of all is it when they invoke the holy power only to mask their iniquity; when the felon trader, who all the week has been besotting and degrading the Indian with rum mixed with red pepper and damaged tobacco, kneels with him on Sunday before a common altar." Among Native Americans, the theme of alcoholic corruption brought by whites has been long widespread, receiving particularly moving expression, in 1805, in an address by the Seneca chief Red Jacket: "We took pity on white men, . . . gave them corn and meat; they gave us poison [rum] in return."[3]

Of Cooper's Indian drinkers, the most pathetic—and sympathetic—is the famous Chingachgook (John Mohegan). When we first meet him in *The Pioneers* (first of the Leatherstocking novels in composition but fourth in chronology), Chingachgook has become the sodden ruin of a once magnificent human being. Like Magua in *The Last of the Mohicans,* whom, as Jane Tompkins points out, whiskey deprives of his identity as a chief, as a Huron, and as a man, the more benign Chingachgook laments his decay through the agency of the white man's firewater.[4]

In the famous scene of the turkey shoot, Chingachgook's pathos gains greater intensity from the fact that, as he speaks, he is too hung over even to participate in the event at which he once excelled. Holding out his trembling hands, Chingachgook says, "See . . . they shake like a deer at the wolf's howl. Is John old? When was a Mohican a squaw, with seventy winters! No! the white man brings old age with him—rum is his tomahawk!"[5] This last phrase encapsulates an entire dimension of North American Indian tragedy, for rum, like whiskey, was in fact consciously used as a weapon in the European domination of Native Americans.[6] Indeed, Chingachgook voices in more graphic and more appropriately violent terms ("tomahawk") the same concept expressed by Benjamin Franklin in a more "civilized" circumlocution: "And, indeed, if it be the design of Providence to extirpate these savages in order to make room for the cultivators of the earth, it seems not improbable that rum may be the appointed means" (Franklin, *Works*, 1:244).[7]

When asked why he uses liquor, since it turns him into a "beast,"[8] Chingachgook replies in a manner striking both for its emotional power and for a stylistic verve unusual in Cooper. The old Indian's words, redolent of bitter self-recognition, self-reproach, and self-justification, begin interrogatively, grow in a steady crescendo of impotent indignation, and close, almost musically, with an echo of and bitterly ironic variation on Chingachgook's opening phrase. The pattern becomes clear if we quote the statement in full:

> "Beast! is John a beast?" replied the Indian, slowly; "yes; you say no lie, child of the Fire-eater! John is a beast. The smokes were once few in these hills. The deer would lick the hand of a white man, and the birds rest on his head. They were strangers to him. My fathers came from the shores of the salt lake. They fled before rum. They came to their grandfather, and they lived in peace; or when they did raise the hatchet, it was to strike it into the brain of a Mingo. They gathered around the council-fire, and what they said was done. Then John was the man. But warriors and traders with light eyes followed them. One brought the long knife, and one brought rum. They were more than the pines of the mountains; and they broke up the councils, and took the lands. The evil spirit was in their jugs, and they let him loose. — Yes, yes—you say no lie, Young Eagle. John is a Christian beast."
> (19:202)

The repetition of the paragraph's first words at its conclusion give Chingachgook's utterance a symmetry, formality, and self-contained coherence. Then, with a smoothness for which he is not usually known, Cooper adroitly continues the theme of Chingachgook's remarks in a verbal cadenza that, while growing directly out of the earlier dialogue, leads to a note of definite closure on the subject of Chingachgook's drinking. Here is how Cooper achieves his transition from Chingachgook's speech back to the larger group of characters before whom Chingachgook and "Young Eagle" (in reality, the young Oliver Effingham) have had their dialogue: "'Forgive me, old warrior,'" cried the youth, grasping his hand. 'I should be the last to reproach you. The curses of Heaven light on the cupidity that has destroyed such a race. Remember, John, that I am of your family, and it is now my greatest pride'" (19:202). Bitter but calm and resigned, Chingachgook gently replies, "You are a Delaware, my son; your words are not heard," and concludes with the simple statement, rich in pathos in light of the foregoing conversation and all the more affecting for its brevity, "John cannot shoot" (19:203).

Before we leave this scene, it is worth dwelling on the full irony of the emotional climax of Chingachgook's comments, occurring at the words "John is a Christian beast." The statement's irony emerges in its contrast to Oliver Effingham's disparaging reference to Chingachgook as a "beast" and to Chingachgook's echo of that very term in the opening words of his reply: "Beast! is John a beast?" As Chingachgook approaches the end of his statement, he achieves a greater understanding of his situation as he attempts to explain it, as much to himself as to Effingham; his tragedy is illuminated by the paradoxical conjunction of two seemingly incompatible terms—"Christian" and "beast." But it is his very Christianization—understood broadly as the exposure to "Christian" (i.e., European) culture—that has ruined Chingachgook.

Cooper's own perspective, of course, is emphatically Christian and European, as he unapologetically and repeatedly makes clear. But Cooper is also sufficiently honest and insightful to recognize that in Native American experience, the supposed benefits of Christian civilization came not merely accompanied by but inextricably fused with elements of genocidal destruction. "Civilization or death to all American Savages," proclaimed the Fourth of July toast made by officers in Sullivan's expedition in

1779, a decade before Cooper's birth (quoted in Pearce, 53). As Chingachgook implies, and as U.S. history has all too abundantly demonstrated, the Europeanization of America brought civilization *and* death to the "American Savages."

Cooper does not, however, follow up on the implications of this view for his own culture—probably because it could only lead to a repudiation of the entire imperialistic agenda of the United States' westward thrust. But modern readers can at least give Cooper his due in recognizing his willingness to acknowledge the bitter ironies of that thrust, as with Chingachgook here, or, most famously, with Natty, who serves as pathfinder for the very civilization whose onward march will make his (and Chingachgook's) way of life impossible.

The alcohol-induced fragmentation of personal and racial identity that is so evident in Chingachgook and Magua appears vividly in the later novel *Wyandotté* (1843), the eponymous protagonist of which is an alcoholic Tuscarora whose condition as a wretched outcast results less from "base meanness" than from "the excess of ungovernable passions" (32:47). First shown scrounging pitifully for drink, Wyandotté, like Chingachgook, has two names—the native Wyandotté and the Europeanized name Saucy or Sassy Nick. Like Magua, Wyandotté has been whipped by his white master, but unlike the earlier Indian, Wyandotté feels no dishonor in a remarkable instance of split identity. "Saucy Nick" is a drunken, groveling, passive-aggressive wretch. Wyandotté is his other self, submerged beneath layers of drink but still strong enough to rise to the surface and displace Saucy Nick, the product of Wyandotté's degradation. It is this quality in Wyandotté that so strongly interested Poe, whose own work, of course, abounds with similar themes.

In a generally favorable review of *Wyandotté,* Poe remarked on the protagonist's "keen sense of the distinction, in his own character, between the chief Wyandotté, and the drunken vagabond, Sassy Nick."[9] As Wyandotté himself explains to Captain Willoughby, "No man—pale face, or red skin, can give blow on back of Wyandotté, and see sun set!" Wyandotté dismisses his earlier whipping by saying, "Dat happen to Nick—Sassy Nick—poor, drunken Nick—to Wyandotté, nebber!" (32:344). Wyandotté's attitude seems to possess greater complexity and psychological validity than would the mere rationalization of a humiliating experience. Unfortunately, however, the "keen distinction," as Poe calls it, between Wyandotté's alcoholic and nonalcoholic selves is never developed beyond the level of intriguing but vague implications about liquor's role in the fragmentation of individual identity. Exploring such implications is, of course, far more the province of Hawthorne and Melville, to whom we turn in subsequent chapters, or of Poe himself, than it is of the less introspective Cooper.

The alcoholism of Chingachgook, Magua, and Wyandotté alike is inextricably connected to their racial identity. Without defining that connection, Cooper nonetheless points it out and presents various attitudes toward it, ranging from Natty's generalization in *The Pioneers* about "savages" invariably making "dogs of themselves" through liquor (19:181) to Magua's bitter denunciations of the white man's firewater to Wyandotté's and Chingachgook's subtler, more complicated views of the matter. Cooper's most extensive fictional treatment of alcoholism, however, deals with a white man, Gershom Waring, in whose drinking problems race is not a significant factor. [10]

*The Oak-Openings* is an important novel for a number of reasons. Yvor Winters remarked that as "a story of simple adventure, it is one of Cooper's best," while Leslie Fiedler has called this late novel, published in 1848, Cooper's "pious last testament" (although much the same could be said of his final fiction, *The Ways of the Hour*) (Winters, 193; Fiedler, *Love and Death,* 198). For our purposes here, *The Oak-Openings* is important also because it contains much of Cooper's most representative thinking on alcohol-related problems. These problems, in fact, take up much of the first third to one-half of the novel, especially in connection with the drinking of Gershom Waring, also known as "Whiskey Centre."

Befriended by the intelligent, intrepid, and sober bee hunter,

le Bourdon—a cross between Natty Bumppo and Cooper's aristocratic heroes—Gershom Waring fits in with the model of
drunkard as immoderate lover of liquor rather than as addict
torn between will and desire. The only solution to this problem,
Cooper implies, is to "make up your mind, like a man, and vow
you'll never touch another drop" (16:72), as le Bourdon piously
advises Gershom to do.

In part, le Bourdon's advice reflects one side of a controversy
current in Cooper's time: whether the drunkard should give up
alcohol at once, as urged by most temperance supporters, or
taper off gradually, as advocated by other observers, such as the
eminent Scottish surgeon Robert Macnish.[11] In an unusual parallel to the temperance movement and in anticipation of Alcoholics Anonymous, Cooper urges the view here that complete
abstinence is the only dependable cure for alcoholism. Cooper
has le Bourdon say of Gershom, "One is never sure of a man of
such habits, until he is placed entirely out of harm's way" (16:83).
It is because of this fear that le Bourdon insists to Gershom's
sister, Blossom (whom le Bourdon eventually marries), that all
liquor in the Waring household be destroyed: when Blossom
thanks the bee hunter for his protection from an Indian attack,
he replies, "That danger is over now, Blossom, but there is still an
enemy here, in your cabin, that must be looked to." Asked by a
puzzled Blossom to identify this enemy, le Bourdon replies, "His
name is Whiskey, and he is kept somewhere in this hut, in casks.
Show me the place, that I may destroy him," as in fact le Bourdon, with Blossom's help, proceeds to do (16:78).

But when le Bourdon urges Gershom to be "a man" and forsake liquor, he also reflects the notion, already old-fashioned in
some quarters in Cooper's day, that Jonathan Edwards expressed
in *Freedom and Will:* a drunkard drinks because he loves to. For
Edwards, there is no real division between will and desire. As the
sociologist of drink Harry Gene Levine has pointed out in an important essay, "Edwards rejected the idea that the drunkard can
be compelled by appetite or desire to do something against his
will." In Edwards's own words, "It cannot be truly said, accord-

ing to the ordinary use of language, that a malicious man, let him be never so malicious, cannot hold his hand from striking, or that he is not able to show his neighbor kindness; or that a drunkard, let his appetite be never so strong, cannot keep the cup from his mouth." In contrast, the disease theory of alcoholism maintains the exact opposite, most notably, of course, in the relatively recent movement, Alcoholics Anonymous.[12]

Old-fashioned as he may be on the issue of a drunkard's will and desire, Cooper is ahead of his time in recognizing the importance of what we now call the "enabler"—a friend or relative of the drinker who tolerates the latter's intoxication and even finds excuses for it. Such is Gershom Waring's wife, Dolly. Defending her husband's drinking, Dolly explains, "Gershom is so troubled with the ague, if he don't take stimulant in this new country" (16:92). She speaks, moreover, "in the apologetic manner in which woman struggles to conceal the failings of him she loves" (16:92) and answers le Bourdon's reproaches about Gershom's drinking and his plans to sell whiskey by saying, "As for the whiskey, I don't grudge *that* in the least; for it's a poor way of getting rich to be selling it to soldiers, who want all the reason liquor has left 'em, and more too. Still, Gershom needs bitters; and ought not to have every drop he has taken thrown into his face" (16:92–93). The reader may well concur with Dolly at this point, after le Bourdon's tireless (and tiresome) comments about how much better off Gershom is without the liquor that he had disposed of earlier, as well as his sardonic jabs at Gershom for sampling the liquor he was planning to sell. Dolly's comments, though transparent rationalizations of her husband's drinking, nonetheless help to place that drinking in a context of greater moral complexity than would have been the case without them, and to present that drinking not merely in terms of le Bourdon's criticisms but from the more intimately sympathetic vantage of a pained, embarrassed, but finally loyal and loving mate.

Dolly is also adept at covering for Gershom's drunkenness with the kind of euphemisms and circumlocutions that seem always to have abounded for the intoxicated state. When Blossom asks Dolly to tell her where Gershom is, for example, Dolly replies, "Gershom is not himself, just now.... [H]e has fallen into one of his old ways, ag'in" (16:111). Cooper here echoes, down to the syntax (forgetfulness on the author's part?), his earlier description (p. 92) of Dolly's attempts to hide Gershom's drinking: she spoke, we are told, in a "low voice, and in that sort of manner with which woman struggles to the last to conceal the delinquencies of him she loves" (16:111).

Cooper's sympathetic awareness of Dolly's perspective, however flawed that perspective may be, clearly tempers the severity of his condemnation of Gershom's alcoholism. A similar purpose is served by Cooper's occasional comic touches, for example, Gershom's amusingly blithe rationalizations of his drinking; his obliging agreement with le Bourdon to forsake whiskey completely, but only after "these two barrels is emptied" (16:72); le Bourdon's tricking some Indians into searching for a whiskey-flowing spring. On the whole, however, the portrait of drink here is a largely dark one. Despite his amusing joviality, Gershom never fully emerges from a life of squalor and irresponsibility; near the book's end, after a brief bout with sobriety, Gershom returns to "his old habits" and dies (16:491).

It may well be that Cooper, writing this novel in the late 1840s, as the nation moved steadily toward the Maine Laws, was viewing an earlier time's heavy drinking through the lens of his own period's increasingly antidrink attitudes. Although by 1848, when *The Oak-Openings* appeared, the temperance movement was rapidly becoming associated with and controlled by the middle classes, with strong infusions of populist sentiment, the earlier nineteenth-century movement of Lyman Beecher and others reflected elite Federalist ideals and upper-class concerns with the rights of property owners.[13] Cooper, of course, was no Federalist, but he was the son of a judge who supported Federalist positions, and, as is well known, he remained a staunch, even obsessive, upholder of property rights throughout his life. Thus the conservative Cooper may well have found some appeal

in the earlier, more property-conscious, aristocratically controlled temperance movement. He may even have absorbed
later temperance influence (no real evidence exists to point us in
this or an opposing direction), despite his constantly proclaim-
ing unrelenting resistance to the official temperance movement.

That resistance was both theoretical and personal. Theoreti-
cally, Cooper opposed what he saw as the puritanistic extremism
and rigidity of temperance in its increasingly teetotal mode. In
more personal terms, Cooper launched unabashedly ad hominem
sallies against the supposed hypocrisy, fanaticism, and uncouthness of temperance supporters. *The Oak-Openings,* which we
have already discussed in relation to drunkenness, is also useful
for understanding the role of temperance in Cooper's work.

However critical of drink Cooper may be in *The Oak-Openings,* he avoids the more extreme positions holding sway in temperance circles. He criticizes the drunkard, Whiskey Centre, not
by contrasting him with some impossibly pure angel of abstinence, but with the temperate though not teetotaling le Bourdon. The absence of extremism in le Bourdon makes him, in
fact, more acceptable to and thus more influential with Gershom (Whiskey Centre). In a pointed comment on teetotalism,
Gershom explains to le Bourdon that one of the reasons he has
"taken so mightily" to the bee hunter is that, although "you're
not much at a pull . . . you an't downright afeard of a jug, neither" (16:58).

Gershom's statement provides Cooper with a natural oppor-
tunity for airing his own attitudes on the more extreme aspects
of temperance ideology taking hold in the 1840s. Lamenting
fanaticism "in politics, in religion, in temperance, in virtue,"
Cooper notes that, in "these days of exaggeration," the one little
jug of brandy le Bourdon does carry on his wanderings "might
have sufficed to give him a bad name; but five-and-thirty years
ago [i.e., in about 1813], men had more real independence than
they now possess, and were not as much afraid of that *croquemitaine,* public opinion, as they are today" (16:60). Cooper's
criticism of "exaggeration" here typifies an attitude toward tem-

perance that we may find elsewhere in his work as well and that can be summarized as the view that drink, as Increase Mather called it, is a "good Creature of God" capable of being used or abused, and that organized, dogmatic temperance, which translates into militant teetotalism, is itself a form of intemperance.

In his preface to *The Pilot,* a novel that we have already discussed in relation to its heavy-drinking characters, Cooper, in an unexpected parallel to Walt Whitman, cites temperance as a misguided attempt to legislate morality, and in *The Sea Lions* (1849), he specifically refers to teetotalism's "*intemperate* cry [my italics] which makes it a sin to partake of any liquor, however prudently" (25:68).[14] In *The Crater* (1847), Cooper uses the occasion of Mark Woolston's recovery—effected largely by the judicious use of wine—to attack the abstinent position, as he writes, "It has been much the fashion, of late years, to decry wine, and this because it is a gift of Providence that has been greatly abused. In Mark Woolston's instance it proved, what it was designed to be, a blessing instead of a curse" (4:145). Significantly, in the same novel Cooper depicts a very different kind of drinker from the moderate Woolston, the frequently drunken and hence unreliable Captain Crutchely. Thus Cooper carefully demonstrates his willingness to condemn the *abuse* of alcohol and also to distinguish such abuse from its proper, moderate *use.*

As if compressing a lifetime's thoughts, experiences, and, admittedly, prejudices, Cooper's final novel, *The Ways of the Hour* (1850), provides his most inclusive, precise assessment of temperance: "Among the liberal, cards, dancing, music, all games of skill and chance that can interest the cultivated, and drinking, in moderation and of suitable liquors, convey no ideas of wrong doing." But, Cooper continues, "an exaggerated morality . . . has the temerity to enlarge the circle of sin beyond the bounds for which it can find any other warranty than its own metaphysical inferences" (29:381–82).

Cooper's last novel also contains salient examples of two other major aspects of its author's objections to temperance— what Cooper sees as the vulgarity and hypocritical sanctimoniousness of its supporters. These examples center on the shrewd but morally obtuse, uncouth country lawyer, Timms. Speaking with the older, more sophisticated Dunscomb—a thinly disguised fictional representative of Cooper's own views—Timms inadvertently reveals the hypocrisy of his involvement with temperance when he corrects Dunscomb's impression that he had begun his career as a temperance lecturer: "I began with the Common Schools, on which I lectured with some success, one whole season. *Then* came the temperance cause, out of which I will own, not a little capital was made" (29:187).

As with Twain's Duke and King from *The Adventures of Huckleberry Finn,* for whom "missionaryin' around" and running temperance revivals are but variations on the same fraudulent theme, reform for Timms is a largely commercial affair. In fact, he goes on to describe to Dunscomb the relative popularity and moneymaking potential of other activities, Cooper thereby suggesting that Timms's interest in temperance was purely mercenary. This implication is heightened by Timms's obvious lack of temperance principles, evident in his eager drinking of Dunscomb's fine Madeira and in his equally eager guzzling of cheap liquor later at Horton's Inn.

Though more likable than Timms, the opportunistic Yankee sailor, Ithuel Bolt, from *The-Wing-and-Wing* (1842), also seems mercenary in his relation to temperance. His conversion to the dry cause at the end of the novel ironically contrasts with his wine-loving character earlier in the book, especially when we first meet him, bawling "Vino!" at the top of his lungs in an Italian tavern (31:61). But more flagrantly hypocritical, if less obviously concerned with temperance for financial reasons, are Jason Newcome from *Satanstoe* (1845) and Steadfast Dodge from *Homeward Bound* and *Home as Found* (1838).

Castigating those who drink or engage in the most innocuous amusements, such as rope jumping, in *Homeward Bound* Dodge suggests organizing a temperance society on board ship for, significantly, the *steerage* passengers only—a fine instance of Cooper's scorn for the plebeian as snob. Yet Dodge's temperance statements are obviously hollow, as shown in his own fondness for tippling that increasingly emerges in his speech and behavior during the ship voyage in *Homeward Bound.* Similarly, in *Satanstoe* the temperance supporter Jason Newcome greedily solicits what he believes will be a spicy strong drink from a street vendor, only to spit out in disgust what is actually a mild white wine, much to the amusement of the novel's protagonist, Cornelius Littlepage.

Repeatedly, Cooper associates the temperance movement with the hypocrisy and venality of such characters—and with their vulgarity. For it is as much a moral as an aesthetic flaw in such characters that they exhibit not only coarseness but a kind of smug, "know-nothing-and-proud-of-it" mentality, yoked to social climbing and pretentiousness. Such characters are, in effect, homegrown varieties of that virtually untranslatable Russian concept, *poshlust,* which D. S. Mirsky renders as " 'self-satisfied inferiority', moral and spiritual," and which is loosely comparable to the English term "philistinism" (Mirsky, 160).[15] In *The-Wing-and-Wing,* the sailor Ithuel Bolt amusingly exemplifies this quality when, as a proud New Hampshire man discussing religion with a group of cultivated, devout Italian Catholics, he declares, "Now, I do wish you could see a Sunday once in the Granite state, Signorina Ghita" (31:163).

As his most famous character, Natty Bumppo, demonstrates, Cooper was capable of viewing lower-class or uneducated people with sympathy, respect, and admiration. But the moral indignation that Cooper obviously feels for the Newcomes, Dodges, and, presumably, the two-faced "goodies," to use Emerson's term, that he saw around him in his society entangled itself with his deeply ingrained elitism. The result is Cooper's use of homely accents, awkward, clichéd speech, and obvious uncouthness of manner as weapons in his attack on temperance, even though the same traits could, when it pleased him, amount to no more than the sometimes amusing or even endearing foibles of other characters, for example, Natty himself, Benjamin Pump, Betty

Flanagan, and some of Cooper's positive Indians. As far as the temperance movement was concerned, its moral positions—which Cooper saw as wrongheaded at best, repressive and petty at worst—seem to have become for Cooper indistinguishable from its other great flaw in his eyes: vulgarity. Thus the same qualities that with a Natty Bumppo or Benjamin Pump might occasion the author's condescending smile, with temperance hypocrites provoke a bitter sneer behind which lies a much deeper, more encompassing frustration over America's deplorable taste and worsening cultural situation.

In this regard it is instructive to compare the very different responses of Cooper and Whitman to the same phenomenon—the increasing links between temperance and the middle and lower-middle classes in antebellum America. As historians of temperance have shown, the early association of temperance with social elites worried about property rights and voting power quickly gave way to middle-class dominance of temperance. "While the urban poor, increasing numbers of whom were immigrants, never responded to anti-liquor appeals and the rich were only marginally involved in the crusade, the middle class—the skilled mechanics and tradesmen—represented the solid force" (Aaron and Musto, 141–42).

Accompanying this middle-class control of temperance was the greater sensationalism and intentionally ungenteel proselytizing of the Washingtonian Temperance Society, organized in 1840, and of such popular, flamboyant temperance lecturers—performers might be a more apt term—as John B. Gough. In contrast to Cooper's fiction, Whitman's temperance novel, *Franklin Evans; or, The Inebriate* (1842), candidly embraces the very qualities from which Cooper so disdainfully recoils. "It seems to me," writes Whitman, "that he who would speak of the efforts of the Temperance Societies with a sneer, is possessed of a very heedless and bigoted, or a very wicked disposition. It is true, that the dictates of a classic and most refined taste, are not always observed by these people; and the fashionable fop, the exquisite, or the pink of what is termed 'quality', might feel not at home among them." But, Whitman continues, the reformers' sincerity and convictions, based on personal experience, make up "for any want of polish, or grace" (in Whitman, *Early Poems and Fiction,* 237).

It is impossible not to see in this disjunction the influence of each author's background. Whitman, with his modest beginnings, odd jobs, and uncertain prospects, as well as his family difficulties (including an alcoholic brother and prostitute sister-in-law), was obviously much closer than Cooper to the socioeconomic realities that such groups as the Washingtonians frequently addressed—and to the common, man-in-the-street tone in which they addressed them. For Cooper, however, it was not simply his wealth and privilege that made the Washingtonians and all they represented alien to him. It was also a deep personal attraction—ultimately inseparable from his wealth and privilege, of course—to an older, stabler, more hierarchical way of life to which he was tied by upbringing, by temperament, and by age, having been born exactly three decades before Whitman. That way of life, at least in theory, was one of noblesse oblige, of easy but well-defined commerce between master and man, with liquor serving as an uncontroversial social and economic lubricant, a phenomenon invested with cheerfulness rather than dissolution. These qualities, described by Paul Johnson, are also implicit in the following remark by Cooper's father, Judge William Cooper: "A few quarts of liquor cheerfully bestowed, will open a road or build a bridge, which would cost if done by contract, hundreds of dollars."[16] Such was the world into which Cooper was born, which evaporated during his maturation and which he nostalgically looked back to in his fiction.

In addition to the points he scores at temperance's expense through characterization, dialogue, and plot, Cooper implicitly distinguishes the social backwardness of temperance from the more sophisticated, morally refined style that is often associated in his work with people who, whether young (like Cornelius Littlepage) or old (like Dunscomb), embody the ideals and values of the earlier world of Cooper's childhood. Toward the end of *The Ways of the Hour,* in a chapter devoted to the drinking establishment known as Horton's Inn, which will be discussed in more detail later, Cooper writes, "Nothing sooner indicates the school in which a man has been educated, than his modes of seeking amusement. One who has been accustomed to see innocent relaxations innocently indulged, from childhood up, is rarely tempted to abuse those habits which have never been associated, in his mind, with notions of guilt, and which, in themselves, necessarily imply no moral delinquency" (29:381).

In contrast, "exaggerated morality" (in Cooper's context undoubtedly a reference to teetotalism) produces "a factitious conscience, that almost invariably takes refuge in that vilest of all delinquency—direct hypocrisy. This, we take it, is the reason that the reaction of ultra godliness so generally leaves its subjects in the mire and sloughs of deception and degradation" (29:382). Referring more specifically to the various kinds of drinking that take place in Horton's Inn, Cooper writes that "the very same acts assume different characters, in the hands of these two classes of persons; and that which is perfectly innocent with the first . . . becomes low, vicious, and dangerous with the other, because tainted with the corrupting and most dangerous practices of deception" (29:382).

It is clear from the foregoing that for Cooper the "how" of drinking depends not only on "what" is drunk but also very much on "who" is doing the drinking. It is also clear that Cooper's moral perspective on drinking becomes as much a matter of *aesthetic* sensibility as of *ethical* probity. For Cooper, then, beauty *is* truth—not in a Keatsian sense, to be sure, but in a sense that accords with Cooper's long-standing dedication to the moral dimension of style.

Style—in the sense of both general manner and particular manners—is central not just to Cooper's evaluations of temperance but to his understanding of abusive and nonabusive drinking alike. Cooper could recognize that some—the fictional Gershom Waring, for instance, or the historical Ned Myers (the old shipmate whose life story Cooper transcribed)—are constitutionally or psychologically incapable of "moderate" drinking; their condition requires them to avoid alcohol completely. But more often for Cooper alcohol abuse manifests itself as a basic ineptitude in the art of drinking. Cooper's emphasis on skilled or successful alcohol consumption testifies to his belief that alcohol, though potentially dangerous, is not in itself evil, a position aligning him with those like Increase Mather who viewed drink as a "good Creature of God," rather than with those who, like the prominent temperance leader Ralph Grindrod, believed that alcohol was inherently evil.[17] Denying in *The Heidenmauer* (1832) that "dram-drinking" is a peculiarly American, and hence peculiarly "democratic vice," Cooper maintains that "it is the misfortune of man to abuse the gifts of God, let him live in what country or under what institutions he may" (7:124, 127).

The "temperance question is that of no use," Emerson observed (*JMN,* 5:440). For Cooper, the question is that of *proper* use, which generally involves convivial drinking in small groups of two or three; larger, more expansive festive celebrations; and, on the highest level, a connoisseurship that blends moderation, moral self-control, and a discerning taste in fine beverages, that is, in things that are nothing less than what, as we have just seen, Cooper calls "the gifts of God."

Even when convivial souls occasionally exceed the bounds of sobriety, as Benjamin Pump does in *The Pioneers,* Cooper is indulgent with those who, like Colonel Van Valkenburgh in *Satanstoe,* love to "have a frolic" involving "large consumption of tobacco, beer, cider, wine, rum, lemons, sugar, and the other ingredients of punch, toddy, and flip" but who commit "no outrageously durable excesses" (24:289). But there is, to be sure, no Rabelaisianism in Cooper. Even where one might most expect it, in the detailed description of a bacchanalian festival procession in *The Headsman of Berne* (1833), one finds no sense of the carnivalesque spirit that Mikhail Bakhtin has so influentially celebrated in Rabelais. Standing in the lofty tower of his own ethicoaesthetic certitude, Cooper gazes as if through a telescope down at the festival known as the Abbaye des Vignerons, paus-

ing now and then to note with disapproval the crude antics of
the "vulgar devotees of Bacchus" whom he describes (6:258). Although the phrase "vulgar devotees" specifically refers to a
group of drunken prisoners rudely commenting on the festival
they observe from their cell window, Cooper's attitude here extends to the rest of his description of the intoxicated cavortings
of the European hoi polloi.

On a far superior level is the drinking Cooper most admires,
and which appears in several related forms in a number of
Cooper novels, especially *Homeward Bound* and *Home as Found,
Afloat and Ashore, Satanstoe, The Redskins,* and *The Ways of the
Hour.* In the first pair of novels just mentioned, it is Captain Truck
who epitomizes Cooper's ideal of moral style and conviviality.
An exuberant, enthusiastic drinker, Truck tempers his Falstaffi-
anism with a discipline that sets him apart from such likable but
irresponsible drinkers as the hapless Manual and Boroughcliffe
in *The Pilot,* or Captain Crutchely in *The Crater,* whose fondness
for the bottle endangers his ship. Truck knows when to refrain,
as well as when to indulge, which he does most delightfully not
in the rather formal drinking passages in *Homeward Bound* but
in the scenes in *Home as Found* where he and the Commodore
blend amiable conversation and generous tippling with good-
natured barbs at the expense of temperance. The first of these
scenes occurs in chapter 19, the epigraph to which (9:314), from
Shakespeare's 1 *Henry IV,* sets up the Falstaffian mood:

> Item, a capon, 2s. 2d.
> Item, sauce, 4d.
> Item, sack two gallons, 5s. 8d.
> Item, bread, a half-penny.

Toying with temperance earnestness, Cooper has Truck and
the Commodore mirthfully murder logic as they discuss temperance while fishing, smoking cigars, and drinking punch. At
one point the Commodore asks, "If liquor is not made to be
drunk, for what is it made[?] . . . [H]ere is liquor distilled, bottled,
and corked, and I ask if all does not show that it was made to be

drunk. I dare say your temperance men are ingenious, but let them answer that if they can" (9:326). Truck's response, while uttered in the same jovial tone, subtly raises the level of the conversation as his discourse encompasses the loveliness and harmony of nature, within which harmony Truck and the Commodore cement their own friendship with, appropriately, a drink. "Commodore," says Captain Truck, touched by their amity and like-mindedness on various issues (of which temperance is one), "I wish you twenty more good hearty years of fishing in this lake, which grows, each instant, more beautiful in my eyes, as I confess does the whole earth; and to show you that I say no more than I think, I will clinch it with a draught" (9:327). The two men's "agreeable hallucinations on the subject of temperance," as Cooper calls them (9:327), come to an end with Truck's toast, but the two share yet another moment of conviviality near the novel's end where, as their drinking increases, Cooper, with affectionate irony, draws the curtain on the scene: "Here the two worthies 'freshened the nip', as Captain Truck called it, and then the conversation soon got to be too philosophical and contemplative for this unpretending record of events and ideas" (9:484).

In both of these scenes, as throughout both novels, Captain Truck understands well the crucial distinction between work and play, or—to use the metaphor that Gusfield applies to drinking attitudes in American society—"lent and carnival."[18] The understanding of this distinction marks Truck's greatest difference from characters like Manual and Boroughcliffe who, though good-natured and capable, drink "on the job," when they should be sober. It is also this understanding that ultimately distances Truck from Falstaff himself, who, as Hal makes clear, blurs the division between work and play, trying indeed to turn all life into carnival, rather than accepting and negotiating the cycles of labor and leisure, and of sobriety and drink, that Truck understands so well and that fit Cooper's own repeated emphasis on moderation in all things—even sobriety. In a sense, then, Truck represents a middle-class link between the thoughtless, frolicsome coarseness of Betty Flanagan's revelers and the more refined merrymaking and almost philosophical mode of connoisseurship that hold so honored a place in Cooper's pantheon of virtues.

The notion of drinking as a pleasurable, convivial ritual of civilized life appears in late and early Cooper alike. And it is significant that such sociable refinement regarding drink often involves women. Being the paragons of propriety that they are, Cooper's "females"—as Mark Twain reminds us Cooper always called them—never drink as deeply as some of his heroes do. Cooper clearly shares the centuries-old double standard regarding male and female drinking that will occupy us more in a subsequent chapter. Thus while women may drink in Cooper, his "ladies" do so very lightly. But the very presence and participation of women in drinking festivities contrasts sharply with many mainstream and virtually all temperance writers of the antebellum period, and contributes to that air of innocent cultivation that characterizes Cooper's most favored forms of drinking.

In the early novel *The Spy* (1821), although the ladies at Miss Peyton's party withdraw after dinner so that the men may smoke, the drinking of excellent wine in toasts, by both sexes, forms a major part of the entertainment, which contrasts in its civility with the wilder carousings of Betty Flanagan and her cohorts. Nearly a quarter of a century later, in *Afloat and Ashore* (1844) and *Satanstoe* (1845), Cooper still looked back fondly at the colonial period described in *The Spy*. In both of these later novels, the first-person narrators (Miles Wallingford and Cornelius Littlepage, respectively) describe elegant drinking rituals in which the atmosphere is festive, genteel, and full of zest without the least shadow of impropriety or hint of disapproval on Cooper's part. Women and men alike drink fine wines and offer toasts; even when the youthful Harris gets drunk in *Satanstoe,* the ladies playfully object not to his inebriated condition but to the fact that his upcoming portrayal of a woman on the stage may result in a "travesty on their sex" (24:122), a tone completely at variance with that of temperance literature.

In three novels from the mid-1840s, in fact—a period that witnessed an intensive marshaling of temperance forces that would culminate in the Maine Law and its equivalents in some other states—Cooper specifically addressed the appropriateness of women drinking. His remarks now seem inconsequential, incidental. But at the time they appeared, they could not help but suggest an opposition to what was already, long before Carry Nation's antiliquor campaign or the founding of the Women's Christian Temperance Union (WCTU), one of temperance's most consistent motifs: that of woman as the model of abstinence and enemy of alcohol.

In *Afloat and Ashore,* Miles Wallingford's description of the festive supper he attends includes the observation that "it was then [the late 1700s] the fashion to drink toasts; gentlemen giving ladies, and ladies gentlemen" (1:368). Such toasts form a prominent part of the banquet where Cornelius Littlepage shyly toasts his beloved Anneke Mordaunt in the next novel Cooper was to write, *Satanstoe,* while in *The Redskins* (1846) Cooper vents his spleen on the custom of separating the sexes after dinner, with the men remaining at table to drink: "Among other customs to be condemned that we have derived from England, is the practice of the men sitting at table after the women have left it." The narrator, Hugh Littlepage, praises his Uncle Roger who "had long endeavored to introduce into our own immediate circle the practice of retaining the ladies at table for a reasonable time, and of then quitting it with them at the expiration of that time," and goes on to show his uncle's theory put into practice: "When my dear grandmother rose, imitated by the four bright-faced girls . . . and said, as was customary with the old school, 'Well, gentlemen, I leave you to your wine' . . . my uncle caught her hand, and insisted she should not quit us" (23:338–39). Greatly approving of his uncle's behavior, Hugh then recounts how much more civilized the evening proceeded than it otherwise would have, with the assembled guests, male and female, sharing the wine and apparently enjoying (as one suspects few persons other than the author himself could have enjoyed!) a lively discussion of that beloved Cooper theme, antirentism.

All of these convivial celebrations could not be further from either the degrading guzzling of liquor we have amply noted in Cooper's fiction earlier or the tight-lipped "ultra godliness" he condemned in *The Ways of the Hour* (29:382). It is this, his last novel, that contains the most direct contrast between "good" and "bad" styles of drinking and all that those styles imply.

That contrast centers on two sections of the establishment known as Horton's Inn. One of these is a wing occupied by the crusty but learned lawyer, Dunscomb, and his friends. Their refined drinking and card play typify the innocent pleasure that, as we saw in our earlier discussion of this novel, Cooper associated with the "liberal" and "cultivated." However, within "twenty feet" of Dunscomb's group we discover "two little parlours" containing "a very different set" from the urbane old lawyer and his guests. This set consisted of the "rowdies," who "chewed, smoked, drank, and played, each and all coarsely" (29:382, 389). Cooper's attack on the vulgar here builds with an intensity that approaches the quality of a vision.

> To things that were innocent in themselves they gave the aspect of guilt by their own manners. The doors were kept locked; even amid their coarsest jokes, their ribaldry, their oaths that were often revolting and painfully frequent, there was an uneasy watchfulness, as if they feared detection. There was nothing frank and manly in the deportment of these men. Chicanery, management, double-dealing, mixed up with the outbreakings of a coarse standard of manners, were visible in all they said or did, except, perhaps, at those moments when hypocrisy was paying its homage to virtue. . . . Everything was coarse and offensive; the attitudes, oaths, conversation, liquors, and even the manner of drinking them. (29:389)

Timms, of course, features prominently in this group, and we may recall, reading of him here, how he behaves when we first meet him in the novel. He is late to Dunscomb's dinner, and we await him with the older man who is shown as the relaxed but alert, natural gentleman, gazing with an aficionado's love "through the ruby rays of a glass of well-cooled Madeira—his favorite wine" (29:176). When Timms finally arrives, Dunscomb fills his guest's glass with iced Madeira. Shortly after drinking it off, Timms refills the glass (on Dunscomb's invitation, to be sure) and does so by unceremoniously filling it "to the brim"—a small but salient detail (29:180). Cooper's implied criticism of Timms here is twofold, perhaps even threefold. First, Timms impolitely takes as much wine as he can. Second, he fails to leave the traditional space between rim and liquid that allows the drinker to savor the wine's aroma—Timms lacks the knowledge of a Dunscomb (or of Cooper himself as a wine-loving connoisseur) that would enable him to enjoy the wine properly. The third possibility is more tenuous. This is that Timms's way of life does not include the cultivated amenities of a Dunscomb, such as fine Madeira—hence his taking as much as he can of a liquor that he would not normally be able to afford, a rather unfair point, if that is what is going on here, since Timms is a man of considerably smaller means than Dunscomb.

Through their drinking comportment, Timms and his cronies enact a moral ugliness, the flip side of which is the "factitious conscience" (29:382) that taints innocent pleasures, turning them into sins. Against this background, Dunscomb's measured conversation, connoisseur's enjoyment of fine Madeira, elegant card play, and cool irony cannot help but shine favorably, even if one feels Cooper's heavy-handedness in opposing patrician Dunscomb to plebeian Timms. Appropriately for the last of Cooper's novels, these two men cap a long line of characters whose relation to intoxicants serves as an index to their larger moral-aesthetic organization. And it is particularly fitting that Dunscomb, the final Cooper protagonist, so thoroughly embodies that gentlemanly savoir faire regarding food, drink, and moral etiquette that constitutes one of Cooper's most deeply cherished values.

The sense of balance, of moderation—in short, of temperance in its etymologically purest sense—consistently informs both Cooper's narrative voice and the voices of his most positive gentlemanly characters, from Denbigh in *Precaution* to Dunscomb in *The Ways of the Hour*. That temperance, however, should not be confused with temporizing, or with the timidity apparent, for example, in Emerson's treatment of intoxication. For Cooper, moderation is not a path of compromise but a narrow strip of proper conduct perched between two vast swaths of vulgar error.

As a moral topographer, Cooper was bent on delineating the exact and sometimes intricate shape of his ideals. The result is that he often sounds pedantic or ambivalent or both—not to mention cantankerous—in the endless qualifications, distinctions, corrections of public views, and labored disquisitions that occupy so large a portion of his books. But on at least two occasions where he describes the moderate ideal, Cooper attained an unusual pithiness of expression. In a statement from *Satanstoe* that could be easily extended to his view of morality in general and of temperance and drinking in particular, Cooper writes, "It has often occurred to my mind that it would be better had New England a little less self-righteousness, and New York a little more righteousness, without the self" (24:20). This sentiment in turn reflects the broader religious principle, articulated in *Miles Wallingford* (1844), that presides over Cooper's entire handling of the intoxication theme: the ideal subscribed to by the Wallingford family, Cooper tells us, is "religion in its most pleasing aspect; religion that has no taint of puritanism, and in which sin and innocent gayety are never confounded" (14:466).

*Chapter 6*

---

# From Conviviality to Vision

---

## Intoxication in Hawthorne

Earnest people, who try to get a reality out of human existence, are necessarily absurd in the view of the revellers and masqueraders.

—Hawthorne, *The Marble Faun*

---

There are people who, either from lack of experience or out of sheer stupidity, turn away from such phenomena, and, strong in the sense of their own sanity, label them [followers of Dionysos] either mockingly or pityingly "endemic diseases." These benighted souls have no idea how cadaverous and ghostly their "sanity" appears as the intense throng of Dionysiac revelers sweeps past them.

—Nietzsche, *The Birth of Tragedy*

Whatever its merits, moderation is not a very inspiring credo. The pulse beats faster to cries of "Be always drunken!" or "Just say no!" than it does to "Nothing in excess." But as our study of Cooper shows, notions of moderation can provide considerable complexity and variety of literary treatment. Like Cooper, Nathaniel Hawthorne offers us a body of work that ultimately upholds moderation rather than excess, sobriety rather than drunkenness. But support it though he may, the concept of right measure simply is not Hawthorne's chief interest with regard to drink. Open-eyed as he is to the problems of intoxication, Hawthorne also recognizes an affinity between the intoxicated state and a more intense, imaginative level of consciousness. In this regard, we may recall Nina Baym's apt comment, made specifically about *The Blithedale Romance* but applicable to much else in Hawthorne, "In the civilized man, passion is already more than adequately controlled. It is control itself that needs boundaries" (Baym, *Hawthorne's Career,* 201).

Moreover, as with other issues, Hawthorne probes far more deeply than Cooper does into the symbolic, spiritual potentialities of intoxicated experience, areas that Cooper ignores in favor of intoxication's effects on behavior. Thus in moving from Cooper to Hawthorne we move from the external world of action, conduct, and appearance to a more intimate world of feelings, thoughts, and perceptions. This is not to deny Cooper's genuinely complex ideas about intoxication or his insights into the psychology of drinking, in characters like Wyandotté, Chingachgook, or Gershom Waring, among others. But Cooper's emphasis remains more on the outer aspects of drink, on the external world of comportment rather than the inner world of consciousness. He is concerned with the dimensional, not the metaphysical, with the convivial, not the visionary. In the external world of Cooper's fiction, intoxicant use is oriented largely to questions of society and civic considerations. Of course, intoxication in the more interior sense that concerns Hawthorne also reveals its own deep links to social realities—as indeed most interior experiences do. But for Hawthorne (and, as we shall see in the next chapter, for Melville), the social realities of alcohol use function as part of larger, more inclusive metaphysical questions of reason versus nonreason, perception and reality, and the nature and meaning of human existence.

Hawthorne clearly shares Cooper's distaste for temperance extremism and his approval of convivial drinking. And in both of these areas, Hawthorne focuses on what he sees as a basic human need for cheer and consolation in a bleak universe. But Hawthorne also goes beyond issues of temperance and conviviality to present a romanticized image of drink, especially wine, as both product and sign of earth's natural, innocent, God-given bounty, and to explore nebulously mystical aspects of intoxication that are utterly absent in Cooper. As our discussion progresses, it will become evident that a subtle but undeniable interrelatedness characterizes these issues in Hawthorne.

Trying to determine a definite stance in Hawthorne regarding drink is a little like trying to locate the beginning or end of an M. C. Escher design. The famous Hawthornian ambiguities fly as thick and fast with intoxication as they do with other topics.[1] Nevertheless, we can identify the following pattern of intoxication as basic to Hawthorne's work. While critical of temperance dogmatism and alcoholic excess alike, Hawthorne affirms drink's indispensable role as a form of "delirious solace" in a fallen world, where transcendent experience is, paradoxically, both necessary to the human spirit and unavailable to it. In his fiction, Hawthorne uses drinking as a tool not so much to assert as to investigate and symbolically express the interpenetration of spiritual and material realms, asking, as he does so, which is more "real" than the other.

In interrogating the distinctions and connections between these realms, Hawthorne pursues what could be described as a Keatsian agenda, examining problems of perception and ontology similar to those so frequently addressed by Keats's poetry. Most notable in this regard is that great work of art in which intoxication plays a crucial role, the "Ode to a Nightingale": "Was it a vision, or a waking dream? / Fled is that music:—Do I wake or sleep?" Such questions connect to the interplay between the real and the imaginary that is so familiar to readers of Hawthorne. Yet intoxication's obvious, important relation to this interplay in Hawthorne's fiction has still to be addressed with any fullness; in fact, the little available commentary on intoxication in Hawthorne consists mainly of brief references to temperance.[2]

In truth, intoxication is both a pervasive and a thematically significant issue for Hawthorne, one that preoccupied him throughout his career, from the early *Fanshawe* to the last great fragments of his *Elixir of Life* and *American Claimant* manuscripts. Attending to this topic will provide us with a more balanced, nuanced, and detailed picture than we have yet had of an important dimension of Hawthorne's work. In examining this dimension, I want to begin with the topics of alcoholism and temperance, before moving on to convivial drinking and, from there, to the visionary or mystical element in Hawthorne's depictions of intoxication.

Unlike most writers dealing with drink, Hawthorne has relatively few depictions of heavy drunkenness or alcoholism, as opposed to the many instances of tippling, tipsiness, convivial drinking, and commentary on drink that abound in his work. Nor are most of these depictions of drunkenness in any way remarkable. In *Fanshawe,* for example, Edward enacts the banal role of "a perfect madman" inflamed by liquor, throwing furniture around and then undergoing the usual morning after, remorse-cum-hangover syndrome.

The few other references to drunkenness in the fiction are trivial; in fact, it is not in his fiction at all but in his late account of English life, *Our Old Home,* that Hawthorne most clearly recognizes the magnitude of alcoholism. In a passage that we will have occasion to return to later, Hawthorne expresses his horror at the "inconceivably sluttish women" and "sad revellers" of both sexes who frequent London's tawdry gin shops, but he tempers that horror with sympathy for the "smothering squalor of both their outward and interior life" (5:278–79). And in more personal terms, Hawthorne poignantly recounts the tale of the dipsomaniacal New Orleans Doctor of Divinity who sought out Hawthorne's services at the American Consulate. Though "shocked and disgusted," Hawthorne recognized in the doctor a spiritual ailment akin to that in many a Hawthorne character: "he bore a hell within the compass of his own breast. . . . It was the deepest tragedy I ever witnessed. . . . The disease, long latent in his heart, had shown itself in a frightful eruption on the surface of his life. That was all! Is it a thing to scold the sufferer for?" (5:29).

One further instance of drunkenness in Hawthorne deserves attention here. It appears, of all places, in a children's story— "Circe's Palace" from the *Tanglewood Tales,* published in 1853. In this charming, slyly ironic tale, the narrator obviously provides an adult subtext to his ostensible retelling of the Homeric myth for children. "Circe's Palace" is, in fact, paradigmatic of Hawthorne's general treatment of drunkenness and parallels his depiction of drinking and temperance as well. The tale shows drink in all its perilous allure, as a double-edged pleasure that can besot and destroy even while it enlivens and delights. Though condemning loutish inebriety, the tale recognizes drink's potential benefit and suggests that total abstemiousness falls short of being the panacea claimed by temperance advocates. Rather, the remedy for intoxication is not abstinence but, as in Cooper, the controlled, skillful handling of wine by those who, like Ulysses with his protective white flower, keep up their guard while drinking.

As in Homer, so too in Hawthorne, Ulysses' men explore Circe's island, come upon the lovely enchantress, make figurative pigs of themselves at her table, and, having become hopelessly drunk through their heavy quaffing of her delightful but debilitating wine, turn into literal pigs at a wave of Circe's wand. This aspect of the Circean legend had a natural appeal for temperance supporters, who could put it to obvious use as a metaphor of the enchantments of liquor. But the usual temperance approach to alcoholic drinks did not, of course, include descriptions that might make such drinks desirable. Temperance references to liquor tend toward either horrific accounts of rotgut concoctions or brief generalized references to the exotic beverages of the jaded rich—or, at most, to the superficial attractions of the brimming bowl. Hawthorne, in contrast, makes clear the genuine appeal of Circe's wine in phrasing whose eloquence betrays his own appreciation of wine: the liquid, we learn, was "as bright as gold" and "kept sparkling upward and throwing a sunny spray over the brim. But, delightfully as the wine looked, it was mingled with the most potent enchantments that Circe knew how to concoct." Hawthorne follows this statement with the ironic comment, "For every drop of the pure grape juice, there were two drops of the pure mischief; and the danger of the thing was, that the mischief made it taste all the better" (7:290–91). This comment plays an important structural and thematic role. It advances the plot for Hawthorne's child readers while simultaneously serving as a knowing aside to adults who may be all too familiar with the mingled delight and mischief that has been and remains so much a part of drinking for many—that is, to those readers who understand that the very same qualities that make drink so appealing are also what make it dangerous.[3]

Offered a goblet by Circe, Ulysses asks, "Is it a wholesome wine?" The question causes Circe's attendants to titter, but it is Ulysses (protected by the magical white flower—Moly in Homer) who plays the trump card by drinking the goblet's contents without submitting to their baleful influence. He then hurls the goblet to the ground, as if contemptuous of its powers, in contrast to his men who greedily want more and become completely undone by the drink. Thus within the confines of a single, seemingly simple tale, we have uncontrolled submission to drink, a prudent use of it rather than an outright rejection (Ulysses gets the wine's benefit without its evil effects), and a clear indication that an awareness of a beverage's "mischief" need not mean *unawareness* of its more pleasurable or positive qualities.[4]

Indeed, "Circe's Palace" gives us the core of Hawthorne's views on drunkenness, controlled drinking, moderation, and the simultaneously beguiling and befuddling nature of liquor. To understand these views more fully, however, we must begin with Hawthorne's relation to the temperance movement and the ways in which his works both reflect and resist its power. We can then proceed to the convivial and visionary aspects of intoxication in Hawthorne, which become clearer when viewed in the context of his reactions to antebellum temperance.

Temperance for Hawthorne assumes a twofold form: temperance as practice, embodied in his images of individual temperance supporters, and temperance as doctrine, revealed in his comments on the beliefs, ideals, and goals of the temperance movement. In general, temperance advocates fare poorly in Hawthorne: at worst, they are pietistic hypocrites; at best, misguided zealots or naive superrationalists who ignore fundamental human needs that the use of intoxicants, however imperfectly, addresses. (I will focus on this particular issue more closely in discussing temperance ideology.) Apart from clear-cut villains, like the hypocritical, sherry-sipping temperance advocate Judge Pyncheon in *The House of the Seven Gables,* most of Hawthorne's temperance characters are akin to the reformers found in "The Hall of Fantasy," whose singleness of purpose is equaled only by their narrowness of mind. The "noted reformers" in the hall are those for whom the "good and true becomes gradually hardened into fact while error melts away and vanishes among the shadows of the hall. . . . It would be endless to describe the herd of real or self-styled reformers, that peopled this place of refuge. . . . Many of them had got possession of some crystal fragment of truth, the brightness of which so dazzled them, that they could see nothing else in the wide universe" (10:180). A perfect candidate for this group is the temperance lecturer of the short story "David Swan: A Fantasy," who "wrought poor David into the texture of his evening's discourse, as an awful instance of dead drunkenness by the road-side" (9:184). Since the reader already knows that David is not drunk but merely asleep, the temperance lecturer's erroneous conclusion, and the alacrity with which he jumps to it, cannot help but suggest a view of temperance as an idée fixe and scapegoat for its supporters. The lecturer's David is, thus, a fantasy (as the story's subtitle suggests), created by a man who, like the reformers in the hall of fantasy, "could see nothing else in the wide universe" beyond his own particular obsession.

But because "David Swan" also includes a clear, strongly negative image of drink, Hawthorne's depiction of the temperance lecturer should not be taken as a merely partisan jab at the drys by one of the wets. In a metaphorical account that could have come straight out of a contemporary temperance tale, the two thieves who plan to kill the sleeping David "draw forth a pocket pistol, but not of that kind which kills by a single discharge. It was a flask of liquor with a block tin tumbler screwed upon the mouth" (9:189). Thus Hawthorne, while mocking the hastily judgmental temperance busybody who spies on David, also recognizes liquor's potential for evil. This delicate balance between mockery of temperance and acknowledgment of the validity of its concerns embodies the gently ironic sense of moderation that also characterizes Hawthorne's basic attitude to drinking.

Ironically, a similar criticism of temperance extremism appears in "A Rill from the Town-Pump," which protemperance readers praised in Hawthorne's own day. The author, however, slyly stands his putative temperance story on its head as he undercuts the usual hydrosophical panegyrics of such fiction with an ironic commentary on teetotal activists' fiery fanaticism. Hawthorne begins toying with his reader early on, shifting between straightforward temperance sentiments and subtle mockeries of temperance rhetoric already in the tale's second paragraph, when the water pump compares itself to a dram seller. But the ironies buried throughout the tale rise to the surface most clearly toward the end, in a playful, clever summation:

> Is it decent, think you, to get tipsy with zeal for temperance, and take up the honorable cause of the Town-Pump, in the style of a toper fighting for his brandy-bottle? Or, can the excellent qualities of cold water be no otherwise exemplified, than by plunging, slapdash, into hot-water, and wofully scalding yourselves and other people? (9:147)

Both here and earlier in the tale, Hawthorne's criticism applies not so much to temperance's basic position as it does to the movement's exaggerated rhetoric and frenzied tone. But temperance does not split easily into form and content in Hawthorne. The reservations his writings reveal about temperance procedures and tone extend to ideology as well. To be sure, indications of sympathy for temperance, traceable perhaps to Sophia's influence, are easy to find in Hawthorne's work, for example, the prowater pronouncements of "A Rill from the Town-Pump," the evil image of alcohol in "David Swan," Edward's drunken fit in *Fanshawe,* the alcohol-induced murder attempt in "Fancy's Show-Box." But such expressions, like the occasional ambivalence to temperance that we can also detect, exist within a more inclusive unity of vision, wherein temperance emerges as a doctrine that, quite apart from the failings of its devotees, is flawed in its fundamental notions of human nature and experience.[5]

Hawthorne himself provides the best gloss on this aspect of his work in a number of statements that while expressing disapproval of temperance, do so in a way that leads us directly to his views of the sometimes salutary, sometimes malign, but always present, inescapable human needs and longings that intoxicants serve. As we will shortly see, to speak of temperance in Hawthorne means also to speak of the consolatory "true purpose" of drinking, as Hawthorne puts it in *The Blithedale Romance.* To speak of that purpose in turn leads us to consider the subtle, sometimes intricate ways in which Hawthorne explores drink's ties to nature and, foreshadowing William James, to the ineffable.

Hawthorne's pithiest critiques of temperance doctrine appear, nearly a decade apart, in "Earth's Holocaust" (1843) and *The Blithedale Romance* (1852). When "the votaries of temperance" hurl "all the hogsheads and barrels of liquor in the world" into the huge bonfire described in "Earth's Holocaust," the narrator sympathizes with the consternation of those who do not share in the teetotalers' joy. Without the solace of liquor, "many deemed that human life would be gloomier than ever, when that brief illumination should sink down." Speaking for his bereaved brethren, the Last Toper exclaims, "What is this world good for . . . now that we can never be jolly any more? What is to comfort the poor man in sorrow and perplexity?—how is he to keep his heart warm against the cold winds of this cheerless earth? and what do you propose to give him, in exchange for the solace that you take away?" The narrator adds, "Preposterous as was the sentiment, I could not help commiserating the forlorn condition of the Last Toper, whose boon-companions had dwindled away from his side, leaving the poor fellow without a soul to countenance him in sipping his liquor, nor, indeed, any liquor to sip" (apart, of course, from the brandy bottle the toper filches from the flames "at a critical moment") (10:386–87).

In a similar vein, a striking passage in *The Blithedale Romance* proclaims,

> Human nature, in my opinion, has a naughty instinct that approves of wine, at least, if not of stronger liquor. The temperance-men may preach till doom's day, and still this cold and barren world will look warmer, kindlier, mellower, through the medium of a toper's glass; nor can they, with all their efforts, really spill his draught upon the floor, until some hitherto unthought-of discovery shall supply him with a truer element of joy. The general atmosphere of life must first be rendered so inspiriting that he will not need his delirious solace. The custom of tippling has its defensible side, as well as any other question. But these good people snatch at the old, time-honored demijohn, and offer nothing—either sensual or moral—nothing whatever to supply its place; and human life, as it goes with a multitude of men, will not endure so great a vacuum as would be left by the withdrawal of that big-bellied convexity. The space, which it now occupies, must somehow or other be filled up. As for the rich, it would be little matter if a blight fell upon their vineyards; but the poor man—whose only glimpse of a better state is through the muddy medium of his liquor—what is to be done for him? The reformers should make their efforts positive, instead of negative; they must do away with evil by substituting good. (3:175)

This passage, which now appears in the Centenary Edition and in most editions of the novel, was crossed out in the manuscript and did not appear in the book's early printings, presumably because of Sophia Hawthorne's temperance inclinations.

That the passage represents Nathaniel Hawthorne's actual views is suggested both by the absence of statements contradicting it and by the presence of similar ideas in the nonfictional *Our Old Home.* In this memoir, while expressing dismay at the sodden drunks thronging London's streets, Hawthorne writes that he "should certainly wait till I had some better consolation to offer before depriving them of their dram of gin, though death itself were in the glass; for methought their poor souls needed such fiery stimulant to lift them a little way out of the smothering squalor of both their outward and interior life, giving them glimpses and suggestions, even if bewildering ones, of a spiritual existence that limited their present misery" (5:279). Here Hawthorne clearly anticipates William James's link between alcohol and mysticism in *The Varieties of Religious Experience:* "Not through mere perversity do men run after it [alcohol]. To the poor and unlettered it stands in the place of symphony concerts and of literature; and it is part of the deeper mystery and tragedy of life that whiffs and gleams of something that we immediately recognize as excellent should be vouchsafed to so many of us only in the fleeting earlier phases of what in its totality is so degrading a poisoning" (James, 13:307).[6]

A common thread through the Hawthorne passages we have just cited is the unfairness of an abstinent ideology that provides drinkers with no alternatives to alcohol. This complaint was echoed by a number of Hawthorne's contemporaries. It is implicit, for example, in the need of Cooper's old naval comrade, Ned Myers, to tap into the liquor supply carried, ironically, by a grogless ship on which Myers was a sailor. More explicitly, it appears in Richard Henry Dana's anger at the practice of depriving sailors of rum without giving them equivalent supplies of coffee or hot chocolate: "When the rum is taken from him [the sailor], he ought to have something in its place." Emerson makes the same point when, in an October 1841 entry, he asks the following of his journal: "Well, now you take from us our cup of alcohol as before you took our cup of wrath. We had become canting moths of peace, our helm was a skillet, and now we must become temperance watersops. You take away, but what do you give me?" (Dana, 352; Emerson, *JMN,* 8:116).

Hawthorne, however, takes the need for alternatives to alcohol to a metaphysical plane. What would truly fill the place of drink is not some alcohol-free beverage but rather the satisfaction of a psychospiritual hunger that no physical substance, including alcohol, can assuage. This belief comes through strongly, if briefly, in "The Old Manse," where Hawthorne notes—in a passage marked, interestingly, by Melville in his copy of the book—that "stimulants, the only mode of treatment hitherto attempted, cannot quell the disease [of ridding ourselves of old delusions]; they do but heighten the delirium" (10:30).

In both "The New Adam and Eve" and *The Blithedale Romance,* Hawthorne is more explicit. In the short story, after Adam and Eve find the champagne bottle, the narrator tells us, "Had they quaffed it, they would have experienced that brief delirium, whereby, whether excited by moral or physical causes, man sought to compensate himself for the calm, life-long joys which he had lost by his revolt from Nature" (10:260). In *The Blithedale Romance,* we have already noted the long passage in which Miles Coverdale laments the lack—the seeming impossibility, even—of a true alternative to liquor, an idea to which Coverdale returns a few passages later, where we find the closest thing to Hawthorne's own definition of the motive for intoxication: "But the true purpose of . . . drinking—and one that will induce men to drink, or do something equivalent, as long as this weary world shall endure—was the renewed youth and vigor, the brisk, cheerful sense of things present and to come, with which, for about a quarter-of-an-hour, the dram permeated their systems" (3:178). From these comments it is clear that in speaking of alternatives to liquor, Hawthorne is thinking in terms of spiritual solace and psychic regeneration—not apple juice or cocoa.

All of this suggests that if the true Bacchus is inaccessible, Hawthorne readily accepts rather than scorns the "Bastard Bacchus" of alcohol, to recall the Coleridgean locution referred to in the introduction. Certainly the passage from "The New Adam and Eve" quoted above ties in perfectly with the notion of drink as a "Bastard Bacchus," as a poor but necessary substitute for, and reminder of, that more natural, innocent mode of being that we can only dimly intuit—like William Wordsworth's "fallings from us, vanishings" in the "Immortality Ode." Such notions of the compensatory "delirious solace" provided by alcohol do not appear in Hawthorne until the late 1830s, but they grow naturally enough out of his earliest, sympathetic descriptions of convivial drinking. Despite Edward's drunken outburst, for example, alcohol in *Fanshawe* is generally pleasant, being usually consumed with the breezy self-indulgence of that good-natured source of anacreontic doggerel, Hugh Crombie, or with the more dignified geniality of Dr. Melmoth—an easy stand-in for any number of gentlemanly Cooper characters with a benign, moderate affection for the wine bowl.[7]

Two years after *Fanshawe*, in 1830, the short story "Sir William Phips" shows wine's warming effect on both the external manner and the internal disposition of the chilly Puritan title character. With "Edward Fane's Rosebud" (1837), Hawthorne provides a fuller sense of drink's compensatory qualities as he moves beyond the straightforward conviviality of his very first works to the view expressed in Emerson's journal entry that reads, "Men want wine, beer, & tobacco to dull or stupefy a little the too tender papillae" (*JMN,* 11:255). Foreshadowing the character of old Moodie in *The Blithedale Romance*, who derives similar soul-warming comfort from drink, the Widow Toothaker feels that her "sad old heart has need to be revived by the rich infusion of Geneva, which is mixed half-and-half with hot water, in the tumbler." The old woman has her "torpid blood warmed, and her shoulders lightened of at least twenty ponderous years, by a draught from the true Fountain of Youth, in a case-bottle. It is strange that men should deem that fount a fable, when its liquor fills more bottles than the congress-water!" The narrator's empathy with the Widow and her potations even leads him to address her directly: "Sip it again, good nurse, and see whether a second draught will not take off another score of years, and perhaps ten more, and show us, in your high-backed chair, the blooming damsel who plighted troths with Edward Fane. . . . But, alas! the charm will not work. In spite of fancy's most potent spell, I can see only an old dame cowering over the fire, a picture of decay and desolation" (9:464–65). Ineffective though it is, alcohol seems acceptable, even welcome to Hawthorne here. It provides, at least, a transitory moment of forgetfulness, of "delirious solace." It gives, in other words, that "quarter-of-an-hour" of ease we have already seen associated with liquor in *The Blithedale Romance.*

Yet Hawthorne also recognizes that drink's anesthetic qualities can be not only therapeutic but also destructive, a form of evasion and escapism from life's challenges. In "The Celestial Rail-road," for example, the deluded denizens of Vanity Fair seek peace of mind in "opium or a brandy-bottle" (10:200); we have earlier noted the reference in "The Old Manse" to humanity's misguided efforts to solve its frustrations with stimulants (10:29); in "The Artist of the Beautiful," Owen Warland hides his head not in the sand but in "the golden medium of wine" through which, for a time, he seeks to shelter his refined sensibilities from the mundane dullards who surround him: Owen "contemplated the visions that bubble up so gaily around the brim of the glass, and that people the air with shapes of pleasant madness, which so soon grow ghostly and forlorn" (10:461).

The linkage of artist with intoxication in the case of Owen Warland recalls similar (but not always such negative) pairings both in romanticism and in the whole tradition of the divinely mad or inebriated poet that stretches back to classical times, as discussed earlier. In Hawthorne, that linkage is particularly explicit in the 1843 story, "The Hall of Fantasy," where it is the "laurel-gatherers"—poets—who are especially heavy partakers of the fantasy-inducing, intoxicating waters of the hall's fountain. Like the concept of drink's "delirious solace," with its foreshadowing of William James's visionary theories of intoxication in *The Varieties of Religious Experience,* Hawthorne's art-intoxication link suggests his interest not only in issues of convivial drinking and temperance but also in the mystical or Dionysian dimensions of intoxicant use. Hawthorne's is, to be sure, a sporadic and muffled Dionysianism at most. He is too ironic, too skeptical of grand, all-illuminating truths, perhaps too timid and definitely too wary of the Janus-faced qualities of drink to yield completely to the Dionysian impulse.

As we will see, even in his most Dionysian work, *The Marble Faun,* the visionary quality is compromised by the sentimental, disingenuously make-believe quality of the characters' references to Bacchus and transcendent experience. That said, Hawthorne's interest in the supernatural and mysterious, in the intersection of dream and reality—the ghostly harpsichord music at the end of *The House of the Seven Gables* that may or may not be real, to cite but one of many possible examples—helps to explain his interest in the manifold relations of drink to altered modes of perceiving, thinking, and feeling.

Certainly "The Artist of the Beautiful" exemplifies Hawthorne's mingled fascination with and skepticism about art as intoxicated inspiration. In Owen Warland we find wine simultaneously acting as complement to Owen's sensitive, genuinely original, artistic perceptions and as the pathetic anodyne of a morbidly self-conscious man incapable of negotiating even simple relations in his own society. Such ambiguity frequently characterizes the visionary dimension of intoxicants in Hawthorne. In "Fancy's Show-Box," for example, the "three figures" (Fancy, Memory, and Conscience) that old Mr. Smith beholds entering his chamber are perceived "through the brilliant medium of his glass of old Madeira": the implicit question here is, are these figures real, or only the hallucinatory vapors of a wine-befogged mind? And if they *are* real, is their presence discernible only because of the effects of the wine? Are there, then, modes of being perceptible only to the nonrational or distorted consciousness, such as that of the tipsy Mr. Smith? The questions remain unresolved, as do the ambiguities surrounding drink in the unfinished *Elixir of Life* and *American Claimant* manuscripts, in which Hawthorne grappled, in part, with intoxication in its mystical or visionary aspects.

None of the fragments included in these manuscripts centers on intoxication, but most reveal a remarkably persistent concern with drinking or related issues. Although this concern never finally coalesces into a coherent, distinct pattern, it is worth noting its tantalizing manifestations throughout the manuscripts. In *The American Claimant,* Hawthorne admiringly comments on hearty English eating and drinking, as compared with the American diet, and makes much of the elaborate drinking ritual known as the Loving Cup. Issues of moderation in drinking and its relation to being "jolly" preoccupy the Warden and Etheredge during their midnight conversation. In the *Grimshawe* section of the manuscript, Hawthorne writes himself a note stressing the importance of intoxicants to Dr. Grimshawe's characterization: "Early introduce Doctor Grim as a smoker & drinker" (12:344). Irascible, eccentric, saturated with the brandy and water he drinks all day long, Dr. Grimshawe is nonetheless kindly and sympathetic, and far preferable to the neighbors who scorn him because of his supposedly disreputable qualities—mainly his unconventional behavior, but also his smoking and drinking. But it is these very qualities that give him such vividness as a character and that, even in their less pleasant aspects, are refreshing in comparison to the homogenized blandness and carping moralisms of the respectable.

The *Elixir of Life* manuscripts include *The Dolliver Romance,* in which the search for the immortality-bestowing elixir inevitably invokes parallels and contrasts with conventional alcoholic beverages. Issues of toxicity and moderate, controlled drinking preoccupy Dr. Dolliver, the apothecary who watches aghast as the blustering Colonel (a kind of Roger Danforth in old age) greedily drinks a huge draught of the magical elixir, instead of taking the single drop recommended to him by Dr. Dolliver, and falls dead. As if in anticipation of further developments along the lines of the nature of the elixir and of its relation to drink and to notions of moderate consumption, the manuscript breaks off with the apothecary guarding the secret of the elixir by explaining that the Colonel died from drinking, against the apothecary's advice, "a dose of distilled spirits" (13:494–95).

Like Dr. Grimshawe, old Aunt Nashoba from the *Septimius Norton* section of the *Elixir* is a crusty but positive character

who drinks continuously out of a mysterious brown jug; one of
Septimius's ancestors is an alcoholic Indian who dies, drunk, in
a snowdrift; the evocatively named Dr. Portsoaken, a brandy-
sipping, spider-loving heavy smoker, is an obvious version of
Dr. Grimshawe but remains undeveloped in the *Elixir.* These
and other scattered references result in a continuum of intoxicant use in which we see various vulgar, mundane versions of
the legendary, secret intoxicant whose consumption renders
the drinker immortal—a true aqua vitae! This search for the
elixir could obviously lend itself well to more visionary associations, and a hint of such associations does accrue to the magical elixir and to the experiences of those whose lips touch it—
like Sybil in the *Septimius Felton* portion of the *Elixir* (an earlier
version of *Septimius Norton*), who consumes an improperly
mixed dose of the elixir: "the drink of death exhilarated her like
an intoxicating fluid" (13:190). For the most part, however, the
mystical dimensions in the manuscripts are as amorphous as
other issues in these beautifully written, hopelessly discon-
nected texts.

But one particular evocation of the mystical here stands out.
In the *Etherege* portion of *The American Claimant,* the young
American (Etherege) drinks Brathwaite's drugged wine and
seems on the verge of a Poe-like, transcendent experience, a vision of ultimate truth.

> Etherege sipped his second glass, endeavoring to find out what
> was this subtile and peculiar flavor that hid itself so, and yet
> seemed on the point of revealing itself. It had, he thought, a sin-
> gular effect upon his faculties, quickening and making them ac-
> tive, and causing him to feel as if he were on the point of pene-
> trating rare mysteries, such as men's thoughts are always
> hovering round, and always returning from. Some strange, vast,
> sombre, mysterious truth, which he seemed to have searched
> for long, appeared to be on the point of being revealed to him;
> a sense of something to come; something to happen that had
> been waiting long, long to happen; an opening of doors, a draw-
> ing away of veils, a lifting of heavy, magnificent curtains, whose
> dark folds hung before a spectacle of awe;—it was like the

verge of the grave. Whether it was the exquisite wine of Brathwaite's, or whatever it might be, the American felt a strange influence upon him, as if he were passing through the gates of
eternity, and finding on the other side the revelation of some secret that had greatly perplexed him. (12:307)

Even Poe never produced language more evocative of otherworldly intoxication. But Hawthorne's little surprise here is that
all this fine rhetoric—like the incipient vision it describes—falls
apart when Etherege wakes to find himself, not united with
some transcendent truth, but locked in the evil Brathwaite's
wretched dungeon.[8] Not an unequivocal denial of visionary experience, perhaps, but clearly an undercutting of the rhetoric of
intoxicated transcendence. And, somewhat like the experience
described in "Circe's Palace," the passage here draws our attention to the duplicitously double nature of the intoxicated state,
in which an enchanting vision can actually signal degradation
and incapacity.

To be sure, Hawthorne is not as extensive in his undercutting
as the next chapter will show Melville to be. But many of the examples I have discussed reveal an ironic manipulation and sub-
version of various discourses, whether of temperance, conviviality, or inspired intoxication. In one crucial area, however—wine's
link to the natural plenty of the earth—Hawthorne engages in no
significant undercutting. Particularly in *The Marble Faun,* we see
Hawthorne interpreting drink, the act of drinking, and even the
making of one particular beverage—wine—as earthly phenomena possessing a more spiritualized, mystically Bacchic dimension. But before turning to this topic in and of itself, I wish to ar-
ticulate its larger philosophical context: Hawthorne's attitude to
the earth and to the interconnectedness of the spiritual and the
physical.

Romantic writers such as Keats, Emerson, and Coleridge all
sharply divide spiritual from merely material, mundane forms
of intoxication. We have already discussed Coleridge's concept
of the "Bastard Bacchus"; similarly, Keats dismisses physical
wine as a vulgar stand-in for the true sublime:

> Away! away! for I will fly to thee,
>     Not charioted by Bacchus and his pards,
> But on the viewless wings of Poesy,
>     Though the dull brain perplexes and retards. . . .

In Emerson, we have seen how intoxicants largely divide between "God's wine" and "Devil's wine," with the former usually being no more than "the semblance and counterfeit of . . . oracular genius." For these romantics, physical intoxication may partake of the sublime but in a way that is ultimately no more than an attempt to "counterfeit infinity," in Coleridge's phrase, and is therefore suspect. Hawthorne fully shares the sense of the "Bastard Bacchus" as we saw earlier, but in general, his work bespeaks far greater comfort with the bastardized sublime than we find in the other writers just mentioned, and indeed conveys the impression of a liminality between wine brewed in what Emerson derisively called "the belly of the grape" and the more spiritual wine for which Hawthorne, like all good romantics, yearns.

Hawthorne's greater acceptance of "Devil's wine" and its comforts matches his sympathetic, unusually tender feelings for what idealists might see as the mere dross of physical existence—especially in the natural world. Thus in "The Hall of Fantasy," a loving pity for the "poor old Earth" exerts claims on the narrator stronger than any abstract principle or creed. Admitting that the earth "has faults enough," the narrator goes on to say that he "cannot bear to have her perish. . . . [T]he root of human nature strikes down deep into this earthly soil; and it is but reluctantly that we submit to be transplanted, even for a higher cultivation in Heaven." Nor is the narrator's fondness for the earth based solely on physical sensation. In a passage anticipating the interfusion of the moral and the material in *The Marble Faun* (but without the wine imagery of the novel), the narrator of "The Hall of Fantasy" asks, "As for purely moral enjoyments, the good will find them in every state of being. But where the material and the moral exist together, what is to happen then? And then our mute four-footed friends, and the winged songsters of our woods! Might it not be lawful to regret them, even in the hallowed groves of Paradise?" (10:182–84).

Attitudes such as those expressed in the passage above show Hawthorne's distance from a Baudelairean, "n'importe-où-hors-du-monde" celebration of intoxicated consciousness. Despite his emphasis on drink's capacity to console and revive, Hawthorne stops short of the full-blown, even if metaphorical, romantic idiom of an Emerson or a Dickinson, a Poe or a Byron. It is as if, like Frost's narrator in "Birches," Hawthorne would go "*toward* heaven," but no farther. This kind of "toward" movement is what Hawthorne prizes most in his treatment of intoxication, as he celebrates that liminal realm in which the physical partakes of the spiritual without ever losing its distinctly physical character. It is, finally, a very earthy *and* earthly jubilation that Hawthorne affirms.

Part of Hawthorne may float away longingly after Clifford Pyncheon's evanescent bubbles or Owen Warland's fragile butterfly, or fantasize about inhaling "jollity with every breath" like the fish in the liquor-spiked aquarium he imagines in *The Blithedale Romance* (3:178). But another part remains as firmly rooted in the tangible world as were the Brook Farm vines that Hawthorne described so admiringly in an 1841 letter to Sophia.[9] However high the intoxicated flight may bear him, Hawthorne never forgets the physical *fact* of the grape. But by the same token, Hawthorne's delight in the tangible assumes a spiritual dimension, often through the metaphoric richness and descriptive lyricism of his language, which, unlike the Etherege incident described above, reveals no subversive irony.

In connection with intoxication, the central image out of which the spiritual-material bond grows is that of the grape. That image appears very early in Hawthorne, before reaching its full growth in the lush, suggestive prose of his last finished romance, *The Marble Faun*.

In the 1841 letter to Sophia, Hawthorne thinks of the grapes in terms of the potential wine they may produce. As early as 1830, the story "Sir William Phips" reveals a similar emphasis on the physical genesis of wine in the earthbound grape: "as the grape-juice glides warm into the ventricles of his heart, it produces a change like that of a running stream upon enchanted shapes" (23:64). The wine thus possesses an almost magical but not sinister power, as it lends a lively, intense aspect to the commonplace, blends with Sir William's very blood ("glides warm into the ventricles of his heart"), and renders him more engaging and humane than he appears in other scenes of the tale.[10]

By the time of *The Blithedale Romance,* the grape image grows in both meaning and intensity. In the chapter "Coverdale's Hermitage," the narrator ensconces himself in the "leafy cave" of a pine tree entwined by a large, "wild grape-vine." "I counted the innumerable clusters of my vine," says Coverdale, and, like Hawthorne in his letter to Sophia, "forereckoned the abundance of my vintage" (3:99). The association of grapes with wine's intoxicating properties becomes more vivid later, when Coverdale, back in town, describes the garden near his hotel, where "grapevines clambered upon trellises and bore clusters already purple and promising the richness of Malta or Madeira in their ripened juice" (3:148). An incipient intoxication appears already in Miles Coverdale himself as he revels in the visual beauty of the grapes and as he anticipates the rich wine those grapes will provide. These pleasant associations of the grape become simultaneously more sensuous and more spiritually meaningful when Coverdale finds himself back in his Blithedale grape arbor, which he experiences all the more closely, even intimately, as he gazes at, fondles, and bites into the luscious grapes redolent with the promise of wine.

> The grapes, which I had watched throughout the summer, now dangled around me in abundant clusters of the deepest purple, deliciously sweet to the taste, and though wild, yet free from that ungentle flavor which distinguishes nearly all our native and uncultivated grapes. Methought a wine might be pressed out of them, possessing a passionate zest, and endowed with a new kind of intoxicating quality, attended with such bacchanalian ecstasies as the tamer grapes of Madeira, France, and the

Rhine, are inadequate to produce. And I longed to quaff a great
goblet of it, at that moment! (3: 208)

In this passage, intoxication inheres in innocent nature itself, as
if in the very earth out of which these wild grapevines grow.
Through Coverdale, Hawthorne seems to intuit a spiritual or supernatural, almost mystical element or presence in the physical—an unprovable, mysterious, indefinite but nonetheless genuine immanence of the spiritual within the organic.

The sense of wine as a life-affirming extension of the earth's
natural abundance and as a mediator between physical and spiritual orders of reality finds its greatest expression in *The Marble
Faun.* Unfortunately, critics have largely ignored the importance
of wine both in its own right and in relation to key issues and
characters in the book. This neglect has not only obscured an
important aspect of *The Marble Faun,* it has also left unexam-
ined some of the most eloquent, lyrical evocations of drinking
and its significance in American literature.

Although it only touches on drunkenness and temperance,
*The Marble Faun* is the most inclusive of Hawthorne's treatments
of intoxicant use, interweaving the topic of drink with a broader
tapestry of myth, nature, art, and connoisseurship. At the heart
of this inclusiveness lies the *transformation* (to echo the book's
British title) of grape into wine. All of the grape and vineyard images we have discussed earlier in Hawthorne are but preludes to
the heightened significance of such imagery in *The Marble Faun.*
Through this imagery, Hawthorne emphasizes the almost al-
chemical process of wine making. But in this process the grape
is not so much changed into something different as it is revealed
in its innermost character. Before examining these issues in *The
Marble Faun,* however, we need first to clarify the attitudes to
mythology and nature that, quite early in the novel, form the
background for the intoxication theme to come.

Already in the preface to the romance, Hawthorne sets up (in
a famous passage) the general attitude to all of his material in
the book, including the natural and the mythological: "Italy, as

the site of his Romance, was chiefly valuable to him as afford-
ing a sort of poetic or fairy precinct, where actualities would not
be so terribly insisted upon, as they are, and must needs be, in
America" (4:3). Within this "precinct," Hawthorne employs a
vaguely Bacchic tone that might well appear ludicrous in a
Salem or Boston setting but that is more consonant with the atmosphere of a grand mythic past and aristocratic decay that
permeates *The Marble Faun.*

The book's Bacchic tone emerges in the partly earnest, partly
facetious references to the wine god, an awareness of whose
spirit and legends seems always to hover around Hawthorne's
American tourists, but whose presence is never quite palpable, except fleetingly in the figure and manner of Donatello.
Throughout the romance it is Donatello, with his Bacchic associations, who embodies Hawthorne's sense of liminality between the ineffable realm of myth and the material realm of
earthbound reality. "I hardly know," says Miriam to Donatello, at
the end of chapter 8, "whether you have sprouted out of the
earth, or fallen from the clouds" (4:76). Much the same could be
said of alcohol use here, as a phenomenon both physical and
moral.

Bacchus—a god—has traditionally been linked with the emphatically physical reality of wine and with the natural world of
forest, stream, and vineyard. His closest companion—whom Donatello physically resembles—is that hybrid of the mythological
and the natural, the faun. Thus mythic spirit and animal materi-
ality fuse in Donatello, whose links to Bacchus receive emphasis
from Miriam's repeated comparisons of Donatello to Bacchus's
faun, and in Kenyon's fantasy "that Donatello was not merely a
sylvan faun, but the genial wine god in his very person" (4:237).
Miriam's and Kenyon's fanciful view of Donatello as Bacchus/
faun reflects the book's continuous expressions of longing for a
pagan sensuality, on the one hand, and a clearer sense of the supernatural or visionary, on the other, and ultimately for a blending of the two in a mythologized, poeticized world of nature.
Such a blend, Hawthorne tells us, seems present in the "discol-

ored marble surface of the Faun of Praxiteles. . . . [A]fter all, the idea [of the faun and the mingled qualities it represents] may have been no dream, but rather a poet's reminiscence of a period when man's affinity with nature was more strict, and his fellowship with every living thing more intimate and dear" (4:10–11).

In the specific cultural context of *The Marble Faun,* these longings evince a potent nostalgia for a European sensual-mythological heritage to which, alas, neither Hawthorne nor his fictional compatriots can ever belong. This nostalgia and its attendant yearnings receive some of their most important formulations in terms of drinking and the harvesting of wine, and of the mythic figure of Bacchus. Pertinent to Hawthorne's treatment of these issues here is the German philologist Christa Karoli's analysis of the concept of *ekstasis* in the ancient world. Observing that ekstasis was "originally a purely bodily heightening of the self" (through physical intoxication in ancient religious cults), Karoli notes that in Greek antiquity, "ecstasy becomes a creative state of excitement as the bodily and spiritual forms of intoxication merge" (die Ekstase zum schopferischen Zustand der Begeisterung, als sich körperlicher und geistiger Rausch verbinden) (Karoli, 7).[11] Although never articulated as explicitly as this, Hawthorne's frequent attempts in *The Marble Faun* to conjoin physical and spiritual through wine are obviously related to the antique concept Karoli discusses. Even more strikingly, Hawthorne's description of the paradoxical designs on the sarcophagus, which occurs in the very next sentence after his first association of Bacchus with Donatello, parallels the ancient understanding of Dionysos/Bacchus's dual nature. Here is the passage from Hawthorne.

> Bacchus, too, a rosy flush diffusing itself over his time-stained surface, could come down from his pedestal, and offer a cluster of purple grapes to Donatello's lips, because the god recognizes him as the woodland elf who so often shared his revels. And here, in this sarcophagus, the exquisitely carved figures might assume life, and chase one another round its verge with that

wild merriment which is so strangely represented on those old
burial coffers: though still with some subtle allusion to death,
carefully veiled, but forever peeping forth amid emblems of
mirth and riot. (4:17–18).

As Karoli points out regarding the ancient cult of the wine
god, "Dionysos is the god of Mania, the ecstatic movement in a
dual countenance of extreme joy in life and insanity, death. In
this the problematic kernel of all intoxicating inspiration is represented: the transport contains joy and pain, fulfillment and destruction at the same time." Thus Dionysos is "the god of two-
faced rapture" (Karoli, 7). This concept of the inextricability of
joy and sorrow—another Keatsian motif in Hawthorne that is
linked to intoxication—remained important to Hawthorne well
into his last creative efforts, as indicated in the following fascinating note to himself in *The American Claimant:* "Now, if this
great bleakness and horror is to be underneath the story, there
must be a frolic and dance of bacchanals all over the surface"
(12:292).

These concepts and attitudes exist not in neatly separable
categories but along a fluid continuum of combinations and patterns. Nonetheless, three basic areas informed by them emerge
in *The Marble Faun.* Of these, the most extensively and inten-
sively treated is the vine itself and the entire viticultural enter-
prise by which its fruits turn into wine. But also important are
the interrelated themes of connoisseurship and of the moral/
material dimensions of the act of drinking.

All three of the above areas appear throughout *The Marble
Faun,* but they are especially concentrated in an eight-chapter
section, beginning with chapter 25 and focusing on Donatello's
ancestral estate, Monte Beni. Appropriately, the very title of the
first chapter in this section is "Sunshine," the nickname given to
Donatello's best wine, more formally known by the name of the
estate itself. For Hawthorne, the harvest and processes that result in Monte Beni wine bespeak a way of life that is harmo-
nious, graceful, and simultaneously sensuous and poetic. Even
though New England cider making might be more picturesque,

and "sweet cider an infinitely better drink than the ordinary un-ripe Tuscan wine" (4:275), the "processes connected with the culture of the grape [especially the Monte Beni grape], had a flavour of poetry about them." Hawthorne hymns the Monte Beni harvest scenes in a rich paragraph that blends matter-of-fact physical description with evaluative commentary, as well as with the lush fantasy that, as his preface explained, the "precinct" of Italy allows.

> The toil, that produces those kindly gifts of nature which are not the substance of life, but its luxury, is unlike other toil. We are inclined to fancy that it does not bend the sturdy frame, and stiffen the overwrought muscles, like the labour that is devoted in sad, hard earnest, to raise grain for sour bread. Certainly, the sun-burnt young men and dark-cheeked, laughing girls, who weeded the rich acres of Monte Beni, might well enough have passed for inhabitants of an unsophisticated Arcadia. Later in the season, when the true vintage-time should come, and the wine of Sunshine gush into the vats, it was hardly too wild a dream, that Bacchus himself might re-visit the haunts which he loved of old. But, alas, where now would he find the Faun, with whom we see him consorting in so many an antique group!
> (4:275)

In this passage, guidebook patter (complained of in some contemporary reviews of *The Marble Faun*) gives way to an admiring vision of a deeply attractive, coherent mode of life and labor. Of course, this vision is suspiciously idealized; one wonders what the laborers in the Tuscan vineyard would have to say about their Arcadian tasks. But then, as often is the case with Hawthorne, the physical reality takes on a more symbolic dimension, which Hawthorne himself alerts us to when he speaks, at the beginning of this paragraph, of the "flavour of poetry" attaching to such scenes as this.

Ever on the watch for the poetic or symbolic association, Hawthorne even turns the wine not merely to Bacchic but to temperance use some pages later, as Kenyon wanders the Tuscan countryside around Monte Beni. "Nothing can be more picturesque," we learn, than an old grape vine, with almost a trunk of its own, clinging fast around its supporting tree. Nor does the picture lack its moral. You might twist it to more than one grave purpose, as you saw how the knotted, serpentine growth imprisoned within its strong embrace the friend that had supported its tender infancy; and how (as seemingly flexible natures are prone to do) it converted the sturdier tree entirely to its own selfish ends, extending its innumerable arms on every bough, and permitting hardly a leaf to sprout except its own. It occurred to Kenyon that the enemies of the vine, in his native land, might here have seen an emblem of the remorseless gripe with which the habit of vinous enjoyment lays upon its victim, possessing him wholly, and letting him live no life but such as it bestows. (4:291–92)

What seems most important to the narrator here is not the question of temperance as such but rather the symbolic possibilities of the vine, which clearly fascinates him not simply because of its relation to wine but because of its mythic associations and the flexibility with which its stages of growth and its various uses can be put to interpretive ends. Hawthorne's hermeneutic of the vine here allows him to have his interpretive cake and *read* it too, since he is himself at several removes from the temperance point the passage makes.

Through Kenyon, Hawthorne obliquely genuflects to temperance, but he distances himself from the cause first by noting, "You might twist it [the vine] to more than one grave purpose." Thus, first, the vine's potential meanings are multiple, not single, and therefore not inevitably or necessarily those that support temperance ideology. Second, any one meaning might be contrived, forced, or imposed—as the word "twist" ever so lightly adumbrates. Third, the narrator notes that the particular temperance interpretation in question occurs to Kenyon, not himself. Fourth, Kenyon thinks of the interpretation that American "enemies of the vine" *might* put on the vine in question, thereby emphasizing the potentiality and provisional nature of the interpretation. The temperance metaphor put forward actually seems to me to be both elegant and apt, but Hawthorne has made sure that it is not the only metaphor possible in the circumstances. In fact, Hawthorne has managed to use a temperance symbol while safely standing behind the barriers that his rhetoric of displacement has erected: the metaphor is only possible ("might"); is potentially wrongheaded ("twist"); is imagined by a fictional character, Kenyon, not by the narrator himself; is imagined about a particular group ("enemies of the vine") who are clearly not to be identified with either the wine-loving Kenyon or his narrative creator.

If anything, for that narrator and for Kenyon both, the vineyard imagery in this romance implies at times the *innocence* of wine as a product of the natural world, and indeed as something that is, according to the narrator, already immanent in nature itself, before human intervention brings wine into actual existence: "The contadini . . . found many clusters of ripe grapes for [Kenyon], in every little globe of which was included a fragrant draught of the sunny Monte Beni wine" (4:274). The vine's connection to innocence comes through as well in its association with Donatello's guiltless, happy childhood and, as we shall now see, in a very specific comparison of Donatello's estate to the Garden of Eden.

As a child, Donatello "was the soul of vintage festivals. While he was a mere infant . . . it had been the custom to make him tread the wine press with his tender little feet, if it were only to crush one cluster of the grapes. And the grape juice that gushed beneath his childish tread, be it ever so small in quantity, sufficed to impart a pleasant flavor to a whole cask of wine" (4:237). Like a little Bacchus, baby Donatello participates in the winemaking process that takes on all the qualities of a benign ritual, his childish presence accentuating the harmlessness of an activity that Hawthorne's readers would, of course, have often heard or seen demonized by the "enemies of the vine." A short time later, as he explores Monte Beni, Kenyon again sees in this place of grape vines and wine barrels the image of a prelapsarian world and feels "somewhat the sensations of an adventurer who should find his way to the site of ancient Eden" (4:275).

This innocence extends even to connoisseurship, which, if properly understood, is not the decadent frivolity perceived by temperance eyes. Rather, connoisseurship blends seamlessly in this romance into a subtler preoccupation with the moral or spiritual nature of the act of drinking. Although no American writer treated in this book approaches the appreciation of wine with the mingled gravity and fervor of Cooper, Hawthorne manifests intense interest in connoisseurship in *The Marble Faun*. And, while we should not make too much of his elevated descriptions of wine, which in part reflect the lavish rhetoric of nineteenth-century connoisseurship, we should not make too little of them, either. The situation with connoisseurship somewhat parallels that of Hawthorne's references to Bacchus. Of course, neither Hawthorne nor any of his characters *really* believes that the actual god Bacchus will suddenly appear and prance around with Donatello—but the Bacchic images are not just figures of speech, either. Rather, they represent the intuition of a mythical or supernatural reality just beyond the reach of reason and sense experience, but also somehow immanent in that experience. So too Hawthorne's praise of Monte Beni wine blends the playful linguistic exuberance of traditional connoisseurship with a deeper sense that the wine and its consumption possess indefinable yet undeniable layers of spiritual value and meaning, in which it is difficult to say where the literal ends and the symbolic begins.

At the Monte Beni estate, familiar details of connoisseurship, like savoring a wine's aroma before drinking it, and observing the gradations of taste over time occupy Donatello, his butler Tomaso, and Kenyon. Yet with no sense of arbitrariness, their conversation modulates into a finer tone, particularly under the guidance of the old butler. That tone, of course, depends in part on the nature of the wine, as well as of the drinker. The most highly refined spirit will be wasted on an unworthy wine. But the worthiest wines involve more than physical taste or monetary worth. A wine like the Sunshine of Monte Beni, resplendent with all the sweet abundance of the vineyards that seem to

Kenyon to have been blessed by Bacchus himself and possessing the power to warm and illuminate the human heart, almost like a kind of sun of the spirit, requires respect, even reverence. The religious implications of my language here derive from the text itself.

In the chapter entitled "Sunshine," we read that the "invaluable liquor" of Monte Beni wine, "if carelessly and irreligiously quaffed, might have been mistaken for a very fine sort of champagne. It was not, however, an effervescing wine, although its delicate piquancy produced a somewhat similar effect upon the palate. Sipping, the guest longed to sip again; but the wine demanded so deliberate a pause, in order to detect the hidden peculiarities and subtle exquisiteness of its flavor, that *to drink it was really more a moral than a physical enjoyment*" (my italics). Kenyon then goes on to tell his hosts, "I feel myself a better man for that ethereal potation. . . . The finest Orvieto, or that famous wine the Est Est Est of Montefiascone is vulgar in comparison. This is surely the wine of the Golden Age, such as Bacchus himself first taught mankind to press from the choicest of his grapes" (4:223). In this passage, metaphor and reality meet, as the wine seems to possess the glowing and warming powers of its namesake, "sunshine." And indeed, when Donatello first calls for the wine, he simply says, "Tomaso, bring some Sunshine" (4:222).

The mysterious spirituality of the wine is again addressed by Kenyon, when he says that he "venerate[s] the Sunshine of Monte Beni" and describes it as "a sort of consecrated juice [that] symbolizes the holy virtues of hospitality and social kindness." But body is never far from soul when Hawthorne treats of wine in *The Marble Faun.* In a striking turn to sensual imagery, Tomaso gives the wine an intensely personal, intimate, and indeed sexual dimension when he tells Kenyon, "That very flask of Sunshine, now, has kept itself for you, Sir Guest, (as a maid reserves her sweetness till her lover comes for it,) ever since a merry vintage-time, when the Signor Count here was a boy!" (4:225). Although Hawthorne balances this potentially melodramatic for-

mulation with a feather-light ironic touch, as Donatello inter-
rupts Tomaso's rhapsodies to say, "You must not wait for Tomaso
to end his discourse . . . before drinking off your glass" (225),
Tomaso's description remains intact, reminding us of the physical dimension of the wine. Yet even that physical dimension,
involving as it does a comparison to tender, long-awaited sexual intimacy between two lovers, complements the spiritual-
religious connotations of the wine given earlier. In this wine,
spirit and body become one in a condition of innocent, even visionary sensuousness. Thus these passages on the Monte Beni
wine convey that same sense of the interrelatedness of vine,
grape, vintage, wine, physical taste, and spiritual perception
that, on a broader scale, has informed all aspects of intoxicant
use in Hawthorne's work.

# Chapter 7

# Too Sober or Too Drunken

## Melville's Dialogics of Drink

But since the too-sober view is, doubtless, nearer
true than the too-drunken; I, who rate truth, though
cold water, above untruth, though Tokay, will stick to
my earthen jug.
　　　　—Herman Melville, *The Confidence-Man*

I won't believe in a Temperance heaven.
　　　　—Melville, letter to Hawthorne, June 1851

Toby: Dost thou think, because thou art virtuous,
there shall be no more cakes and ale?
Clown: Yes, by Saint Anne, and ginger shall be hot i'
th' mouth too.
　　　　—passage in Shakespeare's *Twelfth Night*
　　　　marked by Melville

As far as drink is concerned, Hawthorne clearly has much in
common with Cooper: admiration of convivial pleasures, rejection of temperance dogmatism, disapproval of alcoholic excess.
Sharing Cooper's rich awareness of the physicality of drink,
Hawthorne's texts are also distinctly more cognizant of intoxi-

cation's physical aspects than are those of Emerson, Poe, or Dickinson. Nevertheless, Hawthorne reveals an affinity with a romantic Dionysianism that Cooper does not even acknowledge, much less approve or abjure. Cooper's perspective remains that of eighteenth-century rationalism, anchored in notions of good taste, virtue, decorum, and control of one's ruling passions. Since the issue of visionary intoxication or inspired Dionysianism does not exist for Cooper, he cannot affirm, deny, or even address the topic, let alone deal with it in as full and complex a manner as Hawthorne does. Much closer to Hawthorne in this regard is Herman Melville, who reveals a similar fascination with what Edwin Haviland Miller has called "the Dionysian depths or underworld of the unconscious," but who also retains sufficient skepticism to undercut his own effusive romanticizing of drink.[1]

The name of Melville reminds us how great a role the procurement, consumption, and discussion of drink played in the celebrated Hawthorne-Melville friendship.[2] But more pertinent to my purposes here is the pervasiveness and importance of intoxication as a topic in Melville's writing. In contrast to the surprising paucity of scholarly analysis of this topic for most of the other authors examined in this book, intoxication in Melville has garnered considerable critical attention. That attention, however, has tended to be highly compartmentalized. Thus Edward H. Rosenberry and Jane Mushabac focus on drink and humor; William B. Dillingham, on drink's symbolism in "The Paradise of Bachelors" and *The Confidence-Man;* William Bysshe Stein and Dorothee Metlitsky Finkelstein, on the imagery of visionary intoxication in Melville's poetry; David S. Reynolds, on Melville's fictional exploitation of "dark temperance" motifs.[3] Valuable as the discussions of these critics are, each deals with one particular corner of intoxication in Melville in isolation from its other aspects. In the pages that follow, I seek to bind these partial formulations into a more integrative discussion that will address the topic of Melville's treatment of intoxicant use as a significant human problem in and of itself and that will

clarify the range and depth of intoxication in Melville more precisely and fully than has yet been the case. This project will
place in greater relief the intoxication theme in Cooper and
Hawthorne as well, whose work reveals significant lines of connection and divergence from Melville's with regard to temperance, convivial drinking, and Dionysianism.

No writer has railed against teetotalism as charmingly as
Melville in a letter to Hawthorne written in June 1851—the same
month that saw controversial passage of the first Maine Law
prohibiting the sale of liquor.

> Would the Gin were here! If ever, my dear Hawthorne, in the
> eternal times that are to come, you and I shall sit down in Par-
> adise, in some little shady corner by ourselves; and if we shall
> by any means be able to smuggle a basket of champagne there
> (I won't believe in a Temperance Heaven), and if we shall then
> cross our celestial legs in the celestial grass that is forever trop-
> ical, and strike our glasses and our heads together, till both mu-
> sically ring in concert,—then, O my dear fellow-mortal, how
> shall we pleasantly discourse of all the things manifold which
> now so distress us,—when all the earth shall be but a reminis-
> cence, yea, its final dissolution an antiquity. . . . Let us swear
> that, though now we sweat, yet it is because of the dry heat
> which is indispensable to the nourishment of the vine which is
> to bear the grapes that are to give us the champagne hereafter.[4]

As this passage suggests, Melville fully shared not only Hawthorne's and Cooper's impatience with teetotalism but also their
appreciation of drinking and its accompanying rituals as essential to male bonding and civilized sociability. The passage
conveys as well Melville's awareness of the metaphorical potentialities of drink. But in addition to these qualities, Melville's depictions of intoxication confront the reader with a dizzying variety of attitudinal nuances and plausible but enigmatically
contradictory interpretations.

Repeatedly, Melville seems to mimic, mock, subvert, and
generally toy with the discourses of society and literature alike
on the subject of drink, almost as though he were experimenting with, rather than supporting or advancing them. Protemper-

ance (or are they only pseudotemperance?) sentiments, antiteetotal moderation, anacreontic whimsy, Dionysian inspiration,
sober rationalism, a fatalistic yearning for oblivion, absurdist
skepticism: these are the disparate elements that complement
and clash with one another in Melville's depictions of drink.
Eluding definite categorization, Melville's various modes of talking about intoxicants ultimately suggest the ironic indeterminacy of intoxication's meaning, as well as implying a larger,
more philosophical sense of the absurdity and indeterminacy of
life itself.

   In relation to drink, Melville's work often seems like a variation on Byron's ironic undercutting of his own paean to intoxication in the second canto of *Don Juan*. In a stanza whose opening lines we have seen earlier, in the chapter on Poe, Byron
glorifies the intoxicated state, raising it to the level of an all-
encompassing vision of human existence. But abruptly, the
stanza's concluding couplet brings the impassioned rhetoric
down to earth with a thud.

> Man, being reasonable, must get drunk;
>    The best of life is but intoxication:
> Glory, the grape, love, gold, in these are sunk
>    The hopes of all men, and of every nation;
> Without their sap, how branchless were the trunk
>    Of life's strange tree, so fruitful on occasion:
> But to return—Get very drunk, and when
>    You wake with headache, you shall see what then.
>                                        (*Don Juan*, 2:179)

   This passage typifies the quality in *Don Juan* that so annoyed Hazlitt: "You laugh and are surprised that anyone should
turn round and *travestie* himself. . . . A classical intoxication is
followed by the splashing of soda water, by frothy effusions of
ordinary bile."[5] With Melville, however, intoxication-related
ironies are achieved not only through the contrast of lofty
utterance with mundane event (e.g., bacchanalian rhetoric with
a hangover) but also through the friction of disparate modes of
language—in tone, vocabulary, imagery, and implication—that

suggest conflicting perspectives on such matters as temperance, sobriety, drunkenness, and drink itself. This often unresolved friction between competing voices in Melville exemplifies the Bakhtinian concept of the dialogic, with its openness, flexibility of perspective, and multiplicity of voice, as opposed to the constraints of the monologic mode. As my introductory chapter has shown, nineteenth-century American culture abounded with distinct social languages regarding intoxicant use; rather than subordinate these to one overriding discourse representing the author's superior perspective, Melville presents us with that shifting plurality of conflicting but valid voices that, for Bakhtin, constitutes the truly dialogic work of art.[6] As will become clear, however, this achievement entails artistic results that, in my view, are as uneven as Melville's narrative voices are multiple.

The dialogic quality emerges in the numerous varieties of intoxicant-related discourse present in Melville, often within a single work. These discursive "kinds" generally include the following basic positions or perspectives: temperance; conviviality; the consumption of alcohol as a symbolically charged social ritual; an Epicurean/Aristippean sense of pleasurable moderation; and a visionary dimension to intoxicant use that is especially strong in the poetry. And, except in the poetry, Melville's treatment of the intoxication theme points to a profound, restless skepticism that would seem to place "no trust" either in the pieties of sober, work-ethic rationalism or in the lofty, intoxicated flights of romantic imagination. One gets the sense that temperance, the pains of liquor and its pleasures, its evils and benefits, and the links between intoxication and otherworldly experience are *all* delusions. Even so, Melville brings us back to the need for the kind of psychic solace that Hawthorne associated with drink, for, as Melville expresses it in one of his late letters, "nepenthe seems all-in-all" (14:452). Only Melville's poetry on drinking themes is relatively free of this skepticism, as if in that more lyrical form Melville could allow himself the romanticizing of drink and the optimistic celebration of convivial communion that, in his prose, regularly meet with qualification, contradiction, and satire.

Because the intoxication theme in Melville's poetry has been so thoroughly and ably studied by Stein and Finkelstein, I focus primarily on the patterns outlined above in Melville's prose, especially *Omoo, Mardi, Moby-Dick,* and his last published fiction before his death, *The Confidence-Man.* This satirical novel, with its gleefully contradictory portrayals of drink, I take as paradigmatic of intoxication in Melville. Indeed, *The Confidence-Man* represents the apotheosis of the polyphonic ironies that play so prominent a role in Melville's treatment of intoxication. Pertinent here is a letter of 1877 that recalls the blend of skepticism and metaphysical whimsy that is typical of *The Confidence-Man* and that was already present in many of his earlier depictions of drink. Written some twenty years after *The Confidence-Man* was published, this letter (to John Hoadley) states, "Life is so short, and so ridiculous & irrational . . . that one knows not what to make of it, unless—well, finish the sentence for yourself" (14:454). Although overtly unrelated to intoxication, this spirit of absurdist skepticism may help us to understand the shifting meanings and insistent ironies that frequently characterize the portrayal of drink in Melville's work and that mark its distance from the moral certainties of Cooper and, even, from the often ironic but tonally more consistent complexities of Hawthorne.

*Omoo* is the first of Melville's works to explore intoxication at any length, and the first to present the ironizing diversity of perspectives that defines his treatment of this theme. Like the earlier *Typee,* much of *Omoo* reflects what the book's preface calls "the proverbial characteristics of sailors" (1), including heavy drinking. But while *Typee* contains only fleeting references to drink and to the gentle narcotic "arva," *Omoo* presents a fuller, more many-sided treatment of drink in relation to farcical humor, solace, social ritual, death or incapacitation, genuine conviviality, and the equally genuine but ironic undercutting of convivial ideals. In Melville, drink-related issues assume an irony, breadth, and almost perversely protean quality unsurpassed in antebellum writing.

As with Poe, paradox dominates Melville's depiction of drink in *Omoo*. In one protracted scene of shipboard carousing, death walks cheek by jowl with humor when the sailors "make a night of it," crawling about the deck with all the farcical ineptitude of the stage drunk. A crewman who finally manages to stand erect does so only, we are told, "by holding on to the tiller." This atmosphere of humorously raucous inebriety wears somewhat thin when two sailors drown by stepping "tranquilly over the side" of the ship (2:291–92). Yet these sailors—anonymous and completely unindividuated—are soon forgotten, and the ship coasts (Melville says at one point that it "staggered") along. Within a few sentences of the two sailors' deaths, the comic tone returns as the drowned sailors' rescued shipmates go ashore, "rolling before them their precious cask of spirits"—the contents of which, Melville coyly tells us, "soon evaporated" (2:291–92).

Similar paradoxical qualities appear in Melville's treatment of the alcoholic mate, Jermin, and his relationship to the crew. Clearly unsympathetic in his drunken viciousness, Jermin lacks the charm, wit, and quality of tragic mystery belonging to another copious drinker in the book, Dr. Long Ghost. But the very drinking habits that alternately enrage and incapacitate Jermin on some occasions play a more positive role, particularly when Jermin drinks moderately. "Taken in moderate quantities," says the narrator, "I believe, in my soul, it did a man like him good; brightened his eyes, swept the cobwebs out of his brain, and regulated his pulse. But the worst of it was, that sometimes he drank too much," with the result that he became "an obstreperous fellow" when "in his cups" (2:11). Ironically, however, Jermin's "one failing" (2:11) enables him to control the recalcitrant, violent crew—until, of course, they desert the ship. The narrator observes that "riotous at times as they were, the bluff, drunken energies of Jermin were just the thing to hold them [the sailors] in some sort of noisy subjection. . . . A sober, discreet, dignified officer could have done nothing with them; such a set would have thrown him and his dignity overboard" (2:114–15). In a further irony, the rest of the crew's sufferings at the hands of Jermin, as well as from the inherent hardships of a sea voyage, are eased by the same drink that so inflames the sailors' chief exploiter.

Again as in Poe—albeit on a far different, nonmetaphysical level—alcohol is both poison and cure, spurring Jermin on to his violent behavior but diminishing that behavior's effects among the sailors; the narrator explains, "There was one circumstance, to which heretofore I have but scarcely alluded, that tended more than any thing else to reconcile many to their situation. This was the receiving regularly, twice every day, a certain portion of Pisco, which was served out at the capstan, by the steward, in little tin measures called 'tots'" (2:48). Drink here becomes a precious means of escapism, as it often is in Melville ("nepenthe seems all-in-all").

Drink also serves as pretext for, and necessary adjunct to, the weekly convivial ritual that gives the sailors a sense of occasion that is so dismally absent from their lives the rest of the time. Thus, rather than gulp the liquor down from their "Saturday-night Bottles," the men gather for a bit of ceremony that gives them some semblance of festivity and social communion and that possesses its own set of established procedures: the "oldest seaman" first tastes the liquor from each of the two bottles regularly procured on Saturday nights, then "pours out the good cheer and passes it round like a lord doing the honors of his table" (2:48).

"Good cheer" is ultimately the chief value of drink in *Omoo*, as it is in Melville generally. It is also the chief attribute of the Catholic priests who visit the narrator and his fellow inmates in that travesty of a prison, the "Calabooza Beretanee" (British jail) in a section of the book that must have grated against the largely Protestant, antipapist mentality present among many in the mid-nineteenth-century American temperance movement. While the English missionaries merely leave "a package of tracts" (2:141) for the prisoners, the French Catholic priests and their companion, the Irish Father Murphy, visit the prisoners in person, simultaneously pouring out liquor and gladness for the inmates.

A veritable "club of Friar Tucks" (2:142), the Catholic priests drink long, rise late, and easily attract sailors to their mass.

> We all turned Catholics, and went to mass every morning, much to Captain Bob's consternation. Upon finding it out, he threatened to keep us in the stocks, if we did not desist. He went no farther than this, though; and so, every few days, we strolled down to the priest's residence, and had a mouthful to eat, and something generous to drink. In particular, Doctor Long Ghost and myself became huge favorites with [Father Murphy]; and many a time he regaled us from a quaint-looking traveling-case for spirits, stowed away in one corner of his dwelling. . . . In truth, the fine old Irishman was a rosy fellow in canonicals. His countenance and his soul were always in a glow. (2:144)

Dextrously turning Father Murphy's chronic tipsiness into a virtue—that is, a sign of his good fellowship and hospitality—the narrator continues, "It may be ungenerous to reveal his failings, but he often talked thick, and sometimes was perceptibly eccentric in his gait" (2:144). These traits, of course, are precisely what indicate Father Murphy's humanity, his rapport with the sailors, and his capacity for that ideal, "good cheer"—not to mention his capacity for good liquor. The chapter concludes, appropriately, with a toast to Father Murphy that fleetingly sounds, at first, like a rejection of drink but then turns into undiluted praise of the Irish priest and simultaneously indicates the narrator's own continuing status as a drinker: "I never drink French brandy, but I pledge Father Murphy. His health again! And many jolly proselytes may he make in Polynesia!" (2:144).

The virtues embodied by the "rosy" Father Murphy receive even more emphatic connection to drink in the late chapter called "A Dealer in Contraband," where, on their way to Taloo, Dr. Long Ghost and the narrator seek out the old, liquor-making native hermit, Varvy. After telling us more than we ever wanted to know about Varvy's "poteen"-making techniques, the chapter proceeds to replicate the buildup and ironic demolition of intoxication that I have noted in Byron's *Don Juan*. First, that key Melvillean sign of solace, the pipe, is introduced as a validating accompaniment to the drinking done by the narrator, Long Ghost, and Varvy. Between pipe and calabash, Varvy, Long Ghost, and the narrator grow in fellowship: "After a while, Long Ghost, who, at first, had relished the 'Arva Tee' as little as myself, to my surprise, began to wax sociable over it, with Varvy; and, before long, absolutely got mellow, the old toper keeping him company" (2:274).[7] Brotherly feeling begets more brotherly feeling, with Melville observing, "Every one knows, that, so long as the occasion lasts, there is no stronger bond of sympathy and good feeling among men, than getting tipsy together. And how earnestly, nay, movingly, a brace of worthies, thus employed, will endeavor to shed light upon, and elucidate their mystical ideas!" (2:274).

There is, of course, a definite touch of irony in the reference to the "mystical ideas" of two inebriated, down-and-out adventurers and their quasi-criminal host. But this gentle, almost affectionate irony amounts to no more than do Cooper's bemused comments in *Home as Found* on Captain Truck and the Commodore. Thus the celebration of drinking camaraderie between Varvy and Long Ghost seems, in the main, genuine, and continues with Varvy and the Doctor "lovingly tippling, and brimming over with a desire to become better acquainted" (2:274). But within a few brief phrases, the scene's convivial triumphs tumble down as Long Ghost rises the next morning with a terrible hangover. In a final further twist, his drink-induced agonies turn to outrage, as Long Ghost discovers his boots are missing and, certain of Varvy's deceit, must make his way to Taloo not only hungover but barefoot as well.

Yet the ironic turn Melville gives the Varvy episode functions more as a complementary, corrective view than a wholesale repudiation of the convivial ideal espoused earlier in that scene. In fact, like Byron in the intoxication passage cited from *Don Juan,* Melville here seems not to be promoting one view of drink over the other but to be expressing an ineluctable process of point and counterpoint, finally resulting in a blend that, as Melville says in another context, "is half melancholy, half farcical—like all the rest of the world" (*Journal,* 159).

The multiple perspectives on drink in *Omoo,* as well as the pattern of ardent assertion followed by ironic reversal, especially in the Varvy episode, appear even more extensively in *Mardi.* Melville's echoing of Rabelaisian motifs in *Mardi* and other works has long been a commonplace of Melville criticism.[8] But the representation of that central Rabelaisian preoocupation, drink, has received little attention in discussions of *Mardi.* That representation is anything but fixed. What is intoxication in *Mardi*? A series of assertions and images undercut by ironic subversions that are in turn reversed or subverted themselves, all in that spirit of chaotic playfulness that has delighted and annoyed—sometimes simultaneously—the book's readers from Melville's time to our own. The result is a persistent sense of intoxication's double-edged qualities. Drink's ambiguity in *Mardi* reflects, not the Emersonian uncertainty as to whether liquor is essentially positive or negative, but rather a sense of alcohol's simultaneous capacity for both good and evil. Nor does Melville present drink merely as a foe in the guise of a friend, as temperance authors often did, or as the unalloyed blessing that antitemperance spokesmen, in their resentment of teetotalism, sometimes saw in alcoholic beverages. In *Mardi,* drink is many things, but it is almost always both friend and foe, even at one and the same time.

Like *Omoo, Mardi* robustly proclaims drinking's connections to geniality. Early in the novel, Melville strikingly anticipates the image of a convivial heaven that we saw in his letter to Hawthorne and that appears also in a passage in *Moby-Dick* to which we shall turn later:

> In heaven, at last, our good, old white-haired father Adam will greet all alike, and sociality forever prevail. Christian shall join hands between Gentile and Jew, grim Dante forget his Infernos, and shake sides with fat Rabelais, and monk Luther, over a flagon of old nectar, talk over old times with Pope Leo. (3:13)

Within the framework of this genial ideal, however, Melville exploits multiple perspectives, ironies, contrasts, and modes of talking about intoxicants. The Luther passage itself is not challenged, but later chapters recall the ironizing tendencies of the Varvy episode in *Omoo,* while the shifting associations of drink throughout the book reveal an insistent pattern of ironic sub-version and counterpoint.

Melville's playful procedures regarding both intoxication and his reader are apparent in chapter 33, entitled "Otard," where the narrator defines one of the "cardinal virtues" of Jarl, the Norse ship's mate, as a "detestation and abhorrence of all vinous and spiritous beverages." This seemingly straightforward, protemper-ance statement actually serves as the setup for a most untemper-ance kind of punch line: for Jarl so detested alcohol "that he never could see any, but he instantly quaffed it out of sight." Leading the reader first one way and then the other at almost every turn of his prose, Melville goes on to call this trait Jarl's "weak side" but then has the narrator say, "I earnestly entreat, that it may not disparage him in any charitable man's estimation," and concludes the para-graph in which he introduced Jarl's drinking with the assertion that "the most capacious-souled fellows . . . are the most apt to be too liberal in their libations; since, being so large-hearted, they hold so much more good cheer than others." But the next three paragraphs switch perspective and tone again as they sound pseudosolemn cautionary notes about the ill effects of drink. These paragraphs are then followed by yet a fourth, which an-nounces, "So impressed was I with all this, that for a moment, I was almost tempted to roll over the cask on its bilge, remove the stopper, and suffer its contents to mix with the foul water at the bottom of the hold." Yet here again, temperance-seeming senti-ment is asserted only to be undercut as the narrator concludes the chapter with a brilliant passage of self-ironic rationalization that must be quoted in full to convey its deliberate, sly wit.

> But no, no: What: dilute the brine with the double distilled soul of the precious grape? Hafiz himself would have haunted me!
> Then again, it might come into play medicinally; and Paracel-sus himself stands sponsor for every cup drunk for the good of the abdomen. So at last, I determined to let it remain where it was: visiting it occasionally, by myself, for inspection.

But by way of advice to all ship-masters, let me say, that if your Otard magazine be exposed to view—then, in the evil hour of wreck, stave in your spirit-casks, ere rigging the life-boat. (3:106–07)

Melville's pattern of textual self-subversion is richly developed in a pair of later chapters (84, 85) dealing with Taji's visit to the realm of King Donjalolo. Chapter 84, "Taji sits down to Dinner with five-and-twenty Kings, and a royal Time they have," first appeared as a sample of the forthcoming *Mardi* in the Duyckincks's *Literary World* in 1849. With its quasi-Rabelaisian theme, chapter 84 consorted well with that journal's generally "wet" perspective and self-conscious worldliness. The familiar Melvillean link between wine and cheer, established earlier in the novel, appears almost at once in chapter 84's account of the beneficent effects of "Morando" wine, the drops of which undergo a metamorphosis from physical to psychological form, with the drinker's skull itself transformed into a kind of goblet: "a marvellous effect did it have, in dissolving the crystalization of the brain; leaving nothing but precious little drops of good humour, beading round the bowl of the cranium" (3:254). Continuing with an exuberantly metonymic yoking of the banquet wine with the boatlike calabashes containing it, the text of chapter 84 itself seems intoxicated with its own verbal pyrotechnics.

But soon, the Morando, in triumphant decanters, went round, reeling like barks before a breeze. But their voyages were brief and ere long, in certain havens, the accumulation of empty vessels threatened to bridge the lake [on which the decanters floated] with pontoons. (3:256)

The celebratory tone grows steadily as Taji launches into a hyperbolic apostrophe to yet another wine, Marzilla, the drinking of which "was as the singing of a mighty ode, or frenzied lyric to the soul." In that wine, cries Taji's friend, the king Donjalolo, "a king's heart is dissolved. . . . [I]n this wine lurk the seeds of the life everlasting. Drink deep; drink long: thou drinkest wisdom and valor at every draught. Drink forever, oh Taji, for thou drinkest that which will enable thee to stand up and speak out before mighty Oro himself" (3:257). This crescendo of vinous celebration intensifies with the anacreontic song of Donjalolo, which, despite its doggerel tendencies, suggests not irony but rather a versified version of that "bluff and hearty tone" that Ziff complains of in *Typee* and that frequently characterizes Melville's references to drink (Ziff, *Literary Democracy,* 11). Representative of the song as a whole is its vigorous last stanza.

> Then drink, gods and kings; wine merriment brings;
> It bounds through the veins; there, jubilant sings.
> Let it ebb, then, and flow; wine never grows dim;
> Drain down that bright tide at the foam beaded rim:—
> Fill up, every cup, to the brim!
>
> (3:258)

But to what, finally, do these vinous ecstasies lead? To stupefaction, sleep, and a royal hangover, as Taji and company find the king pale and trembling the morning after. It is through Donjalolo that Melville most explicitly addresses the double-edged quality of alcohol, as the king, in chapter 85, entitled "After Dinner," calls the wine he celebrated and consumed the night before a "treacherous, treacherous friend! full of smiles and daggers." There is no question here but that, as Bruce L. Grenberg has said, Donjalolo's is a "sodden, degraded existence" (Grenberg, 38). But just as Melville seems about to expose the hollowness of Donjalolo's pseudo-Dionysianism, he qualifies his prior qualification by having Donjalolo explain wine's usefulness in terms that seem free of any sardonic subtext. Rather, Donjalolo's words point to the profound sadness that underlies his desperate quest for gaiety: "Yet for such as me, oh wine, thou art e'en a prop, though it pierce the side; for man must lean. Thou wine art the friend of the friendless, though a foe to all. King Media, let us drink. More cups!—And now, farewell" (3:261). Even Donjalolo's presumably alcohol-induced stupor, as he falls back after delivering these lines, serves not to debunk drinking as such but to conclude the merry exuberance of the Donjalolo scenes with a subdued sense of the paradoxes and ironic limitations of humanity's longing for that elusive good cheer and sense of the ineffable that Melville's characters so often seek, and sometimes even find, but never manage to keep.

Further chapters in *Mardi* continue the techniques of multiple reversal and of ironies within ironies; like Russian nesting dolls, many a Mardian scene contains within itself some surprising or ironic twist on the intoxication theme that in turn contains yet another such twist. The Nora-Bamma scenes of chapters 87 and 88, for example, tellingly illustrate this pattern. Unnerving in its eerie lassitude, the isle of Nora-Bamma is nonetheless described in terms of unquestionable beauty, its seductive dreaminess evocatively rendered by Melville's prose: "But as we floated on, it looked the place described. We yawned, and yawned, as crews of vessels may; as in warm Indian seas, their winnowing sails all swoon, when by them glides some opium argosie" (3:266). The slow, drawn-out phrases full of long vowels and protracted nasals and sibilants (*m, n, s, z*), coupled with the absence of harsher consonant clusters and with the Lotos-land topic, produce an aptly languorous, somnolent effect. Yet the opening sentence of the next chapter powerfully qualifies the graceful drowsiness on which this chapter closed. Encapsulating the enigmatic doubleness of the seemingly sweet oblivion of Nora-Bamma, Babbalanja cries, "How Still! . . . This calm is like unto Oro's everlasting serenity, and like unto man's last despair" (3:267). What is most significant here is Melville's refusal to "take sides" on the condition of Nora-Bamma; rather, he insists on its dual nature, as a place that at once evokes both serenity and despair.

A very different kind of intoxication from Nora-Bamma's appears in the Falstaffian character Borabolla, whose drunken roistering and robust praise of wine are attended by a sudden attack of gout, cursings of wine, a vow never to drink again, and, within moments of the passing of his attack, a shameless return to the bottle. There is no question that, as Milton R. Stern has said, Borabolla is a "gout-ridden caricature of a man"—as, for that matter, is Falstaff (Stern, 130). And the obviousness of

Melville's mockery of Borabolla's short-lived, gout-inspired reformation needs no belaboring. But less obvious, and more important, is the fact that Melville does not leave us with one simple instance of comic irony. Instead of contenting himself with making Borabolla the butt of his own (Borabolla's, that is) inconsistency, Melville gives us a seemingly straightforward restatement of drink's geniality-inducing virtues.

> As the affinity between those chemical opposites chlorine and hydrogen, is promoted by caloric, so the affinity between Borabolla and Jarl was promoted by the warmth of the wine that they drank at this feast. For of all blessed fluids, the juice of the grape is the greatest foe to cohesion. True, it tightens the girdle; but then it loosens the tongue, and opens the heart. (3:292)

With Donjalolo and, in *Omoo*, with Varvy, Melville reverses the celebrations of drink through images of hangovers and other alcohol-related misfortunes: but in this passage on Borabolla, Melville reverses the condemnation of drunken folly with a hymn to wine as an inspirer of friendship.

Despite his greater intelligence and sophistication, Taji's friend Babbalanja reminds one of Borabolla when his frequent calls for a sane, balanced, Epicurean moderation are undercut by his bacchanalian oratory and drunkenness. But even so, Melville's text refuses to be pinned down to any definite position. In chapters 176 and 181, for example, what are we to make of Babbalanja proceeding to get drunk right after his own praise of moderation? Is it the professed ideal that is being mocked, or the person who fails to live up to it? The point of the contrast between word and deed is perversely inconclusive. Similarly Media, whose name suggests a kind of median or a medium, balanced path, speaks with forceful eloquence of many things just before he passes out drunk. But here too nagging questions remain: "muttering to himself," Babbalanja wonders at the fallen Media's sudden silence, and says, "Is this assumed, or real?—Can a demi-god be mastered by wine? Yet, the old mythologies make bacchanals of the gods. But he was wondrous keen! He felled me, ere he fell himself." Just after this, however, we read the following: "'Yoomy, my lord Media is in a very merry mood today,' whispered Mohi, 'but his counterfeit was not well done. No, no, a bacchanal is not used to be so logical in his cups'" (3:490). Was Media merely pretending to be drunk? Or has he succumbed to the strain of being "so logical in his cups"? Is the median philosophy of Media no more reliable than the Dionysian babblings of Babbalanja? These are among the unresolved possibilities raised but not resolved by the text.

Similar equivocations appear throughout *Mardi*. In chapters 191 and 192, for example, the rhetoric of Circean deception displaces that of hearty male conviviality when Hautia enchants Taji with her druglike wine, and in chapter 111, the life-enhancing properties of drink extolled elsewhere in the novel give way to associations with grotesqueness and deathly lamentation: containing "gourds of old wine," the obelisk to the god Mujo also holds three bizarre figures who, at first "holding stout wassail"— the kind of phrase that often in Melville signifies vinous good fellowship—disappear into the obelisk's inner recesses, from which there emerge only "a sepulchral chant, and many groans and grievous tribulations" (3:344). Thus *Mardi* continuously doubles back on itself, eluding any single, dominant view of intoxication, instead reveling in intoxication as a mirror of humankind's enigmatic, inconsistent nature.

The blatantly self-consuming ironies of *Omoo* and *Mardi* take on renewed force in Melville's last, darkly satirical novel, *The Confidence-Man*. But in *White-Jacket, Redburn,* and *Moby-Dick,* Melville treats intoxication more through ironic undercutting of earlier scenes or statements than through the presentation of multiple perspectives, be they complementary or conflicting, on drink and the drinker. In *White-Jacket,* scenes of drunken tragedy are balanced by drunken farce.[9] In *Redburn,* we may smile at the eponymous hero's temperance priggishness and may also note such things as the author's praise of ale and of grog's power to soften rough sailors' temperaments, but we must also recognize alcohol as the source of violence, even of death, as with the American sailor Danby who beats his

English wife, or the carpenter's boy who harms no one but drinks himself to death. In *Moby-Dick,* however, this range of associations appears most vividly in relation to temperance and conviviality.

Already in the novel's prefatory material, Melville introduces drink in relation to characterization, as he dismissively addresses the sub-sub-librarian: "Thou belongest to that hopeless, sallow tribe which no wine of this world will ever warm; and for whom even Pale Sherry would be too rosy-strong" (xvii). Curiously, however, the narrator's seeming scorn for the tepid-hearted Sub-Sub turns into sympathy and a surprising promise of joy in an afterworld whose nature Melville describes through a single oblique but nonetheless lucid image drawn from the social rituals of drink. "But gulp down your tears" says Melville, addressing all of the world's Sub-Subs, "and hie aloft to the royal-mast with your hearts; for your friends who have gone before are clearing out the seven-storied heavens, and making refugees of long-pampered Gabriel, Michael, and Raphael, against your coming. *Here ye strike but splintered hearts together—there, ye shall strike unsplinterable glasses!*" (6:xvii–xviii; my emphasis). Melville's phrasing here recalls the "temperance heaven" letter to Hawthorne written the same year that *Moby-Dick*—and the first Maine Law—came into being: 1851. Both Melville's masterpiece and the letter to Hawthorne use the notion of paradise itself as a vale of boon companionship and unsullied, freely quaffing conviviality.

A similar spirit informs numerous other passages in the book, where the text, though not overtly celebrating drink, seems sympathetic to those who do, such as the bottle-brandishing Captain of the Bachelor, and the seriocomic character Stubb, in whose anacreontic jingles and alcoholic enthusiasms Bacchus seems to meet W. C. Fields. That sympathy is also implicit, in a *negative* way, in Melville's scornful reference to the character of Dives who, "being a president of a temperance society . . . only drinks the tepid tears of orphans" (6:11). But Melville also has Ishmael declare, "Better sleep with a sober cannibal than with a drunken Christian" (6:24), and actually incorporates the rhetoric of temperance reform at several points, most notably the Spouter Inn scene, where the "little withered old man . . . for their money, dearly sells the sailors deliriums and death" (6:14). In this regard, we may also recall that seemingly sincere temperance tale in miniature, the chapter in *Moby-Dick* devoted to the alcoholic blacksmith, Perth; however, as Reynolds has shown, the Perth chapter, while drawing on temperance motifs, subverts the conventional perspective and tone. Noting that Melville eschews the typical temperance tale's didacticism, Reynolds points out, "In the story of Perth, Melville is showing how an ostensibly moralistic mode (the temperance narrative) in fact carries the seeds of a cynical portrait of human despair. The Perth episode shows that the dark-reform mode can be used as an appropriate entrance to gloomy message and mythic imagery" (Reynolds, 152). Melville's own, "real-life" views of drink, of course, lie primarily with the wets and the kind of jovial conviviality that his poetry and prose often depict.[10] But that convivial ideal appears in constant, ironic, and thought-provoking friction with other ways, positive and negative, of talking about drink.

For all their dialogic vitality, the examples I have been discussing reveal a clear relation to temperance and, especially, conviviality. But in *Moby-Dick* we find too a scene unique in Melville in its fusion of the demonic with the daimonic: Ahab, who scorns the jovial lubricity of the Bachelor's Captain, binds his sailors together in an emphatically *uncheerful* mode when he has them seal their fealty to his pursuit of the white whale by drinking a ritual toast.

In an inversion of Stubb's whiskey-soaked sentimentality, Ahab swears his crew to loyalty as he calls for the pewter measure bearing drink. The entire scene (in the same chapter in which Ahab nails the doubloon to the mast) exudes a sense of primitive, irrational bonding between master and men, with a latent Dionysianism seething beneath the somber ceremony. The drink itself is devilish—"hot as Satan's hoof," Ahab calls it, linking the drink further to the Satanic serpent as he says, "It spiralizes in ye; forks out at the serpent-snapping eye" (6:165). Ahab foreshadows the infernal baptism of his harpoon with the pagan harpooneers' blood when he has them drink. In light of the primordial symbolic relationship between alcohol and blood, manifested in the Christian eucharist, for instance, it is all the more appropriate when Ahab has the men use the sockets of their death-dealing harpoons as goblets, for it is those very harpoons that will draw *literal* blood out of Moby-Dick. [11]

Ahab calls his mates "cup-bearers to my three pagan kinsmen" (the three harpooneers), but he also calls them "my sweet cardinals" (6:166), and his ritual appears not only as some reenactment of paganism but also as a diabolical parody of Christian communion. Like communicants, the three harpooneers are ranged in front of the priestlike, officiating Ahab and await the ceremonial liquor. Paralleling the harpooneers, the three mates stand, like so many acolytes, ready to assist Ahab as he fills the harpoon/communion cups to the brim. That the entire ritual is a form of demonic communion is made explicit when Ahab calls the harpoon goblets "murderous chalices!" (6:166). And this demonism receives further emphasis from the serpentine sound of the whole crew drinking the fiery liquor from the sockets of their harpoons. "The long, barbed steel goblets were lifted; and to cries and maledictions against the white whale, the spirits were simultaneously quaffed down with a hiss" (6:166).

Unlike *Omoo* and *Mardi,* Melville's most famous work does not rely greatly on ironic undercutting of drinking discourses, but it does resemble the earlier novels in its assimilation and recasting of the imagery and language surrounding questions of intoxicant use and temperance. To be sure, Melville's diapason of reference does not include conventional temperance, but, as the Spouter Inn and Perth episodes show, it comes close to doing so, and certainly makes use of temperance's more sensationalistic elements. Moreover, among the various discursive modes that it does employ, *Moby-Dick* never gives unquestioned primacy to any one perspective on the topic of intoxication. The same breadth of interpretive possibility regarding intoxication typifies Melville's final novel, which returns to, indeed outdoes, the whimsically ironic, undercutting procedures of *Omoo* and *Mardi*.

Drinking in *The Confidence-Man* is treated with a pervasive skepticism whereby virtually every instance of drinking or temperance is countered with an ironic inversion. Throughout the book, the various colloquies on drink are not resolved in favor of any of the participants. The stranger, the bachelor, and the cosmopolitan all make eloquent, forceful assertions that reflect prominent traditions of discourse about intoxication in Melville's culture: ideals of male sociability and hospitality, disciplined moderation, high-toned abstinence, openness and trust as embodied in the willingness to share drinks in the established tradition of "hobnobbing." But then, just as forcefully, each statement is undercut, making a definite, unambiguous conclusion impossible.

This inconclusiveness is reflected in the divergent reactions that some have had to the novel's presentations of drinking. In a recent article, Rosenberry argues that the bachelor's comment—"the too-sober view is . . . nearer true than the too-drunken" (10:135)—represents Melville's own views. "Everywhere in Melville," writes Rosenberry, "the drunken man is a self-evading figure of comedy, the sober man open to the insights of tragic truth" (Rosenberry, "Melville's Comedy and Tragedy," 608). In a book published the same year as Rosenberry's essay (1986), Dillingham maintains almost the exact opposite, claiming that in *The Confidence-Man* the "great praise of wine drinking is in actuality a commendation of truth seeking. . . . For both [Melville and Rabelais], imbibing is the metaphor for discovering the hidden sun" (Dillingham, *Melville's Later Novels*, 319).

But does *The Confidence-Man* truly support either of these positions? Does it, in fact, promulgate a definite position about anything, as opposed to playfully presenting a range of ideas and perspectives, with the author as a noncommittal, ironic puppeteer? Granting, for the sake of argument, that the book does promote certain ideas about drinking, may it not be promoting a far more chilling, pessimistic possibility than those proposed by Rosenberry and Dillingham—namely, that neither drunkenness nor sobriety makes any sense? Such an attitude finds support in the ways that the author veers from one position to the other, tongue firmly in cheek at all times; if temperance never receives the last word here, neither does geniality or connoisseurship or the kind of good fellowship that we know Melville admired in private life and that, despite his various ironies, shines through his other works. For example, in the chapters devoted to those "boon companions," Charlie Noble and Frank Goodman, neither man trusts the other. Both praise drink and its supposedly benef-icent effects, and urge the other to drink, but scarcely take a sip themselves. Their cagey pseudoconviviality perfectly embodies, in fact, a comment that Melville underlined in Sa'di's *Gulistan:* "at table enemies assume the appearance of friends" (Cowen, 288). But never does Melville take sides, any more than, say, Twain does, in the admittedly broader, more unambiguously and flagrantly spurious dialogues between the Duke and the King in *The Adventures of Huckleberry Finn.*

The implications of all this for our topic are an indetermi-nacy more profound than anything else we have seen in Mel-ville—or any other writer. For if, as the bachelor maintains, "Ra-belais's pro-wine Koran is no more trustworthy than Mahomet's anti-wine one," neither is the Koran of "Mahomet" superior to that of Rabelais (10:135). Both of these "Korans" would seem only to testify to that larger problem of life's perplexing nature, indicated by Melville's reference, in one of his late letters, to "these inexplicable fleshly bonds" (14:454).

Intoxication in Melville encompasses so broad—even unsta-ble—a range of nuances that his treatment of the theme might itself seem as inexplicable as the fleshly bonds of which Melville complained. "Oh you man without a handle!" said Henry James, Sr., to Emerson (quoted in Feidelson, 119). Much the same could be said of Melville on the subject of intoxication, except that Melville's very elusiveness in this area *is* the handle, in a sense.

Shuttling between satire and sympathy with regard to drink, Melville never drops anchor at any definite interpretive port. As a result, Melvillean intoxication becomes not so much a topic as a field of discursive possibilities whose deconstructive play undermines any notion of thematic consistency or fixed ideological bearings. Experimenting with these possibilities, Melville exhibits an alternately happy and melancholy abandon, seeming to find that with intoxication as with so much else, "truth is ever incoherent," as he once wrote to Hawthorne (14:213). The result is less a quest for intoxication's hidden truth than a sometimes exuberant, sometimes resigned exploration of the manifold rhetorical positions that the intoxication theme so abundantly provides.

At times, that exploration led Melville into what seem to me to be wrong artistic turns. Some passages in *The Confidence-Man*, in fact, sound strangely like self-parody, for example, the feeble Rabelaisianism in parts of *Mardi* and *Omoo*, the coy humor and painfully labored jocularity of the "stranger" in *The Confidence-Man*. In reaching for the Falstaffian note, Melville's authorial voice sometimes broke, and even in so "uninhibited" a novel as *Omoo* (Rosenberry, *Melville and the Comic Spirit,* 20), some of his celebrations of drink have all the conviction of a department store Santa Claus's "ho-ho-ho." But then Melville rises above these banalities to moments of powerful vision involving intoxicants, as in the Nora-Bamma passage in *Mardi,* the perfectly paced Byronic ironies of that novel and of *Omoo,* the drinking of the infernal toast that seals Ahab's covenant with his crew, and the use of wine imagery in Melville's later poetry to suggest communion with an alternative reality to that of the everyday world. All of these instances, and others like them, testify to the remarkable discursive diversity of intoxication in Melville.

This diversity is composed of voices that, whatever their differences, share one fundamental trait: they are distinctly, even emphatically male. It would be easy (and partly accurate) to attribute this fact to the often mentioned overwhelming maleness of Melville's characters, themes, and settings, whether these involve the voices of bardic poets and fantastically convivial kings in *Mardi,* grog-guzzling old tars in *Omoo, Redburn, White-Jacket,* and *Moby-Dick,* or sensitive spirits seeking brotherly communion through wine in *Clarel* and other poems. But the roots of the matter extend deeper than this. They reach down, as Captain Ahab might say, into the "little lower layer" of social-literary relations, and of the conventions governing permissible authorial discourse for men and women in Melville's day.

However disparate Melville's voices of intoxication may be, their range of tones and associations—like the range we find in Hawthorne and even the more narrowly genteel Cooper—was possible only for male authors. The full import of this statement will become clearer after we understand the discourses available to, practiced by, and sometimes defied by antebellum female authors. To attain that understanding, however, we must now turn to a very different aspect of our topic—the relationship between intoxication and the politics and poetics of gender in nineteenth-century America.

# Chapter 8

# Forbidden Fruit

## Nineteenth-Century American Female Authorship and the Discourses of Intoxication

The path of poetry, like every other path in life, is to the tread of woman, exceedingly circumscribed. She may not revel in the luxuriance of fancies, images and thoughts, or indulge in the license of choosing themes at will, like the Lords of creation.

—Sarah Josepha Hale, *Lady's Magazine*

Drunkards are death to the women—to the wives and mothers and sisters; but some of 'em are more lovable than lots of the moral skinflints that go nagging about.

—Dr. Knox in Constance Fenimore Woolson, *Jupiter Lights*

Come drunks and drug-takers; come perverts un-
    nerved!
Receive the laurel, given, though late, on merit; to
    whom and wherever deserved.
Parochial punks, trimmers, nice people, joiners true-
    blue,
Get the hell out of the way of the laurel. It is deathless.
    And it isn't for you.

—Louise Bogan, "Several Voices out of a Cloud"

In *Drinking in America,* Lender and Martin tell the old story of the American congressman who was "asked by a constituent to explain his attitude toward whiskey. 'If you mean the demon drink that poisons the mind, pollutes the body, desecrates family life and inflames sinners, then I'm against it,' the Congressman said. 'But if you mean the elixir of Christmas cheer, the shield against winter chill, the taxable potion that puts needed funds into public coffers to comfort little crippled children, then I'm for it. This is my position, and I will not compromise'" (Lender and Martin, 169).

This amusing anecdote neatly encapsulates the ambivalence that, as we saw earlier, has long been characteristic of American attitudes toward intoxicants, especially alcohol.[1] But the story is also significant in suggesting the widely differing ways of talking about alcohol and drugs, the disparate discourses of intoxication that have been prevalent in American culture. The congressman replies not with a comment about any reality called whiskey but rather with a menu of signifiers that he can manipulate with little or no regard for anything so mundane as an actual signified beverage. Within his response we can detect implied discourses of economics, morality, medicine, social ritual, and various possible subdiscourses buried within some or all of these (e.g., within the larger framework of the discourse of "morality," there are the associations of heavy drinking with sexual misconduct implied by phrases like "pollutes the body," "desecrates family life," and "inflames sinners").

Embodied in the entire first half of the Congressman's statement is one of the most pervasive, influential discourses in American history—that of militant temperance, within the larger scope of which some of the subdiscourses mentioned above are contained. And it was this discourse that dominated nineteenth-century American writing about drink that was produced by women.

In earlier chapters we saw that American male authors, despite the pervasiveness of temperance ideology, were free to write of intoxicated experience from a variety of viewpoints, whether positive or negative. Among the perspectives available to male authors, temperance was important, but still it was only one of several. This diversity of approaches is apparent in the complex tensions between Dionysianism and self-control in Emerson's and Hawthorne's ideas about intoxication; in Poe's ambiguous explorations of altered states of consciousness and perception; in the celebrations of Falstaffian drinking in Cooper; in the impingement of temperance views not only on such overtly propagandistic works as Whitman's temperance novel, *Franklin Evans,* but also on more mainstream works of literature; in alcohol as a source of violence, tragedy, humor, and physical enjoyment in Cooper and Hawthorne; and in the manipulation of nearly all of the above modes in the unpredictable, ironic, relentlessly protean prose of Melville.

Women authors, in contrast, tended overwhelmingly to write from a rigidly protemperance perspective, in which almost any use of intoxicants was defined as addictive and in which teetotalism and prohibitionism edged out other approaches to intoxicant use and abuse. The reasons for this pattern in American women's writing were twofold: the existence of strict socioliterary codes governing the permissible bounds of female expression and a predisposition of many women from the 1820s on to view nearly all drinking as inimical to their own interests and welfare. Emily Dickinson, as we have discovered, was the major exception to this pattern. Dickinson was capable of showing fully the despair and sordidness of alcoholism, and attacked as illusory the clinging to anodynes of any kind: chemical, psychological, religious. Yet at the same time Dickinson employed a Dionysian discourse that echoed romantic views of poetic inspiration as itself a kind of intoxication and that used positive, celebratory images of intoxicant use to suggest that distortion can sometimes be a means of illumination. But Dickinson was virtually unknown and unpublished (except for eight poems) in her lifetime. Apart from Dickinson and a few other exceptions, women's writing followed the temperance orientation outlined above. Only near the turn of the century do we find a significant shift toward greater pluralism in women's discourses of intoxication, as evident in the work of Kate Chopin, Edith Wharton, and Willa Cather.[2]

Our examination of changing images of intoxication in women's writing will enable us to understand more fully the overall literary-historical context of this theme in nineteenth-century American literature; it will put into greater relief the variety of discourses used by Emerson, Dickinson, Poe, Melville, and such "fellow travelers" of temperance as James Fenimore Cooper, Nathaniel Hawthorne, and William Gilmore Simms; and it will illuminate the work of those writers who challenged the codes governing female authorship at century's end. We must begin, however, with a closer look at the reasons behind the temperance-based pattern of literature produced by women in the United States. We can then discuss the essential features of that pattern, and the few exceptions to it, in representative works of fiction by Mary Jane Holmes, Harriet Beecher Stowe, Louisa May Alcott, Elizabeth Stuart Phelps, and Elizabeth Drew Stoddard. By way of contrast, we will conclude by exploring the turn toward the more varied depiction of intoxication by Chopin, Wharton, and, especially, Cather.[3] This project will, thus, necessarily involve a consideration of more authors than earlier chapters, as well as a more detailed consideration of social context. It will also take us somewhat further chronologically than other chapters, thereby pointing toward the epilogue and its discussion of later developments in the literary depiction of intoxication.

Earlier I mentioned the existence of socioliterary codes restricting topics and attitudes permissible for women authors. These codes sprouted from deep, intertwined roots: the long-established double standard regarding male and female use of intoxicants in Western culture; the increasingly dominant cult of female domesticity and "purity" (i.e., the American version of the "angel in the house" syndrome familiar in Victorian England); and the special moral scrutiny given by reviewers and readers to female authors' private lives and reputations in contrast to those of their male counterparts.

The double standard for men and women drinkers throughout Western history has been amply documented by such historians of alcohol use as Marian Sandmaier, Gregory Austin, and Mark Edward Lender, all of whom have shown that, even when male drunkenness has been condemned, female inebriety is often singled out for particular criticism.[4] This "special stigma," to use Lender's phrase, was powerfully felt in nineteenth-century America, which witnessed a sentimentalization and rigidification of concepts of "ladylike" behavior and appropriate female roles. For middle-class Americans, "the ideal woman" was a "paragon of social virtue and a guardian of the home," while the "alcoholic" embodied all that threatened the ideal woman. Thus a drunken woman became a particularly disreputable, almost unthinkable phenomenon.[5]

Prominent temperance spokesmen and physicians did much to promulgate such views, despite increasing perceptions of addiction as a disease. Addressing the Ladies' Temperance Society of Sandy-Hill, New York, in 1832, Dr. W. K. Scott could speak only tentatively of women's alcohol abuse, thereby implying its relative heinousness to that of men: "I have before adverted to the practice of furnishing wine and other liquor, for the entertainment of our friends. And I firmly believe, that many a man, and many a child, have been ruined by so doing (and if I *dared* to, I would whisper, some women too)." Similarly, the Harvard Medical School professor H. R. Storer expressed long-familiar sentiments when he wrote in 1867 that "a drunken woman would have made purgatory of Eden," ominously adding, "she would make such of heaven." Continuing in this vein, Storer maintained that "a debauched woman is always, everywhere, a more terrible object to behold than a brutish man. We look to see them a little nearer to the angels than ourselves, and so their fall seems greater."[6] A few years later (1873) a temperance tract made the then-common connection between an alcoholic woman and sexual immorality, since alcoholism "was a likely sign that a woman had left 'the paths of virtue . . . to spend a dreadful and pitiable life of sin'" (quoted in Lender, 48). Similarly, the threat to women from drinking and from associating with men who drank was apparent in an 1878 treatise, "Opium and Alcoholic Inebriacy": "The musical alliteration, women and wine, has crystallized in the world's memory. For ages, these words have been on the lips of the bacchanal, and in the song and toast of revelry, and always to the hurt of women."[7]

The deeply ingrained taboos on female intemperance, and often even on female drinking of any kind, would make it unlikely for a woman author to write about intoxication other than from the narrow perspectives of temperance. Indeed, anything other than a temperance-oriented account might be construed as somehow reflective of the morals of the author herself. This could be a genuine concern for American women writers, as they came under much closer personal scrutiny than did men who wrote—at least for much of the period under consideration here. In the words of Nina Baym, "While reviewers almost never considered the private lives of male authors, they did discuss the lives of women," a fact that must have constrained women's writing in ways that we will never fully know. Baym observes that American women writers struck a bargain with their society that may be summarized thus: "Women may write as much as they please providing they define themselves as women writing when they do so, whether by tricks of style—diffuseness, gracefulness, delicacy; by choices of subject matter—the domestic, the social, the private; or by tone—pure, lofty, moral, didactic" (Baym, *Novels,* 254, 257).[8] Such a "bargain" would, of course, militate against any treatment of intoxication that went against the grain of narrowly conceived ideals of womanhood and temperance.

Even women condemning male intemperance could encounter criticism for overemphasizing unsavory details. In 1848, a reviewer for the *Literary World* attacked Anne Brontë's *Tenant of Wildfell Hall* as unrealistic, because the novel showed the heroine's drunkard husband mistreating his wife with impunity. In maddeningly circular reasoning, the review asserts that "the same natural law that decrees the dependence of women guarantees their happiness and safety in the arrangement" (quoted in

Baym, *Novels,* 171). In 1854, another reviewer, this time for the popular *Godey's* magazine, warned that too many women authors, "women of literary reputations, of refined sentiments and delicate nerves—are employing their talents in describing minutely the scenes of drunkenness which are said to occur at public hotels." Such scenes should better be left in darkness, because of the danger of introducing young female readers "to the companionship of the vulgar, the obscene, and the vicious," even when the professed aim is to "teach morality."[9]

The great irony of such idealized notions of female purity and of its connection to teetotalism was the undercurrent of female addiction running throughout nineteenth-century American society. As Dr. William Sweetser put it in 1829, "Many females would regard it as grossly vulgar to drink a glass of rum and water, but disguise it under the alluring shape of a cordial or stomachic elixir, and conscience is at once quieted" (Grob, *Nineteenth-Century Medical Attitudes,* 72). Nearly sixty years later, female addiction to drugs too freely prescribed by doctors, or to various home medications generously laced with alcohol, opium, and other addictive substances, was still a major problem. Indeed, "during the nineteenth century, the typical opiate addict was a middle-aged white woman of the middle or upper class" (Courtwright, 1). But while such addiction was frowned upon, it did not bring the kind of opprobrium that female alcoholism did; the lassitude and passivity induced by the opiates generally used by women were perceived as more "feminine" than the effects produced by liquor, the masculine intoxicant "of choice." Although fewer women than men abused alcohol, many more women drank than people realized or admitted, and many women who did drink excessively were forced to hide their problem, thus becoming "invisible alcoholics" whose condition would go undiagnosed and untreated.[10]

In a distinguished essay on women and temperance in the United States, the sociologist Harry Gene Levine notes that "during the nineteenth century, the restrictions against women's getting drunk were so strong among Protestant middle class supporters of the temperance cause that the *topic* of women's in-temperance was itself almost taboo" (Levine, "Temperance and Women," 33). This attitude extended to much literature, despite the occasional depiction of female drunkenness or addiction, as in Sarah Josepha Hale's *My Cousin Mary* (1839), Ann Stephens's *The Old Homestead* (1855), or Mary Nichols's *Agnes Morris* (1849). Even writing about so sophisticated and artistic a work as George Eliot's "Janet's Repentance," Henry James questioned the selection of a "heroine stained with the vice of intemperance. The author chose it [the topic] at her peril" (quoted in Shaw, 174–75).[11] Thus the social discourses that defeminized and damned drunken and often even nonteetotaling women, together with rigid codes regulating the subject matter and tone of women's writing, created a cultural climate distinctly unfavorable to the female expression of anything but high-minded revulsion toward drink and drugs.

But while the codes restricting female discourses of intoxication were powerful, they accounted for only part of the picture. Even in the absence of such codes, it is doubtful that many women *would* write about intoxication other than they did (although we will shortly examine some exceptions to the temperance-dominated pattern of women's writing). The line between what is permitted and what is desired can sometimes blur, but it seems that the Dionysian was not only not a permissible mode for female authors, it was one that not many antebellum women would find either plausible or desirable. For one thing, as Joanne Dobson observes, "the structures of their [women's] socialization were in direct conflict with the doctrine of American individualism then widely promulgated by Ralph Waldo Emerson and other influential cultural arbiters" (Dobson, 225).

The individualism and rebelliousness often associated with drinking was not a viable mode for women, as it could be for even the most strictly raised men. But there was also just too much enmity felt by women toward the bitter fruits of male intoxication for many women to find the stance of Dionysian rebellion appealing. In this regard, an obscure detail from ancient history becomes powerfully suggestive of the relations of women to intoxication in Victorian America. Dionysos, god of wine, appeared for the first time among twelve gods of Olympus in 432 B.C., when his statue in the frieze of the Athenian Parthenon replaced that of Hestia, goddess of the hearth (Austin, 22). This fact is almost uncanny in its applicability to the tension between women and drink in American society of the 1800s. From the very beginnings of the temperance movement, women battled against liquor in the name of hearth and home, and the phrase "home protection" eventually became the motto of the Women's Christian Temperance Union.

In part, women's opposition to alcohol stemmed from a gradual but inexorable change in the status and meaning of alcohol in America's social structure. Paul Johnson has shown that during the 1820s masters and workmen began to grow farther apart socially and economically, with female piety dominating the middle class. Whereas drinking had once served as an important symbolic bond between the owning and laboring classes, under the influence of that piety masters drank less and less with workers; by 1830, "the doorway to a middle-class home separated radically different kinds of space: drunkenness and promiscuous sociability on the outside, privacy and icy sobriety inside" (Johnson, *Shopkeeper's Millennium,* 57–58). But women's opposition to alcohol also stemmed from the genuine pervasiveness of male alcohol abuse, which often resulted in the physical, emotional, and economic suffering of women. In many states, despite some reform in property laws, women were powerless against a drunken husband's waste of property and money. Quite naturally, temperance linked itself with women's rights issues and provided many women with "a sense of collective purpose and solidarity" (Aaron and Musto, 146).[12]

At times, temperance itself could become a veritable addiction, as indicated in this comment of a female crusader: "I began going [to women's temperance meetings] twice a week, but soon got so interested that I went every day, and then twice a day in the evenings. I tried to stay home to retrieve my neglected household, but when the hour for the morning prayer meeting came around, I found the attraction irresistible. The Crusade was a daily dissipation from which it seemed impossible to tear myself. In the intervals at home, I felt as I fancy the drinker does at the breaking down of a long spree" (Aaron and Musto, 147).

In light of this historical situation, it is understandable that despite some flagging in the late 1850s and the Civil War years, the temperance movement soon picked up momentum again, fueled in large part by women's activism. By 1869, four years after the end of the Civil War and five years before the founding of the powerful Women's Christian Temperance Union, the *New York Herald* predicted that "the next war in this country will be between women and whiskey" (quoted in Furnas, 232).

As far as mainstream literature was concerned, the chief weapon in that war was a sticky compound of tears, treacle, and temperance. And most women writing about intoxication followed the same basic pattern, incorporating some or all of the following motifs: alcoholism as a disease, albeit tinged with moral overtones; the danger even (or especially) of moderate drinking; the use of intoxicants as something alien or unnatural to women; alcohol as a poisonous, literally in*toxic*ating substance; drunkenness as the cause, not the result, of poverty; the disastrousness of being married to a drinking man; weddings arranged by force or trickery, whereby an innocent young woman is chained to an abusive drunkard; and the importance of female influence on drinkers—provided, of course, that the influence be well within the boundaries signified by the catch phrase, "woman's proper sphere." These patterns, or slight variations on them, were common in the works of popular, influential female authors like Sarah Josepha Hale, Susan Warner, E. D. E. N. Southworth, Ann Stephens, Mary Jane Holmes, Harriet Beecher Stowe, Frances Ellen Watkins Harper, and Louisa May Alcott.[13]

None of these particular authors was a temperance writer per se, although some, like Hale, Stowe, Harper, and Alcott, readily lent their pens to the temperance cause.[14] Sometimes, as in the epigraph to this chapter from Constance Fenimore Woolson, or in Stephens's *The Old Homestead* (1855), we even find some criticism of temperance self-righteousness. But in the main, female authors were thoroughly committed to the temperance movement and all that it implied: rationalism; middle-class respectability; respect for established order; industriousness; self-discipline; emphasis on the communal over the individualistic. These values are epitomized in Harper's pithy conclusion to "The Two Offers" (1859), generally considered to be the first short story published by an African-American. Lauding restraint and the sober pursuit of duty rather than pleasure or passion, Harper writes that "true happiness consists not so much in the fruition of our wishes as in the regulation of our desires and the full development and right culture of our whole natures" (70).

The commitment to such self-discipline, of which temperance became a venerated emblem, was a solemn matter. In an essay published in 1843, for example, Stowe expressed indignation at Charles Dickens for having a clergyman in *The Pickwick Papers,* the Reverend Mr. Tiggins, appear drunk at a temperance meeting. Stowe went on to take the famous British novelist to task for ignoring American drunkenness even though he attacked American slavery. Indeed, because Dickens could "burlesque temperance speeches, temperance hotels, and temperance societies," Stowe concluded that the published author of *Sketches by Boz, The Pickwick Papers, Oliver Twist, Nicholas Nickleby,* and *The Old Curiosity Shop* was "a person of no very profound habits or capacity of reflection on moral subjects" (quoted in Gossett, 57–58).

For authors like Stowe, it was simply impossible to make light of so weighty an issue as the battle against intoxication, a single experience of which was, in the eyes of many, a fate literally worse than death. A striking but not untypical instance of this attitude is found in *Meadow Brook,* an 1857 novel by the immensely popular Mary Jane Holmes.[15] The fictional narrator shows us the reaction to a young man's drunkenness at a family gathering.

"Merciful Heavens! it's as I feared!" was Aunt Charlotte's excla-
mation, as she sank upon the lounge, moaning bitterly, and covering her face with the cushion, that she might not see the disgrace of her only son—for Herbert was *drunk!*

At this point, the narrator thinks of her own mother, who had recently mourned the death of her infant boy.

My mother, as she looked upon the senseless inebriate resting
where once had lain the beautiful, inanimate form of her
youngest born, thought how far less bitter was *her* cup of sorrow than was that of the half-fainting woman, who would
rather, far rather, her boy had died with the dew of babyhood
upon his brow than to have seen him thus debased and fallen.
(35)[16]

While this novel's main story centers on the maturation of
the narrator—the young woman, Rosa—into a high-minded
schoolteacher, its major subplot concerns the sorry fate of the
dissipated Herbert and his wife, Rosa's sister Anna. Throughout
*Meadow Brook* we learn of the immense power of women to influence men for good or evil. Herbert's alcoholism, it turns out,
like that of the ill-fated Charles in Alcott's *Rose in Bloom* (1876),
results from maternal overindulgence. Later, after a temporary
period of abstinence, the hapless Herbert finally succumbs to
the temptation of a drink taken at a wedding feast. And once
again, the explanation of Herbert's tragedy offered by the author
might be summarized by the phrase, "cherchez la femme." At the
wedding party, the unbelievably insistent young bride callously
demands that Herbert, as a gentleman and a guest, drink to her
health. The drink Herbert reluctantly consumes takes him on a
binge that ends in fits, delirium tremens, and death. Before he
dies, however, Herbert manages one more attack on the female
sex as he deliriously fantasizes about killing his little son so as
to send him to heaven "where women, with witching eyes and
luring words, never tempt men to drink" (208).

But if woman is poison in this novel, she is also antidote. Despite its condemnation of women who lead men astray, *Meadow
Brook* is not some bizarre instance of female-authored misog-

yny but rather a zealously admonitory piece of propaganda for woman's power correctly used. Stressing the point that women possess vast potential for good or evil, Holmes directs them toward the former, whether as mothers, sisters, lovers, or wives. It is especially to mothers that the book addresses its main message about drink, as articulated in a temperancelike sermonette that warns, "little know they what they do, who set before their sons the poisonous cup, and bid them, by their own example, drink and die." Parents—particularly mothers—must vigilantly teach the lesson, " 'touch not, taste not, handle not'; for therein alone lieth safety" (155).[17]

Holmes's emphasis on the need for women to exercise their beneficent influence on men is common among nineteenth-century female writers (and among a goodly number of male authors too) and is frequently related to alcohol in the work of the century's most popular author, Harriet Beecher Stowe. This concern with woman's influence is already apparent in one of Stowe's earliest publications dealing with drink, the short story "The Coral Ring" (1843), where a young woman's friendly admonitions bring a man back from the brink of alcoholism. But it is in Stowe's later works, beginning with *Uncle Tom's Cabin,* that the theme of intoxication, and of intoxication's relations to women, gains greater depth and interest—even if Stowe's basic message is still reducible to Holmes's echo of Stowe's own father's famous warning: "TOUCH NOT, TASTE NOT, HANDLE NOT" (Beecher, *Six Sermons,* 40). Indeed, Stowe's archvillain Simon Legree (arguably the most infamous figure in nineteenth-century literature) owes much of his viciousness to his youthful flouting of his mother's temperance ideals. Like the mother in Lydia Huntley Sigourney's temperance story, "The Widow and Her Son," Mrs. Legree could well exclaim of Simon, "He despised my woman's voice, my motherly love" (quoted in Douglas, 47). In denying his mother and embracing liquor, Legree follows a path leading to crime, rapacity, slave dealing, and, appropriately, death in delirium tremens, during which visions of his abused, dead mother haunt him.

Legree's embodiment of the drunken male denial of everything female, already suggested in the rejection of his mother,
emerges tellingly in his attempts to intoxicate his concubine,
Emmeline. Both slave and woman, and a sexual slave to Legree,
the helpless Emmeline is forced to violate not only her own will
(not to drink) but also that of her mother, who had forbidden her
to taste alcohol. Thus a double denial of the feminine is at work
here. At the center of that denial lies the manipulation of women
through liquor dispensed by a man enacting the multiple roles
of racial and sexual exploiter and, in effect, drug pusher, the
drug in this case being alcohol. Nowhere is this phenomenon
more forcefully dramatized than in the following dialogue between Emmeline and Cassy, late in the novel.

> "He wanted to make me drink some of his hateful brandy," said
> Emmeline; "and I hate it so———"
> "You'd better drink," said Cassy. "I hated it too; and now I can't
> live without it. One must have something;—things don't look so
> dreadful when you take that."
> "Mother used to tell me never to touch any such thing," said
> Emmeline.
> "*Mother* told you!" said Cassy, with a thrilling and bitter em-
> phasis on the word mother. "What use is it for mothers to say
> anything? You are all to be bought, and paid for, and your souls
> belong to whoever gets you. That's the way it goes. I say, *drink*
> brandy; drink all you can, and it'll make things come easier."
> (2:157)[18]

Cassy here despairs of the impossibility of any finer "feminine" spirit or ideals, represented by "Mother," in Legree's world.
It is as if alcohol and motherhood become two antithetical principles, incapable of sharing the same space; drink usurps the
mother's protective authority, so that it is no use for mothers to
"say anything." Where the drinker reigns, the mother is banished. But in Cassy's embittered speech we also find a sympathy
for the drunkard that became increasingly evident throughout
Stowe's career. We learn here that Cassy drinks not out of sensual indulgence but as an escape from her brutal circumstances.
Similarly, when Tom asks a wretched slave woman why she

drinks, she replies, "To get shet o' my misery" (1:285). This sympathy for the victims of drunkenness grows into a deeper, more complex sense of the power of addiction in two otherwise undistinguished novels of the 1870s, *My Wife and I* and its sequel, *We and Our Neighbors*. Doubtless impelled partly by her own experiences as mother of an alcoholic son and morphine-addicted daughter, Stowe attempts to convey some sense of the inner workings of an alcoholic's mind through the character Bolton, who appears in both books.

Stowe's depiction of Bolton reflects what, as we saw in the introduction, Gusfield has called the "assimilative" aspect of temperance reform, which perceives the object of reform sympathetically; "coercive" reform, by contrast, which eventually replaced more assimilative approaches in the nineteenth century, views the object of reform as an enemy, as an unwilling resister of the reformers' values (Gusfield, *Symbolic Crusade*, 7, 69). Stowe uses Bolton to make the following points: the alcoholic is not to blame for his susceptibility to drink; alcoholism is enormously difficult to overcome, no matter how hard one tries; and certain personalities are more prone to addiction than others. All of these positions are subsumed within and grow out of Stowe's insistence on alcoholism as a "disease."

Obviously impatient with the pietistic approach to alcoholism that was present in many contemporary novels, such as Henriette Newell Baker's *Cora and the Doctor* (1855; see Baym, *Woman's Fiction*, 267), Stowe stresses the physical, *medical* nature of chronic drunkenness. Stowe's chief spokesman in both *My Wife and I* and *We and Our Neighbors*, Harry Henderson, exclaims at one point in the latter novel that Bolton's susceptibility to drink is "a disease of the body. Fasting, prayer, sacraments, couldn't keep off an acute attack of dipsomania; but a doctor might" (13:137). Similarly, Bolton's beloved, Caroline, who has studied medicine, urges him in the same novel to treat his drinking problem "as you would the liability to any other disease, openly, rationally, and hopefully" (13:207).[19]

In connection with this medicalized view of alcoholism,

Stowe also raises the alcoholic (at least in the case of the gentlemanly Bolton) from the temperance stereotype of the drunken wastrel to the level of the tragic, destiny-driven figures of classical myth and literature. In a fascinating passage in *My Wife and I*, Bolton compares the drunkard's lot to that of a person stricken with some disease from on high, like those "men and women [in ancient Greek tragedy] who were smitten with unnatural and guilty purposes, in which they were irresistibly impelled toward what they abominated and shuddered at!" (12:331).

However sympathetic Stowe may be to the unfortunate Bolton, alcohol itself remains almost exclusively a bane in her work. True to conventional temperance perspectives, Stowe treats each liquor bottle as a Pandora's box of evils that fly out with each uncorking. Despite her recognition in *Uncle Tom's Cabin* that some drink to "get shet" of their misery, Stowe steadfastly holds to the temperance movement's party line about drink as the source of poverty, rather than the reverse. Indeed, Stowe reflects the contemporary tendency to turn drinking into "an all purpose explanation for social problems . . . a scapegoat" (Levine, "The Alcohol Problem," 1). This attitude becomes most apparent late in *We and Our Neighbors,* where Stowe inveighs against liquor, "which brings on insanity worse than death; which engenders idiocy, and the certainty of vicious propensities in the brain of the helpless unborn infant; which is the source of all the poverty, and more than half the crime, that fills almshouses and prisons, and of untold miseries and agonies to thousands of families" (13:420).

In Stowe's fiction as in most other work by women authors, there is strikingly little "normal" drinking—that is, of drinking unaccompanied by dire consequences. True, *Uncle Tom's Cabin* opens on a peaceful enough scene, in which two men sit together sipping wine (though one of them is, admittedly, the repugnant Haley). And in *My Wife and I* Bolton's friend Westerford is not an alcoholic despite his collection of fine wines. In Southworth's *India,* the gallants drinking a toast to the heroine's health at the beginning of the book are no villains, and similar isolated examples could be located throughout nineteenth-century literary texts by women. But repeatedly the emphasis is on the unmitigated evils of drink, even in small amounts. This emphasis mirrors the vehement exhortations of temperance leaders like Stowe's father, Lyman Beecher, for whom total abstinence was the only truly temperate course. For Beecher and many other temperance advocates, in fact, moderate drinkers incurred even more wrath than drunkards. Samuel B. Woodward, a hospital superintendent in Worcester, Massachusetts, voiced a familiar theme when he asked, in a pamphlet-essay published in 1838,

> Is, then, intemperance any more criminal than gout, rheumatism, or other diseases that may follow the inordinate use of alcohol . . . ? The criminality lies not in the intemperance, nor in these diseases, but in the *use* of spiritous liquors, that *moderate use,* when the individual is a free agent, which leads to all these consequences. . . . Ten years ago, a man might be a temperate drinker, and be innocent; that day is gone by, and never will return. (Woodward, 5).[20]

To the extent that normal, nonaddictive, nonabusive drinking would be shown, it was almost always a male activity. Those women who did drink were generally shown either as pathetic victims (the slave woman queried by Uncle Tom), tragic grotesques (Mary's vicious mother in *The Old Homestead*), sinister sophisticates or corrupters of youth (the pretentious Mrs. Farnham in *The Old Homestead,* the seedy Mother Moggs in *We and Our Neighbors*), or ludicrous absurdities (Audacia Dangyereyes in *My Wife and I*), or masculinized exotics (like such heroines of dime-novel fiction as 'Shian Sal or Calamity Jane). The general relation of positive female characters to alcohol is one of rejection, as typified by resolute little Ellen in Susan Warner's bestseller, *The Wide, Wide World* (1853). When Ellen's high-handed new guardian, Mr. Lindsay, presses some wine on her, we learn that "that glass of wine looked to Ellen like an enemy marching up to attack her," and the girl steadfastly refuses to drink, only finally touching her lips to the glass.[21]

Even when a character like Southworth's Capitola, the refreshingly spunky, irreverent heroine of the novel *The Hidden Hand,* defies the conventional pieties of Victorian femininity, she remains staunchly dry. Offered a sip of wine by her crusty old guardian, Capitola firmly refuses. She will never, she says, touch a drop, because "my life has shown me too much misery that has come of drinking wine" (Southworth, 52).

Such, indeed, would be Capitola's impression had she read many of the novels by her own creator or other prominent nineteenth-century American women authors. But not all women sang in the temperance chorus. At least two authors, Rebecca Harding Davis and Elizabeth Stuart Phelps, portrayed the alcoholic or heavy drinker not as a moral weakling or even as a diseased unfortunate but as a casualty of soul-destroying poverty and labor. In her *Life in the Iron Mills* (1861), which a curious Emily Dickinson requested from her sister-in-law, Davis refuses to veil the ugliness of alcoholism, but equally refuses to blink at the social and economic conditions that can drive people to the oblivion of drink. Davis describes a life of "incessant labor, sleeping in kennel-like rooms, eating rank pork and molasses, drinking—God and the distillers only know what" (15).[22]

Davis goes on to assess the lot of the as-yet-nonalcoholic female laborer, Deborah Wolfe, who exemplifies a human spirit inexorably drawn to the bottle not by depravity or perverseness or weakness of will but by the ghastly circumstances of her day-to-day life.

> She [Deborah] was hungry . . . and not drunk, as most of her companions would have been found at this hour. She did not drink . . . nothing stronger than ale. Perhaps the weak, flaccid wretch had some stimulant in her pale life to keep her up,— some love or hope, it might be, or urgent need. When that stimulant was gone, she would take to whiskey. Man cannot live by work alone. (17)

In her short book, Davis anticipates the apostasy of the WCTU president Frances Willard, who shocked her organization by acknowledging poverty as a major cause, not always a result, of abusive drinking.[23] In more literary terms, Davis also anticipates Jack London on the relationship between one's working and living conditions and one's drinking patterns. As Martin Eden's workingman/hobo friend Joe Dawson puts it, "When I work like a beast, I drink like a beast. When I live like a man, I drink like a man—a jolt now an' again when I feel like it, an' that's all" (London, *Martin Eden*, 3:394).

Though less explcit than Davis's novel about the connection between poverty and drink, Phelps's *The Silent Partner* (1871) implies that drink is the only release from toil available to the deaf-mute laboring girl, Cathy Garth. Taking on temperance attitudes themselves in the short story "Jack" (1887), Phelps denies that she is writing a temperance tale, even as she depicts the ravages of drink on her young fisherman protagonist.[24] (By the time she wrote this story, Phelps would be reacting to the increasing dominance of the coercive wing of temperance that she sees as self-righteous and hostile in its attitudes toward the drinker.) Showing Jack's alcohol abuse to be largely conditioned by environment and heredity, Phelps scoffs at temperance devotees who (in a wonderful image) held Jack "out on a pair of moral tongs and tried to toast his misdemeanors out of him, before a quick fire of pledges and badges; and when he tumbled out of the tongs, and asked the president and treasurer why they didn't bow to him in the street when he was drunk, or why, if he was good enough for them at the lodge-room, he wasn't good enough to shake hands with before folks on the post-office steps, or propounded any of those ingenious posers with which his kind are in the habit of disturbing the benevolent spirit, they snapped the tongs to, and turned him over to the churches"—and the churches do no better by him (223).

Unlike the social commentary apparent in "Jack," but nonetheless unusual in terms of women writing about intoxicants, is a scene from another of Phelps's novels, *The Story of Avis* (1877).[25] Here we come, in a brief, tentative passage, as close as nineteenth-century women's domestic fiction gets to a sense of Dionysian power in intoxication. Despairing of inspiration, the would-be painter, Avis, drinks some orange liqueur from France.

Avis's demure sip is followed by an incredible series of halluci-
nated potential topics for her languishing brush: sunsets, land-
scapes, religious and social scenes, battles, and miscellaneous
fantasies. Finally, Avis chooses her subject—that of the sphinx
as a symbol of the "mystery of womanhood" (150).[26]

Improbable as Avis's reaction to a sip of liqueur is, its description arouses interest through its verbal evocativeness and
its hints at a Dionysian sensibility. What Avis lacks, here and
elsewhere in the novel, is an inspiring power. A room of one's
own, painting equipment, a little time, even a little money: these
things she possesses. But alone in her studio, Avis feels powerless to bring her canvas to life. She is still hampered by her upbringing in "social and intellectual conditions whose tendency is
strictly to the depression of novelty in conduct or opinion" (449).

Sensing her difference from male artists, Avis wonders, "Was
that what the work of women lacked?—high stimulant, rough
virtues, strong vices, all the great peril and power of exuberant,
exposed life?" (143). She continues to think, trying to shut out the
noise of boys singing army songs in the street. And then "with a
firm step, and half-amused, half-curious lighting of the face, she
unlocked a little French dressing-case that stood upon the bu-
reau, and took from it a slender bottle, bearing the trade-mark
of a house in the south of France, and the label, 'Eau de Fleurs
d'Oranger'" (143–44). The wine she has found is a lovely, jewel-
like fluid, as described in Phelps's lushly evocative prose: "She
poured the liquid out, holding it to the light. Each drop was an
amber bead, sluggish and sweet" (144). The drink seems more
than drink; it is both flower and wine, a potion and a beverage,
and is deeply feminine in character: "Leave men their carousal,
their fellowship, the heart's blood of the burning grape," proclaims Phelps. She goes on: "In the veins of the buds that girls
wear at their bridals runs a fire of flavor deep enough for us. The
wine of a flower has carried many a pretty Parisian to an intrigue or a convent. Could it carry a Yankee girl to glory?" (144).
The feminine qualities of this particular intoxicant emerge not
only through Phelps's overt description but also in the drink's

associations with flowers, its French name (which includes the word "fleurs"), in its location in a "slender bottle" demurely locked away in "a little French dressing-case."

For all of its floweriness, Frenchness, and delicacy, the "sluggish" drink has its dangers—what kind of intoxicant would it be without them? That such a wine has "carried many a pretty Parisian to an intrigue or a convent" can only add to its appeal and mystery for Avis. Mild as it may seem, this delicate orange liqueur, secreted away among a lady's personal effects, gives its sheltered, almost stifled owner some small sense of spiritual adventure, of her own imaginative possibilities, of the "exuberant, exposed life" taken for granted by men. And in fact, the drink bestows the longed-for power on Avis. Feeling as though whirled by a Titan, she then becomes calm and settles down to a "self-articulate hour" (144–45) of watching the visions that, eventually, enable her successfully to complete a major painting of the sphinx that she later sees as an extension of her very soul (454).

The entire incident of the hallucinations takes up only a few pages of a good-sized novel, the descriptions of the liqueur and its consumption only a few paragraphs. And the intoxication presented is innocuous. Moreover, one does not want to claim more for this passage than it merits. Still, the drink here possesses a multiplicity of associations, some possibly not consciously conveyed by Phelps but certainly complementing the general meaning and functions of the drink as overtly described in the text.

Whether intended or not, Phelps's leisurely account of the bottle and of the procedure of taking the drink as well as her elaborate language (e.g., references to amber beads, the alliteration of "sluggish and sweet," the metaphorical fusion of flower and wine) imply the discourse of wine connoisseurship found in innumerable (male) writers. To take only three that would have been familiar to Phelps: Byron in his famous apostrophe to burgundy's "sunset glow" in *Don Juan;* Keats on the "beaker full of the warm south" in "Ode to a Nightingale"; Hawthorne in the chapter entitled "Sunshine" that celebrates wine in *The Marble*

*Faun.* What is more, Phelps adapts this usually male-centered discourse to the private, enclosed, explicitly female space of Avis's studio, adding to it the essentially romantic discourse of empowerment through the ingestion of some form of "the milk of paradise." The result of this adaptation is that, in an admittedly modest way, the liqueur and its consumption take on associations that distinguish Phelps's text from the narrowly polemical discourses of drinking found in most other American women writers in the nineteenth century.

Far more unusual and probing than *The Story of Avis,* however, is Stoddard's novel, *The Morgesons* (1862, 1889).[27] As with everything else she wrote, Stoddard dealt unconventionally with intoxication. In her early newspaper journalism, published in the *Daily Alta California,* Stoddard skillfully satirizes temperance reformers in general and the Maine Law in particular. In the following representative passage, from 1855, Stoddard takes her cue from temperance leaders' boundlessly optimistic predictions of a dry utopia in the future:

> The cup is thrust from the lips of the drunkard: he is saved. The rum seller receives his reward for evil-doing; wives will cease to mourn; and children will grow up virtuous. I doubt, Tribunely speaking, whether there will ever be any more orphans. We may expect that all unlawful appetites will be entirely eradicated from the citizen of the temperance zone. (316)

In a more serious vein, Stoddard goes on to say,

> [Just as I doubt] whether purity can be legislated into men by the imprisonment of lewd women, so do I doubt whether law can keep a man sober. . . . The tendency of all life is to excess; and if a man is cribbed and confined one way, he will break out into another. (316)

Stoddard's ironic view of the temperance movement reappears in her most highly regarded work, *The Morgesons,* both in the novel's original 1862 version and in its revised form (1889). In the scene where the freethinking Cassandra Morgeson encounters two pompous temperance men on a train, they are taken aback by her drinking wine from a flask. Cassandra's reaction is disarmingly eloquent in its simplicity and poised self-assurance: when the men spit "vehemently out of the windows" on seeing her sip her wine, she silently offers them a drink. Their refusal is to be expected, but more surprising is their suggestion that Cassandra, though obviously possessed of a "good head," could benefit from electronic treatments—presumably for the nervous disorder indicated by such braininess and eccentricity in a young woman (204)!

Although the temperance movement does not appear significantly elsewhere in *The Morgesons,* the novel as a whole reveals a number of suggestive, often arresting references to alcohol and drinking, as well as an awareness of the different cultural values that can attach to alcohol. Throughout *The Morgesons,* Stoddard interweaves incidents and conversations with the theme of problem drinking in two important characters, the alcoholic brothers, Ben and Desmond Somers. When, for example, Cassandra is a guest at the Somers family dinner table, Stoddard's depiction of familial tension about the brothers' drinking resembles less the formulaic patterns of nineteenth-century domestic fiction than it does Evelyn Waugh's subtle handling of a similar scene involving the drunken Sebastian in *Brideshead Revisited* (1945).

As in the later novel, so too in *The Morgesons* the family masks its painful awareness of the drinking problem by behaving as if all is normal, with wine plentifully available at the table. Desmond's steady drinking does, however, elicit an oblique comment on the situation from his mother. By pointedly asking the servant what wine is being served and by taking a demonstratively minute sip of the wine with a teaspoon, Mrs. Somers inevitably draws attention to Desmond's heavy drinking. And, despite his own silence, Mrs. Somers's other alcoholic son, Ben, uses his unusual abstinence on that particular occasion as a weapon in the endless rivalry between the two brothers. As Cassandra observes, Ben stares fixedly at Desmond, while the latter casually empties the decanter. Meanwhile, social chatter continues all around the table, which has become the stage for an alcoholic mini-drama, in which mute accusation and mute denial of alcoholism are simultaneously present. With a remarkably light touch, Stoddard shows the entire family enacting a piece of theater in which all the nonalcoholics pretend not to be watching alcoholic number one (Desmond) get drunk, while alcoholic number two (Ben) assumes the mantle of an abstainer and alcoholic number one himself acts as if oblivious to all those who are themselves pretending not to notice his heavy drinking (164–65).

In a later scene, alcohol enters in a small but interesting way into the developing sexual dynamic between Cassandra and Desmond, who will eventually marry. Asked to sing, Cassandra chooses "Drink to me only with thine eyes," a song that, when performed by someone in love with an alcoholic, acquires special resonance. In a passage foreshadowing his eventual victory over addiction and his subsequent union with Cassandra, Desmond joins her in singing the lines, "The thirst that from the soul doth rise, / Doth ask a drink divine" (173–74). This marks Desmond's first, indirect statement of love for Cassandra, in terms that establish her as a "drink divine"—superior to the pallid palliatives and chemical avenues to transcendence with which he has besotted himself. As their voices merge, Cassandra feels her own consciousness altered—not, significantly, by brandy or wine, but by a transporting love for Desmond: "As the tones of his voice floated through the room, I was where I saw the white sea-birds flashing between the blue deeps of our summer sea and sky, and the dark rocks that rose and dipped in the murmuring waves" (174). It is appropriate to Cassandra's character that this lyrical description has some darker, even foreboding elements—the deeps of the sea, the dark rocks in the murmuring waves; earlier in the novel, Cassandra has been described as one "possessed," and in explaining her own rebellious, difficult nature, Cassandra says, "I like devils," and calls the blood in her veins "mulled wine" (110).

In the 1889 version of the novel, Stoddard retained the incidents described this far, even as she pared many of the original edition's more explicit passing references to alcohol. The most notable change concerns Ben Somers. Whereas Ben "died in delirium tremens" in the 1862 version, twenty-seven years later Stoddard leaves the exact nature of his death unspecified. At this remove, we can do no more than speculate on the reasons for the change, but it seems plausible that Stoddard might have wanted to minimize the chance of an oversimplified, temperance-dominated interpretation of the unusual sexual and psychological dynamics of her novel. Certainly in the second version Ben Somers cannot be written off as just another drunken reprobate. As a result, his death, like his unpredictable, darkly menacing yet paradoxically attractive personality, becomes more mysterious, more complex and tinged with tragedy than in the earlier version.

From one perspective, the revised version, as Lawrence Buell and Sandra Zagarell observe, focuses more on Ben's moral weakness than on the symptom of it (Stoddard, 4). But looked at in another way, the alcoholism itself in 1889 actually becomes more of a *symptom* than it was in the first edition—and less of an explanatory *cause* of Ben's problematic behavior and character. Such a revision may have seemed especially appropriate to Stoddard in the wake of the increasingly militant tone of the "coercive" branch of temperance described earlier.

Elizabeth Stoddard did not turn alcohol into a major theme in her fiction, though obviously she came close to doing so in *The Morgesons* and decided, in the 1889 version, to lessen rather than expand the theme. Nonetheless, this now virtually unknown writer left us unusually fresh, original, and memorable portrayals of the multiple meanings that drink can assume.

The examples of Davis, Phelps, and Stoddard show us that female writing on intoxication was not an undifferentiated monolith, despite the fact that a single, powerful perspective dominated women's writing on intoxication far more than it dominated men's work. At times, even an enthusiastically pro-temperance writer like Stowe or Alcott sounds as if she just might be breaking away from temperance-dominated codes; as if she just might begin to be exploring intoxication more adventurously or unconventionally—to probe the nature of altered states of consciousness, to explore the various layers and forms of addiction, to uncover various meanings of drink and drug use embedded in conventional discourse. We saw a glimmer of such a departure in Stowe, but the glimmer was ultimately submerged in a discourse of abstinence and in the transformation of alcohol into a scapegoat. With Alcott, however, the situation is a bit more complicated. Only a bit, perhaps, but a bit worth pursuing.

Though Alcott herself enjoyed an occasional glass of champagne and though her favorite Dickens character, one whose name her own family affectionately bestowed on her, was the comic dipsomaniac Sairy Gamp from *Martin Chuzzlewitt,* Alcott's views on alcohol generally paralleled those of the conventional domestic female novelists.[28] Many of her works contain temperance as a theme, and many stressed a woman's power to influence men for good or evil. Thus Meg in *Little Women* warns the dashing young man, Laurie, against drink. Many years later, in *Jo's Boys,* Jo similarly warns the sybaritic "Stuffy" of the dangers of dissipation. Though Alcott is sometimes sympathetic to the drinker's struggles to withstand "temptation," to use one of her favorite words, she is much less explicit about alcoholism as a disease than, say, Stowe. And in economic terms, as one scholar has pointed out, it apparently "never occurred to her . . . that alcoholism might be more the result of poverty than its cause" (Strickland, 155).

Representative of Alcott's general approach to alcohol is the novel *Rose in Bloom* (1876). In many ways, this book's message is a nineteenth-century American version of the slogan Just Say No. The author clearly shows the pressure to drink in her society and the difficulties facing a problem drinker who is trying to quit. But Alcott lets stand without challenge statements that the novel's hopeless drunkard, Charlie, is "pitiably weak" and a "brute," incapable of the moral fortitude or willpower to reject the drinks frequently offered him (178, 231, 272).

The conjunction of young men and drink in this novel invariably spells trouble. The convivial crews gathering at parties and balls exhibit a shallow, gratingly forced gaiety, but have no sensitivity to Charlie's susceptibility to alcohol. Among the young men, only the noble sobersides "Mac" is clearly positive, as he plays the role of a veritable John Wayne of sobriety, incredibly blending mildly feminist sympathies with a relentless projection of earnestness, masculinity, and rational self-control.

Less clear but more intriguing, if ultimately frustrating, are Alcott's depictions of drug use as opposed to drinking. As we have seen earlier, not only the WCTU, but some antebellum authorities voiced concern with drug use, especially by women. Some authors, like Mary Nichols, turned addiction into a serious literary theme, but drugs appeared little in literature and were usually relegated to the often sensationalistic confessional genre, exemplified by F. H. Ludlow's *The Hasheesh Eater* (1857). The theme of drugs was particularly unusual for an author beloved for wholesome, sunny tales that were considered entirely appropriate for that most tender of Victorian reading audiences, female children. But, while there have been comments on the treatment of drugs as a surprising side of Alcott's imagination, no one has yet gone beyond pointing out the existence of this theme to examine it in literary terms.[29]

It is a theme that obviously fascinated Alcott, but from which, finally, she retreats to fairly one-dimensional interpretation and conventional denunciations. The result is a considerable and tantalizingly puzzling ambiguity in the three Alcott works in which drugs most prominently appear: the short stories "A Marble Woman" and "Perilous Play" and the novella *A Modern Mephistopheles*.[30]

In each of these texts, the most significant drug taking is done by a woman. In each a man is ultimately responsible, directly or indirectly, for the woman's drug use. Finally, in each work drugs function as paradoxical sources of both power and enervation. Drugs empower but also stupefy, endanger, and weaken the woman; the drug experience may illuminate some truth or open up certain possibilities, but it also serves to suppress the woman and to enclose her within psychic walls. In "A Marble Woman," for instance, there is the refreshingly defiant power of the usually subservient Cecil (Cecilia), who challenges her husband Yorke's authority by insisting on her right to go out alone during a stormy night, even if he forbids her to do so. Though not actually intoxicated at the time of this incident, Cecil is motivated by drugs, for her secret supply of laudanum has run out, and she is desperate to obtain more. In *A Modern Mephistopheles,* there is the hashish-induced, almost mystical performative power and grace of Gladys's singing. And in "Perilous Play" there is a sense of liberation, excitement, and even romance linked to hashish. But in each case, drugs ultimately weaken the woman more than they strengthen her, depriving her of control, of reason, and, thus, of power.

Certainly none of Alcott's characters attain the lucidity and power of Lucy Snowe in her opium-induced night walk in Charlotte Brontë's *Villette* (1853), during which she sees and behaves with a clarity and vigor denied her elsewhere in that novel.[31] True, Cecil enjoys a drug-inspired moment of strength and insight: "everything seemed strange. I don't know what I did, but nothing seemed impossible to me, and it was a splendid hour; I wish it had been my last" (190). But after her laudanum habit is discovered, Cecil's embarrassment and guilt turn her back into a depressingly docile spouse of an only slightly chastened husband. And in any event, Cecil took laudanum originally not to obtain power but to accept psychically the powerlessness forced on her by the imperious Yorke. Similarly, any compensatory power that Gladys receives in the beautiful performance of her song comes at the cost of unveiling her mind before the prying, Svengali-like Jasper Hellwyze. Yes, hashish makes possible Gladys's passionate, unconstrainedly beautiful song, endowing her with an aesthetic power she has never known before. But hashish is primarily Hellwyze's tool for committing an act that, as Alcott reminds us, is the equivalent of the "unpardonable sin" (241) described in Hawthorne's "Ethan Brand"; hashish becomes the lever with which Hellwyze pries pitilessly into Gladys's mind, "deliberately violat[ing] the sanctity of a human soul, and robbing it alike of its most secret and most precious thoughts. Hasheesh had lulled the senses which guarded the treasure" (204–05).

Thus if, on the one hand, hashish bestows a certain power, on the other, it robs the user of the more important power of reason, which guards one's consciousness against invasion by another. In "Perilous Play," hashish is not so spiritually sinister but is equally deceptive. The "heavenly dreaminess" (306) it offers causes the befuddled Rose St. Just and Mark Done to lose control of their little boat and nearly to lose their lives. "Heavenly dreaminess" becomes a "cursed folly" (306). In what is, however, the most surprising twist in any of Alcott's drug tales, "Perilous Play" ends with Mark's exuberant praise of hashish. Since the drug's consumption ultimately led Mark and his beloved Rose into greater intimacy, he cries, "Heaven bless hashish, if its dreams end like this!" (315).[32]

The conclusion of "Perilous Play" together with some of our other examples from Alcott suggest a persistent ambivalence, even an irresoluteness about drugs that is not at all evident in Alcott's treatment of alcohol. As she circles uneasily around the drug theme, Alcott sounds as if she might be breaking away from temperance-dominated codes of intoxicant description. But just when her work hints at a more multilayered, complex treatment of drugs than we find in most nineteenth-century American literature, Alcott pulls back into conventional, merely external descriptions of stupefaction, loss of rational control, and personal embarrassment. There is little or no rendering of the actual inner experiences or complexities of the intoxicated mind or of altered states of consciousness. Alcott does reveal some of the intriguing doubleness of drugs found in De Quincey's notions of the pleasures *and* pains of opium, but she only touches this concept and backs away. In her work on drugs we do not find the visionary decadence of the Gautier-Baudelaire variety, or the Dionysian exuberance, even when highly metaphorical, of Dickinson, or the complex sympathy of an Edith Wharton (for Lily Bart's attraction to chloral in *The House of Mirth*), or the sense of grotesque illumination found in Poe. There is certainly none of the energetic confidence present in Alcott's vivid, vigorous condemnations of alcohol. Alcott herself was familiar with drugs from personal experience, and her descriptions of women's drug use draw on situations that were not anomalous for women of her own class. But with the literary topic of drugs she seems irresolute, pulled in different directions, following the path of conventional attitudes but with a notable lack of conviction.

This ambivalence toward drugs may be ultimately inexplicable, but several ways of understanding it do suggest themselves. For one thing, there is Alcott's own drug experience. An apparent regular user of opium, she movingly expresses satisfaction in a journal entry of 1870 at having slept without recourse to "opium or anything—a feat I have not performed for some time."[33] In light of this entry, Alcott's mixed feelings might well reflect the experience of someone reliant on opium for sleep and relief from pain, even while resenting that very reliance. But Alcott's wavering on drugs also ties in with the curious tension between primness and rebellion evident in her career as a whole.[34] It may also remind us of Dobson's suggestion that some of the most properly didactic nineteenth-century American women's fictions covertly subvert their own message. According to Dobson, "these rebellious subtexts most often coexist with a sincere affirmation of the surface text, allowing the novels a peculiar doubleness that says both 'yes' and 'no' to the values of the culture." Such subversions can accomplish "both deliberate *and* inadvertent undercutting" of conventional ideals (Dobson, 241, 224).[35]

Dobson's general argument about subversive subtexts is powerful and suggestive. That it may apply to the theme of intoxication is intriguing but uncertain, given the slightness of the evidence suggesting such subtexts on this particular theme in women's writing. Slight though it may be, however, such evidence does exist, and not in Alcott alone. Throughout nineteenth-century American women's fiction there are some intriguing scattered wisps of potential undercutting or problematization of the surface text's homiletic temperance position on drugs and alcohol. Thus, when Warner's Ellen Montgomery finally caves in before the glass of wine that we saw "marching up to attack her" in *The Wide, Wide World,* and gingerly touches her chaste lips to the noxious liquor forced on her by Mr. Lindsay, she thinks to herself, "I wonder what in the world they will make me do next. If he chooses to make me drink wine every day, I must do it!—I cannot help myself. That is only a little matter. *But what if they were to want me to do something wrong?*" (2:273; my italics). Considering how vehemently Ellen resists Mr. Lindsay's insistence that she drink, it is puzzling that she does not consider the wine drinking to be "something wrong." And earlier in the novel, one of the teetotaling Ellen's most cherished fantasies is that she and her beloved Alice would one day go off to Europe, live among peasants, and learn from them—how to make wine (1:280).

Similar contradictions—or subversions?—with regard to drinking and abstinence occur in Southworth's *India,* another novel we have already mentioned. Southworth's hero, handsome and virtuous Mark Sutherland, is described as "habitually abstemious" when Southworth uses him as a favorable foil to India's loutish drunkard husband, St. Gerald Ashley. But when we first see him, and Southworth needs to establish Mark as an elegant and eligible bachelor, she describes him surrounded by his college classmates, a group of aristocratic, gentlemanly, gay young blades. Mark is clearly part of their merry drinking set when he suavely proposes the toast to India that opens the novel. In the same author's *The Hidden Hand,* Capitola's husband-to-be, Herbert Greyson, is approvingly presented as a teetotaler who promised his dying mother (a figure than which nothing could be more sacred in the culture) never to use alcohol. (Their teetotalism seems to be the only thing in common between bland Greyson and the disarmingly free-spirited "Capitola the

Madcap.") But when Capitola's guardian, "Old Hurricane" War-field, reacts in amusing and disbelieving astonishment to Greyson's abstinence, calling him a "young prig" (55), he ex-presses a sentiment with which most modern readers, at any rate, would probably agree.

These tensions between a text's putative position and the apparent undercutting of that position, though minor, nevertheless imply a veiled qualifying or questioning of the dominant discourse expected of women writing about intoxication. Such questioning may partially explain the indeterminacy underlying Alcott's fictional depictions of drug use. In light of the doubleness characteristic of Alcott as we now see her, Dobson's paradigm of a conventional surface text undermined by a more honest sub(versive)text is particularly plausible.

Yet however much Alcott may be covertly questioning conventional notions of intoxicant use, at the surface level her views replicate those of her society. For Alcott, Stowe, and most other mainstream American women writers, the intoxication theme was simply not available other than as a whipping boy for social and personal ills. It was not available for subtle characterization or complex symbolic purposes or for what, with apologies to William James, I called the varieties of intoxicated experience in chapter 1. Even the reform-minded Emerson as well as Dickinson, Poe, and Melville—and in some ways Stoddard and the less talented Phelps—show a willingness to explore the realm of intoxication deeply and adventurously, to endow their imagery of intoxication with multiple layers of significance and interpretive possibility. These authors reflect the spirit of William James's comments in *The Varieties of Religious Experience* on intoxicated consciousness as one part of the mystic consciousness and as possessing a meaning larger than we are accustomed to give the mere act of drinking a beverage. But the other writers we have been considering never approached this Jamesian view, although Stowe and especially Alcott gave some tentative signs of doing so.

By and large, the authors of female domestic fiction did not probe into such questions as consciousness, perception, illumination, distortion, revelation, madness, apocalypse. Perhaps because of the realistic domestic orientation of their work, they were interested not in consciousness but in behavior, principally in negative behavior resulting from too much alcohol. Such an emphasis naturally precluded any sense of Dionysianism as positive—no delirious eye could ever be discerning for the upholders of, in Dickinson's resonant phrase, "dimity convictions."[36]

The literature guided by such convictions was not likely to result in complex or probing analyses of intoxication, whether seen negatively or positively. Nor was it likely to depart, in tone or subject matter, from narrowly defined notions of what constituted propriety for female authors and readers. Thus, apart from passages of occasional power and complexity in, for example, *Uncle Tom's Cabin,* or in the unconventional work of a Stoddard or a Phelps, nothing in American women's writing on intoxication attained the richness of, say, George Eliot's description of the alcohol-soaked marriage of the Dempsters in "Janet's Repentance," or of Eliot's frequent metaphoric use of opium imagery, or of Anne Brontë's exploration of Lowborough's addictive personality, with its compulsions to drink, laudanum, and gambling in her novel *The Tenant of Wildfell Hall.* In both Eliot's story and Brontë's novel, intoxication and its ill effects are roundly condemned. Yet neither work betrays the heavy-handed didacticism, one-dimensionality, and bathos (as opposed to genuine pathos) that characterize so much temperance-dominated literature, particularly in the United States. To find the kind of depth and complexity we find in Eliot and Brontë in American women writers' treatments of intoxication, we must turn to the late 1800s and early 1900s, specifically to the work of Kate Chopin, Edith Wharton, and Willa Cather.

It is important to note that none of these writers shies away from the negative aspects of intoxication. At the same time, none relies on simplistic formulas or predictable judgments; instead each breaks out of the constricting channels through which most earlier women's writing on intoxication had run. As with most other changes in literary history, this shift arrived gradually, with no apocalyptic burst on the scene. While Chopin, Wharton, and Cather were expanding the possibilities of women's fiction, many other women continued to write about intoxicant use from the perspectives that had dominated women's writing on the subject since the 1820s.

So too in society, even among the largely temperance-supporting middle classes, proper women at the turn of the century often continued to drink, although "woman" and "temperance" (i.e., teetotalism) had become almost synonymous. Thus only a decade before the passage of the Eighteenth Amendment—widely perceived as a woman's victory—the eminently respectable *Woman's Dictionary and Encyclopedia* contained fifty-eight recipes for cocktails, besides mentioning numerous other drinks and cordials with alcohol as a main ingredient (150–52).[37] Such variations in drinking patterns within the larger basic unity of a society's conventions testify to the applicability to social history of a comment Baym has made in a literary context: "At any historical moment, the old-fashioned, the current, and the advanced exist together" (*Woman's Fiction,* 276). Nonetheless, in the late 1800s and early 1900s such major voices as Chopin, Cather, and Wharton achieved a liberating expansion of women's discourses of intoxication that I wish to consider briefly here.

Kate Chopin shows drinking's destructive side in stories like "In Sabine," where the problem drinker is a male, and *At Fault,* where a major female character, Fanny, is alcoholic. But she also depicts drinking as festive and romantic at the Bacchic dinner arranged by Edna in *The Awakening,* and as a mere fact of life in numerous other places in the novel. Drugs appear rarely in her work, an exception being the slight tale, "An Egyptian Cigarette," where the female protagonist casts some tantalizing, mysterious, vision-inducing threads of tobacco to the winds. Chopin's work as a whole amply illustrates Ziff's observation:

The community about which [Chopin] wrote was one in which respectable women took wine with their dinner and brandy after it, smoked cigarettes, played Chopin sonatas, and listened to the men tell risqué stories. It was, in short, far more French than American, and Mrs. Chopin reproduced this little world with no specific intent to shock or to make a point. . . . Rather, these were for Mrs. Chopin the conditions of civility, and, since they were so French, a magazine public accustomed to accepting naughtiness from that quarter and taking pleasure in it on those terms raised no protest. (Ziff, *The American 1890s,* 297)

As we would expect, nowhere in her depictions of drink does Chopin repeat the pietistic platitudes of, as she put it in *At Fault,* "those prolific female writers who turn out their unwholesome intellectual sweets so tirelessly, to be devoured by the girls and women of the age" (Chopin, 2:798).

Like Chopin, Wharton presents alcohol as a normal though significant part of life in many of her stories and novels. In the novel *Summer* (1917), she confronts us with Mr. Royall's drunken boorishness to Charity but refuses to demonize him. In a reversal of the usual formula where the drinker either wins the girl and leads her down the path to ruin or loses to a virtuous teetotaler, Wharton ironically has Mr. Royall emerge as a far more appropriate, likable, and dependable suitor than his impeccably proper but bland rival. At turns surly and kind, lustful and restrained, Mr. Royall is unquestionably superior to the feckless drug addict, Mr. Ramy, in "Bunner Sisters" (1916). But as far as drugs are concerned, Wharton can also be sympathetic to the drug taker and complex in depicting the allure of drugs, as we see in her most familiar depiction of the intoxication theme—the concluding passages of *The House of Mirth* (1905), showing Lily Bart's increasing dependence on and death from chloral.

Like Chopin and Wharton, Willa Cather helped to pave the way for a more varied, multilayered presentation of intoxicant use by women writers in America. In the early short story "On the Divide" (1896), for example, Cather expands on alcohol's significance as something more than simply addictive substance or personal vice. Rather, she connects the drinking of the male protagonist, Canute, to the profound madness that in one form or other afflicts all dwellers on the bleak prairie: "Canute Canuteson was as mad as any of them," writes Cather, "but his madness did not take the form of suicide or religion [as the author informs us with an ironic jab at the conventional prairie pietism of her childhood] but of alcohol" (39). And she also shows how the madness of drink becomes entwined with the artistic expression of Canute's personal anguish in the grotesque, aesthetically powerful figures that he carves while drunk. Refusing either to demonize or sentimentalize the alcoholic, Cather ends the story by having Canute's wife, Lena, turn to him not in any denial of his drinking or of her own sense of self but in a touching display of emotionally complex, humanly credible ambivalence.

A later and better-known work, the novel *A Lost Lady* (1923), again reveals Cather's distance from the discourses of "teetotalitarianism."[38] Published during Prohibition, *A Lost Lady* presents drinking in ways that differ both from the official dogma of its own time and from the temperance perspectives of the 1880s and 1890s, the period in which the novel is set and in which Cather herself grew up. Throughout the book, Cather depicts the drinking and even the intoxication of her protagonist, Marian Forrester, on a continuum with her spontaneity and fresh, unpredictable nature. Moreover, Cather unequivocally and positively contrasts Mrs. Forrester's inclination for the elegant paraphernalia of drink with the vulgarity of the petty, grasping, teetotaling townswomen who gloat over her financial misfortune. Although we learn at the novel's end that Mrs. Forrester dies, Cather gives her the last laugh over her narrow-minded neighbors. Considered by most of them to be a fallen woman—the scandalous "lost lady" of the book's title—Mrs. Forrester leaves them behind to marry a rich Englishman and to live the rest of her days in palatial comfort in South America.

What accounts for the shift represented in Cather's, Wharton's, and Chopin's work? In the case of Chopin, the main explanation lies in the set of particular social and cultural circumstances noted, as we have seen, by Larzer Ziff. For Cather and Wharton, several factors are plausible: the generally increasing emancipation of women in society; the parallel loosening of strictures on women as writers and readers of fiction; the sympathy with European attitudes, including Europeans' relative tolerance of drinking, evident in both Cather and Wharton; the upper-class tastes of both writers, the upper classes having been traditionally less sympathetic, on the whole, to temperance values than was the bourgeoisie. One could also add the Bohemianism of Cather's milieu in Greenwich Village of the 1920s, toward which she already seemed to be heading, as toward a magnet, from her days as a beginning author in the 1890s. In that milieu, Prohibition and all it stood for were, at best, a joke.[39]

For all these reasons—as well as her own individualistic nature—Willa Cather was able to pluck the forbidden fruit of a discourse on drinking often deemed unsuitable for women, even as late as the 1920s. Like Stoddard, Wharton, Sarah Orne Jewett, Ellen Glasgow, and such lesser figures as Gertrude Atherton and Elizabeth Stuart Phelps, Cather helped to expand what, in 1829, Sarah Josepha Hale called the "exceedingly circumscribed" world of women's writing. This expansion anticipated—and to some degree, probably made possible—the richly significant, varied depictions of intoxicant use produced by modern American women writers. The varieties of intoxicated experience play an important role in the work of such twentieth-century American women as Djuna Barnes, Dorothy Parker, Ann Petry, Carson McCullers, Joyce Carol Oates, Anne Sexton, Joan Didion, Lorna Dee Cervantes, Leslie Silko, and Erica Jong, to name but a few. As we turn now to the modern period in the epilogue of this book, it is appropriate to recall that it was not so long ago that intoxication was one of the most severely restricted of topics for women authors. The diversity of discourses on intoxication evoked by the names mentioned earlier in this paragraph began to be possible for women authors only relatively late in literary history—on the threshold of the now rapidly disappearing twentieth century.

# Conclusion

Mr. Leavenworth had apparently just transferred his specious gaze to the figure. "Something in the style of the Dying Gladiator?" he sympathetically observed.

"Oh no," said Roderick, seriously, "he's not dying, he's only drunk."

"Ah, but intoxication you know," Mr. Leavenworth rejoined, "is not a proper subject for sculpture. Sculpture shouldn't deal with transitory attitudes."

"Lying dead drunk's not a transitory attitude. Nothing's more permanent, more sculpturesque, more monumental."

"An entertaining paradox," said Mr. Leavenworth, "if we had time to exercise our wits upon it. I remember at Florence an intoxicated figure by Michael Angelo which seemed to me a deplorable aberration of a great mind. I myself touch liquor in no shape whatever. I have travelled through Europe on cold water."

—Henry James, *Roderick Hudson*

Be always drunken. Nothing else matters; that is the only question. If you would not feel the horrible burden of Time weighing on your shoulders and crushing you to the earth, be drunken continually.

Drunken with what? With wine, with poetry, or
with virtue, as you will. But be drunken.
—from Arthur Symons's translation of Baudelaire's
"Enivrez-vous," quoted in Eugene O'Neill,
*Long Day's Journey into Night*

Certain key themes emerge in antebellum literature's portrayal
of intoxicant use. These are the duality between a lower, physical intoxication that debilitates and coarsens and a higher, spiritual one that expresses transcendent experience and insight;
the additional duality whereby intoxicants can serve as both
poison and cure, a concept paralleling the paradoxes inherent in
the classical notion of pharmakon; the idea of the individual act
of intoxicant consumption, especially drinking, as a meaning-
laden social ritual that binds human beings to one another and
to the natural world; the engagement (whether pro or con) with
the temperance movement; the longing for escape or oblivion.
As we have seen, various combinations of these themes are crucial to an understanding of such major and diverse American authors as Emerson, Dickinson, Poe, Cooper, Hawthorne, Melville,
Stowe, and Alcott, and of their relation to the social and cultural
structures within which they lived, wrote, and published. For
these authors, as for many other antebellum Americans, intoxication's portrayal became enmeshed with larger cultural and
philosophical matters. Thus the works of imaginative literature
examined here (along with less self-consciously "literary" texts)
frequently employed various aspects of intoxicant use as lightning rods for questions of individual and national identity, of the
relation between the spiritual and the physical, and of the very
riddle of human existence.

Why did intoxication prove so thematically useful to these
authors? On the most general level, the topic is a potent one because of the extremes to which human beings under the influence of intoxicants can be led. Moreover, intoxication is simultaneously an affirmation of power and an abandonment of

responsibility. Herein lies part of its often disturbing effect in real life; even in the absence of any overt misconduct, we often feel uneasy around those we know to be intoxicated (especially by alcohol, as opposed to more lassitude-producing drugs). To the sober, the drunken seems capable of anything—the unexpected, the unpredictable, the dangerous. The very condition that makes all of this possible also renders the intoxicated person frighteningly not "responsible" in the sense of being unable or unwilling to "respond" or to be answerable for his or her behavior. Obviously such a condition provides rich material for the exploration of human relations and of the individual's relation to society at large.

In the American cultural context, to be intoxicated is to throw down the ultimate challenge to traditionally (or at least stereotypically) American ideals of practicality, rationality, and self-reliance. The intoxicated person is in one sense an annoyance, but in another a rebel (even if no less an annoyance for that) demonstrating individuality through the rejection of sobriety and all it stands for. Thus intoxication becomes a perfect vehicle for expressing the perennial American tension between the demands of conventional society and, in Norman Mailer's phrase, "the rebellious imperatives of the self" (Mailer, 304). This conflict between the values of conformity and community and those of radical self-determination and individualism would be of clear interest to writers concerned with describing and defining "the American," as were most of the authors discussed in this study.

It would also be natural for American writers to turn to intoxicant use simply because of its prominence as a major ideological and political issue from the mid-1820s on up to the Civil War, and because of its obvious relation to temperance, the enormous importance of which I have already pointed out. No writer of the antebellum period could ignore the vocal arguments on both sides of the total abstinence question, or fail to note how both the adherents of drinking and of teetotalism claimed true Americanism and patriotism for their own. Finally, intoxication's age-old links to the desire for transcendence, its presence as image and theme in the literary legacy of romanticism (an important influence for many antebellum authors), and its richly varied symbolism as social ritual all help to explain its thematic attraction for the American writers I have discussed. A central assumption of this book is that intoxicant use does not belong solely to the category "social problems," regardless of whether the emphasis falls on the first or second of these terms. But since the pathological wafts so unavoidably over my topic, I want to flesh out the importance of that assumption here. In addition to their commonly recognized societal dimensions, drinking and drug use involve numerous cultural, semiotic, and literary associations. While these associations go hand in hand with societal concerns—for example, intoxicated comportment, public consumption of intoxicating substances, social class, economics, and legal guidelines and prohibitions—they are not reducible to such factors alone. *Pace* Henry James's squeamish Mr. Leavenworth, whose views seem to be mirrored in the critical neglect that, until recently, has met intoxication in literature, the use of psychoactive substances extends far beyond the social worker's casebook to all areas of culture and experience. From the squalid to the sublime, intoxication has permeated the full breadth and depth of artistic representation. Moreover, if not exclusively social, intoxicant use is also not exclusively a *problem,* though this is still the mode in which even its sociohistorical and anthropological study continues to be stereotyped. As Mark H. Moore and Dean R. Gerstein observe in the introduction to their study of alcohol and public policy, "a simple equivalence of drinking with problems, and more drinking with more serious problems, while often true, can be somewhat misleading" ("Nature of Alcohol Problems," 19). Much depends on the physical and social contexts of intoxicant use, on its results, and on the degree of intoxication in determining the extent to which such use is a "problem."[1]

In the literary depiction of intoxicant use, the social and the personal, while sometimes easy to separate, often interact in ways that blur their distinctions. And that interaction can include both the positive and the pathological as well as various shadings in between. Even in the relatively straightforward work of Cooper, which lacks the Dionysian ambiguities of, say, Hawthorne or Emerson, intoxicant use functions not only as a problem or even as a mere given of social reality, but as a subject of remarkable moral complexity and semiotic richness.

The multiplicity of intoxication's various forms, settings, and meanings suggests that no totalizing explanation or category of intoxicant use can account for its myriad functions in literature—even the literature of a given nation or period. But one issue comes closer than any other to constituting a unifying thread in the literary portrayal of intoxicant use. This issue, which I call "the argument with reality," runs throughout the antebellum texts discussed here. But it also continues in modern literature, connecting to many different types and conditions of intoxicant use.

The argument with reality often springs from negative motives, in the sense of wanting to escape pain, anguish, or boredom; it can also proceed from a more positive motive, such as the wish to reach higher levels of consciousness or emotional experience. Intoxicants have always been used, by some, either to escape a hell or to create a paradise (albeit an artificial one). But even in their most positive manifestations, such uses of intoxicants, and their literary imagery, proceed from a sense of the inadequacy or incompleteness of existing conditions. Life need not be hellish or even unpleasant for one to wish it more exciting, meaningful, or rewarding than it is.

A desire to alter reality lies behind the "delirious solace" found in Hawthorne and the longing for oblivion or, at least, for psychic respite that is so much a part of Melville. That desire also informs the bulk of Emerson's, Dickinson's, and Poe's texts on intoxication. In fact, the quest for Eden that we have seen as crucial to these three authors' work, and that in its imagery parallels their treatment of intoxication, itself implicitly suggests a dissatisfaction with everyday reality. Those who search for Eden seek a higher plane of being and perception than that on which they currently find themselves. A longing for such a plane

repeatedly appears in antebellum, as in much romantic literature, often expressed through the medium of intoxication both
as literal subject and as metaphor. Of course, the powerful example of British romanticism, with its elevation of a nonrational
creative imagination and of visionary experience generally,
along with the ancient Dionysian tradition I have discussed earlier fit in well with the argument with reality, permeating the
very rhetoric of transcendentalism, even if many transcendentalists were themselves committed to reform and reason.

Of the writers examined here, Cooper is farthest from either
the Dionysian mentality or from the motif of the Edenic quest,
but the issue of reality is important to his work as well, serving
as a touchstone of truth and good judgment. For all his emphasis on connoisseurship and conviviality, Cooper clearly shows
abusive drinkers losing touch with objective reality and therefore bringing on suffering or ignominy to themselves and others. Yet some of Cooper's most charming scenes (such as those
involving Captain Truck and the Commodore in *Home as Found*)
reveal a gently indulgent view of good-natured drinking as a
harmless act that blurs the sharper edges of actual life. Cooper
never argues with reality, but he does seem willing, at certain
times, and through certain of his characters, to take a short va-
cation from it.

For many Americans of Cooper's time, one of intoxication's
chief ills was its interference with citizens' ability to be efficient
and productive within the "real world" of business and industry.
Those for whom "reverie" or "extempore novel-making" were as
dangerous as, in an earlier chapter, we saw Lyman Beecher
claim, would never tolerate anything that produced such results.[2] For antebellum women (as for women in later eras, of
course), a male's indulgence in drunkenness and its fantasies
could lead to domestic chaos, poverty, and violence—elements of
an all too real nightmare for the wives and families of many alcoholics or periodic "drunks." But many women themselves also
sought chemical paths to oblivion or transcendence, whether of
self or circumstance or both.

"To get shet o' my misery" cries the old slave woman to Uncle Tom, when asked why she drinks. "Men want wine, beer, and tobacco to dull or stupefy a little the too tender papillae," writes Emerson in his journals. "To get away from ourselves" is wealthy Bessie Lynde's explanation of drinking in Howells's *The Landlord at Lion's Head*. "Liquor was medicine for the anger that made them hurt," writes Leslie Marmon Silko of the alcohol-abusing Laguna Pueblo youths in *Ceremony*. And long before any of these statements, the author of Proverbs wrote, "Give strong drink unto him that is ready to perish, and wine unto those that be of heavy hearts. Let him drink, and forget his poverty, and remember his misery no more" (31:6–7).[3] Escape through intoxication, even if such escape leads to the prison of addiction, links the texts discussed in this book with innumerable depictions, ancient and modern, of human beings striving to change the reality in which they find themselves.[4]

Stepping back to compare antebellum and contemporary literary relations to the argument with reality, we find certain shared features: the depiction of intoxicant use as a failure to face reality, as an anodyne against pain, whether psychic or physical, and as a partly metaphorical, partly actual means of suggesting an alternative mode of being to that found in a rationalistic, convention-bound society. But in many recent examples of the serious literary treatment of intoxicants, it is the nature of reality itself that has changed. In the antebellum period, and still in much contemporary work, intoxicant use constitutes an escape from or rejection of things as they are. In recent writing, especially of a postmodern or experimental nature, the external world itself has assumed the hallucinatory qualities of a drug-induced dream. For a writer like Cooper, reality was solid, objective, verifiable. And while "reality" was much less clear-cut for Poe, Emerson, Hawthorne, or especially Melville, whose sense of absurdity so strikingly anticipates postmodern perspectives, reality retained an implicit validity in their work, however difficult it may have been to understand or know or describe.

But in much of the most interesting work of recent years, reality has ceased to be a reliable reference point or standard of judgment, having itself become bizarre to the point of seeming *un*real. Such is the reality encountered in novels like Thomas Pynchon's *V.* (1963), with its grotesque (although not humorless) description of blind, unreasoning appetite in the bar where dozens of drunken sailors hurl themselves at beer-dispensing, foam rubber breasts, or the same author's *The Crying of Lot 49* (1966), where Oedipa Maas, herself often inebriated, constantly confronts a society in which the taking of LSD, multifarious pills, and huge amounts of alcohol seems merely incidental to the irrationality and emotional unresponsiveness writ large across America.

Similar patterns of grotesque or distorted reality appear in John Cheever's *Bullet Park* (1969), in which intoxication fits in with patterns of compulsive behavior and disorientation in American society at large. Both in Joan Didion's *Play It as It Lays* (1969) and in Robert Stone's *Children of Light* (1986), the Hollywood milieu and scenes of extensive drug and alcohol abuse convey a sense of an often bizarre, hallucination-haunted world in which any meaningful, lasting, or transcendent experience proves as illusory as the fleeting images on celluloid. And in that infamous blend of factual reporting and fictional technique, Hunter S. Thompson's *Fear and Loathing in Las Vegas* (1971), the narrator, describing Las Vegas novelties and entertainments, says, "No, this is not a good town for psychedelic drugs. Reality itself is too twisted." Yet that twisted reality is a concentrated form of a more diffuse madness that pervades the country as a whole. "We came out here to find the American Dream," says the narrator to his faltering, drugged-out companion and attorney. "'You must realise,' I said, 'that we've found the main nerve'. 'I know,'" the attorney replies. "'That's what gives me the Fear'" (47–48).

Closely interwoven with these views of American reality as itself intoxicated or mad is a greatly expanded sense of addiction, of which chemical addiction is only one variation. This idea, of course, has appeared before, as the Baudelaire epigraph to this chapter indicates. But in recent work the idea of love or power or sex as addiction has moved away from metaphor to a much more literal plane.[5] In the externally placid 1950s, George Mandel's novel, *Flee the Angry Strangers* (1952), draws frequent parallels between drug addiction and other, subtler forms of addiction: "Everybody chose his own dream world. Mrs. Lattimer and her cynical godliness, Wengel and his dollar worship, poor Edna and her focus on sex, a whole nation of people suspending consciousness in whatever way they could: in churches and movie houses, before television sets, in barrooms and in books. . . . The whole world sought hard for its narcosis" (208). I have already mentioned Cheever's somewhat later *Bullet Park,* which shows a similar range of druglike, addictive entities: alcohol, tobacco, television, cars, even freeways. Summarizing this catholicity of addictions, one of Cheever's characters (Mrs. Hammer) declares, "Never, in the history of civilization, has one seen a great nation single-mindedly bent on drugging itself" (168).

The preceding statements extend the notion of addiction far beyond the usual suspects of alcohol, opiates, heroin, cannabis, and the like. But although such an extension is not new, it has achieved unprecedented intensity and breadth of expression in modern American literature and culture. Appropriately enough, this expanded view of addiction recently received explicit articulation from modern American literature's most notorious addict-author, William S. Burroughs, who points out that his many drug-suffused works (e. g., *Naked Lunch,* 1959) are actually not so much about addiction to any particular drug as they are about the power of addiction that manifests itself, among other ways, *through* that drug. Acknowledging that specific drugs "play a part in all my subsequent work" after the publication of *Junky* (1953), Burroughs asserts, "from the beginning I have been far more concerned, as a writer, with addiction itself (whether to drugs, or sex, or money, or power) as a model of control" (Burroughs, 9).

The conjunction of addiction-related themes and modernity

is not surprising. After all, we expect a concern with alcohol and drugs in a society still reeling from the advent of the sixties drug culture and bombarded daily with news reports about drug abuse by the young, Colombian cocaine cartels, the domestic "war on drugs," the proliferation of addictions and treatment centers and AA offshoots, and the alcohol and drug-related travails of contemporary celebrities. The abuse of alcohol and other substances seems to fit in with the fragmentation, stress, and socioeconomic turmoil that so often appear as givens of the modern condition. An interest in drugs and drug-related imagery accords also with modern and postmodern artistic tendencies toward heightened or expanded consciousness or, more often, toward qualities of absurdity, distortion, and grotesqueness that seem to reflect similar qualities in society itself. But intoxication in American literature, far from being a solely modern phenomenon, receives some of its most rewarding portrayals from the authors treated in this book. And between those antebellum portrayals and more recent depictions of intoxication stretch complex lines of continuity and change.

The United States has, of course, never had the kind of intimate, overt national link with a particular intoxicant that, for example, we find in France—a venerable link recently receiving new corroboration from an unlikely source. Lamenting the cultural isolation of Muslims in France, Sheikh Abdelkabi Sahraoui, a Paris-based Muslim cleric, observes, "You have to drink wine, or you cannot become French" (quoted in Mabry, 33). The power of cultural semiotics has never been more pithily expressed, and probably could *not* be so expressed with regard to any single intoxicant in this country. Nonetheless, the history and literature of the United States illustrate the subtle but profound importance, metaphorical and literal, played by intoxicants throughout the evolution of American culture. Both now and in the antebellum period that seems at once so close and so remote intoxication has proved to be an astonishingly many-sided and fertile issue for American writers. In the study of both modern and antebellum literature, intoxication's links to actual human experience, its ancient mythic heritage, and its ramifying symbolic associations with good and evil make it a powerful tool with which to explore lesser-known works and to see long-familiar ones afresh. But whether the texts we examine be obscure or well known is less important than what a study of their portrayal of intoxication gives us. That gift is not just the clarification of a socially and literarily significant theme, or of individual works themselves, but the clarification of literature's larger relation to the beliefs, attitudes, and practices that it both reflects and shapes.

# Notes

## Chapter 1. Introduction:
## The Varieties of Intoxicated Experience

1.   Lamenting this pervasiveness in a quaint but erudite volume, the nineteenth-century American temperance scholar Daniel Dorchester observed that "people of every clime and age, savage or civilized, have found methods for gratifying the propensity for stimulants"; see Dorchester, *The Liquor Problem,* 12. From a very different perspective, Aldous Huxley also notes this propensity, seeing in it the human longing for self-transcendence that "has always been one of the principal appetites of the soul"; see Huxley, *The Doors of Perception,* 62. More recently, the anthropologist Ronald Siegel has described intoxication as a phenomenon far more encompassing than that suggested by conventional notions of bars, cocktail parties, or rock houses: "Recent ethological and laboratory studies . . . and analyses of social and biological history, suggest that the pursuit of intoxication with drugs [including alcohol] is a primary motivational force in the behavior of organisms." Of all species, however, it is humans who are "the most eager and reckless explorers of intoxication"; Siegel, *Intoxication,* 10.

2.   Anecdotal commentary about authorial intoxicant use is plentiful, but the first full-scale biographical approaches to the subject have been Donald W. Goodwin's *Alcohol and the Writer* and Tom Dardis's far more detailed and probing *The Thirsty Muse,* which deals with Faulkner, Fitzgerald, Hemingway, and O'Neill. A brief but often-cited earlier biographical discussion of drinking writers is Alfred Kazin's "Giant-Killer." For incisive comments on the biographical analysis of drinking

writers, see Roger Forseth, "'Alcoholite at the Altar'" and "Ambivalent Sensibilities."

As far as the literary depiction of drinking is concerned, two useful early articles, both written from a social science perspective, are Dimitre Bratanov, "Le problème de l'alcoolisme dans la littérature mondiale," and the more focused, detailed analysis by Mairi McCormick in "First Representations of the Gamma Alcoholic in the English Novel." An engaging lecture published in book form is Everett Carter's *Wine and Poetry*. The first book-length study is Thomas B. Gilmore, Jr.'s *Equivocal Spirits;* see also John Crowley's *The White Logic*.

On drugs, see R. A. Durr, *Poetic Vision and the Psychedelic Experience,* and especially Alethea Hayter's excellent *Opium and the Romantic Imagination*. A brief discussion of opium use by English and German romantics may be found in Reiner Dieckhoff, "Literarische Avantgarde und Drogenkonsum von der Romantik bis zum Surrealismus." An early semiotic approach to intoxicants that, alas, has been little followed up appears in "Wine and Milk," Roland Barthes's analysis of the totemic significance of wine and opium in French culture. See also the articles dealing with intoxication in the following collections: Enid Rhodes Peschel, ed., *Intoxication and Literature;* Evelyn J. Hinz, ed., *Literature and Altered States of Consciousness,* Nicholas O. Warner, ed., *Alcohol in Literature*. Since 1989, the journal *Dionysos: The Literature and Addiction Triquarterly* has been a valuable forum for critical analysis of intoxication in literature.

3. The importance of intoxicant use in literature—as in other areas of scholarly investigation—has not always received its due: there is something not quite respectable about the topic of intoxicant use, linked, on the one hand, with lower-class stereotypes and, on the other, with the intolerance suggested by Prohibition and, more recently, with the moralistic oversimplifications associated with the slogan Just Say No. Commenting on this problem, the drug and alcohol sociologist Robin Room notes that for the past half century in North America, many people believed "that it was somehow old-fashioned and reactionary to have or show any concern about drinking. For two generations, in a reaction against Prohibition and what temperance had come to stand for, few progressive, urban, middle-class Americans—let alone intellectuals or bohemians—were willing to give much credence to alcohol problems"; see Room, "Discussion," 52.

4. Joseph Gusfield provides a comment highly relevant to this

issue from the perspective of alcohol research: "Whether as a dialectical response to capitalist culture and industrial organization or as historical continuity, the romantic resistance to rationalization has been a recurrent theme of modern thought. Drinking has become, especially in the United States, a symbol of the irrational, the impulsive, the 'free' side of life. Its association with the uncontrolled and irresponsible, with the unpredictable appearance of trouble, is part of its appeal and danger"; see Gusfield, "Benevolent Repression," 418.

5.    Mather's phrase occurs in his *Wo to Drunkards,* 7. For "the sober eye of reason," see Edgar Allan Poe, "The Premature Burial," in *Collected Works of Edgar Allan Poe,* 3:969. The idea of a deeper truth lurking within drunkenness—*in vino veritas*—is a variant of the "reason in madness" theme brilliantly explored by Lillian Feder in *Madness in Literature.* From the unlikely pair of Michel Foucault and Jack London we may derive remarkably similar points related to this issue. Madness, writes Foucault, possesses "at a deeper level . . . a rigorous organization dependent on the faultless armature of a discourse"—that is, the mad often reveal a rigorous logic within a state of dementia, and the "voice" of madness "obeys its own grammar." A similar order is discernible in Jack London's concept of white logic, the "pitiless, spectral syllogisms" of which dazzle the drunken mind with truth, but a truth that "is not normal"; for Foucault, see *Madness and Civilization,* 96, 188; for London, see *John Barleycorn,* 14, 307–08. "White logic" is London's phrase for the uncannily lucid but perverse, bleak, and suicidal thought processes that drunkenness visits on the more than usually imaginative mind.

6.    A fascinating discussion of Dionysos in the ancient world, as well as a thorough bibliography relating to this figure, may be found in the recent biography by John Maxwell O'Brien, *Alexander the Great;* see especially pp. 1–4. Recent valuable studies of the diverse aspects of Dionysian myth appear in Thomas H. Carpenter and Christopher A. Farsone, eds., *Masks of Dionysos.*

7.    See also Jellinek's earlier essay, "Cultural Differences in the Meaning of Alcoholism." Jellinek touches briefly on cultural matters in his most influential work, *The Disease Concept of Alcoholism,* 149–50. On the various meanings that attach to alcohol and its use, see also Lisa M. Heilbronn, "What Does Alcohol Mean?"

8.    In the words of the anthropologist Dwight B. Heath, "Members of different societies hold different beliefs about drugs and their uses, the effects of such drugs, and associated behaviors, as well as about the

meanings and values that attach to all of these"; see Heath, "Sociocultural Perspectives on Addiction," 223. Other discussions of sociocultural approaches that have been particularly germane to my work are Heath, "The Sociocultural Model of Alcohol Use"; Susanna Barrows and Robin Room, "Introduction"; Craig MacAndrew and Robert B. Edgerton, *Drunken Comportment;* David T. Courtwright, *Dark Paradise;* and Victoria Berridge and Griffith Edwards, *Opium and the People.*

9.   Hawthorne, "My Kinsman, Major Molineux," in the *Centenary Edition of the Works of Nathaniel Hawthorne,* 11:212–13. John Allen Krout, *The Origins of Prohibition,* 26; see also William Bradford, *Of Plymouth Plantation,* 205–06, 316. In point of fact, the concern with intoxication predates Bradford's journal: already in 1622, the notorious drinking in Virginia "caused the governor of that colony to issue a proclamation against drunkenness"; see Norman H. Clark, *Deliver Us from Evil,* 16. Memorable testimony to the ubiquitousness of heavy drinking in the early nineteenth century is provided by Abraham Lincoln, reminiscing about his own youth: "Intoxicating liquor [was] used by everybody, repudiated by nobody. It commonly entered into the first draught of the infant, and the last draught of the dying man. From the sideboard of the parson, down to the ragged pocket of the houseless loafer, it was constantly found. . . . [T]o have a rolling or raising, a husking or hoedown, any where without it, was *positively insufferable,*" quoted in Clark, 22; see also Lincoln, *Abraham Lincoln,* 135. For an excellent starting point on the history of American drinking and attitudes toward it, see Mark Edward Lender and James Kirby Martin, *Drinking in America.*

10.   H. Wayne Morgan, "Introduction," 34; on the "alcoholic republic," see W. J. Rorabaugh, *The Alcoholic Republic;* on other references to drugs in this paragraph, see David F. Musto, *The American Disease,* 5, 279 n 3.

11.   John W. DeForest, *Kate Beaumont,* 57–58; Leslie Fiedler's phrase occurs in his *Return of the Vanishing American,* 57.

12.   Clark's position does not mean that a culture lacking America's individualistic traditions could not also possess a tradition of heavy drinking but rather that in the American context, certain attitudes and tensions peculiar to American culture help to foster abusive drinking patterns. For additional discussions of America's supposed sociocultural predisposition to heavy intoxicant use, see MacAndrew and Edgerton, *Drunken Comportment,* and Clark, *Deliver Us from Evil;* Paul Johnson, *A Shopkeeper's Millennium;* idem., "Drinking, Temperance, and the

Construction of Identity"; Paul Aaron and David F. Musto, "Temperance and Prohibition in America," esp. pp. 134–45.

13. On Harrigan's exploitation of the "lovable sot" character for comic purposes, see Joan L. Silverman's "'I'll Never Touch Another Drop,'" 124–26. For the Twain passages, see Samuel L. Clemens, *Adventures of Huckleberry Finn*, 27, 34.

14. On ambivalence and drinking, see Abraham Myerson, "Alcohol"; Morris Chafetz, "Introduction," 1–4. A comprehensive, skeptical discussion of ambivalence as a sociological explanatory concept is found in Robin Room, "Ambivalence as a Sociological Explanation." For ambivalence regarding drugs as well as alcohol, see Charles E. Goshen, *Drinks, Drugs and Do-Gooders*, as well as H. Wayne Morgan, ed., *Yesterday's Addicts*.

15. The phrase is Charles Warriner's, quoted in Room, "Ambivalence," 1062. A minor but apt illustration of cultural ambivalence to drink in America was Charles A. Dana's popular *Household Book of Poetry*. In the late 1850s, following the push to temperance legislation earlier in the decade, this text included a section called "Convivial Songs," consisting mainly of poems celebrating drink. Yet the various editions of this handsome volume graced the shelves of many family libraries, including that of Emily Dickinson's temperance-supporting father.

16. "Periodization is a necessary evil of all historical study. Anything short of universal history must periodize"; Lawrence Buell, *New England Literary Culture*, 11.

17. Writing in 1837, Emerson pithily expressed the ubiquitousness of temperance concerns in antebellum society: "The Temperance question is that of no use [i.e., of total abstinence from drink], a question which rides the conversation of ten thousand circles, of every Lyceum, of every stage coach, of every church meeting, of every county caucus, which divides the whole community as if one party wore Blue coats and the other Red, which is tacitly present to every bystander in a bar room when liquor is drunk and is tacitly heeded by every visiter at a private table drawing with it all the curious ethics of the Pledge, of the Wine Question, of the equity of the Manufacture and of the Trade"; see Emerson, *Journals and Miscellaneous Notebooks*, 5:440.

Temperance literature is not part of my subject for reasons both practical and theoretical. On the practical side, there is the need to keep the scope of my discussion manageable, especially since I already cast my net fairly widely, including some neglected as well as more traditionally "canonical" authors. On the theoretical side, there is the fact that temperance literature constituted a "genre to itself," as Nina Baym has observed more specifically of the temperance novel; see Baym, *Woman's Fiction*, 267. Temperance works existed primarily as vehicles for the dissemination of abstinent or near-abstinent propaganda and often were explicitly identified as temperance works by their publishers (many of whom published temperance materials exclusively) and/or by their title pages and covers. Thus such works tended to be clearly distinguishable from mainstream literature.

18.    Stephen Crane, "Opium's Varied Dreams," in *The Works of Stephen Crane*, 1:365. On "assimilative" and "coercive" reform, see Gusfield's influential *Symbolic Crusade*, 6-7, 69, as well as Harry Gene Levine's comprehensive article, "The Discovery of Addiction," esp. p. 158. The temperance historian Jack S. Blocker, Jr., however, warns that while temperance reform "began . . . with methods more suasionist than coercive . . . its history reveals no simple progression toward coercion." Still, Blocker acknowledges that each movement or cycle of reform within the larger span of temperance history "followed a progression that led it toward a more coercive policy than that with which the movement began. . . . In each generation some Americans have confronted the problem of drinking; again and again they have begun by trying to persuade their fellow citizens to act in ways calculated to solve the problem; again and again the intractability of the problem has led them to entertain more coercive approaches"; see Blocker, *American Temperance Movements*, xv-xvi.

Influential as the above studies have been, several alternative or supplementary interpretations have appeared. Specifically challenging Levine's argument that the concept of alcoholism as a progressive disease developed only in the late 1700s, Jessica Warner, in "'Resolv'd to Drink No More,'" asserts that "what we identify as the 'modern conception of alcohol addiction' dates not from the late eighteenth century but from the early seventeenth century at the very least. It is in the religious oratory of Stuart England that we find the key components of the idea that habitual drunkenness constitutes a progressive disease, the chief symptom of which is a loss of control over drinking behavior" (685). See also Roy Porter, "The Drinking Man's Disease," and Nicholas O. Warner, "The Drunken Wife in Defoe's *Colonel Jack*." In another recent essay, Linda Schmidt, while acknowledging the validity of the sociopolitical approaches of Gusfield, Levine, and Rorabaugh, emphasizes the impact of religious ideas on the American temperance movement: "The crusade against vice and intemperance, then, was powerfully conceived as a domestic holy war that would extend the War for Independence onto the spiritual plane." See Schmidt, "'A Battle not Man's but God's,'" 119; for a similar argument, see James R. Rohrer's call for greater attention to the role of evangelical protestantism in his "The Origins of the Temperance Movement."

19.   Similarly, the antebellum scientist and reformer Edward Hitchcock expatiates on the patriotism of abstinence as opposed to the unpatriotic practice of tippling; see Hitchcock, *An Essay on Alcoholic and Narcotic Substances,* 35–42.

20.   Responding to attacks on his supposed drunkenness in the *New England Washingtonian,* Poe mockingly referred to the temperance publication as the *Washingtonian Reformer,* the *Jeffersonian Teetotaler,* and the *Washingtonian Teetotaler;* see Burton R. Pollin, "The Temperance Movement and Its Friends Look at Poe," 124–25.

21.   Royall Tyler's celebration of Adams in terms of drinking had no serious repercussions, but the famous "Log Cabin and Hard Cider" campaign of 1840 witnessed a conjunction of partisan politics, campaign advertising, and candidates' supposed taste in alcoholic beverages that had most serious results on a national election. Mocking Martin van Buren as an effete, champagne-sipping elitist, Whig supporters of William Henry Harrison portrayed their candidate as a log-cabin-dwelling, cider-drinking man of the people. The irony behind this aspect of the successful Whig campaign was that Harrison himself belonged to an old, aristocratic family far removed from the down-to-earth image that helped propel him to the White House. See Norma Lois Peterson, *The Presidencies of William Henry Harrison and John Tyler,* and Robert G. Gunderson, *The Log Cabin Campaign.*

22.   On the music, text, and early history of "The Star-Spangled Banner," see P. W. Filby and Edward G. Howard, *Star-Spangled Books,* 24, 60–61, 132.

23.   A compilation of many of the Wine-Press's humorous pieces, as well as similar essays from other sources, may be found in Frederick Swartout Cozzens, ed., *The Sayings of Dr. Bushwhacker.*

24.   For Mather, spiritual drunkenness is also evil, taking the form of "Corrupt Doctrines" that "as it were intoxicate & inebriate the Souls of them that do imbibe or embrace them"; see *Wo to Drunkards,* 3–4. Philo speaks much of drunkenness both literal and figurative, positive

and negative. The most influential instance of his thinking on intoxication is the concept of "sobria ebrietas," a "sober drunkenness" in which the soul is filled with an ecstatic love for and consciousness of the divine; see Philo Judaeus, *Allegorical Interpretation of Genesis* 203, and "On Drunkenness," 395–99; probing analyses of Philo's complex notions of physical and spiritual intoxication include Hans Lewy, *Sobria Ebrietas;* Harry Austryn Wolfson, *Philo,* 2:50; and Mari-Madeleine Davy, "La *Sobria ebrietas.*" Paralleling the "two wines" concept is Plato's idea in *Phaedrus* 265A of "two kinds of madness: one resulting from 'human sickness,' the other from the liberating influence of the gods"; see Lillian Feder, *Madness in Literature,* 287 n 5.

25. The issue of literal intoxication's connections to spiritual "intoxication" has earned its share of controversy. R. C. Zaehner, for example, sneers at William James's famous passage on drunkenness as the great exciter of the "yes" function: "To the average frequenter of cocktail parties this may come as a revelation. That there is a grain of truth in it may be conceded, but to state that by drinking three or four gin-and-tonics the drinker becomes one with truth would surprise no one more than the drinker himself"; see Zaehner, *Zen, Drugs and Mysticism.* To begin with, of course, James never makes the silly claim Zaehner implicitly attributes to him. Moreover, Zaehner's comment misses the fact that observations about cultural patterns are not invalidated merely because participants in the culture may not acknowledge or even recognize those patterns. Rather than imply that cocktail drinkers are seeking Nirvana at the bottom of a gin and tonic glass (though some, undoubtedly, do), James is concerned with pointing out the deeply buried roots that "regular" drinking and the achievement of altered consciousness share.

In a statement that makes James appear tame by comparison, the contemporary Russian author and celebrated dissident, Andrei Sinyavsky, says vis-à-vis drinking: "Drunkenness is our [Russia's] national vice and moreover our *idée fixe.* It is not from poverty nor from sorrow that a Russian drinks but from an eternal inclination towards miracles and the unusual; he drinks, if you will, mystically striving to lead his soul out from earthly equilibrium and return it to its blessed incorporal condition," quoted in Boris M. Segal, *The Drunken Society,* 507–08. Specifically addressing Zaehner (in a context other than the James comment), I. M. Lewis writes that he has no "ambition to follow Zaehner or other ethnocentric writers in seeking to distinguish between 'higher' and 'lower', or 'more' or 'less' authentic forms of ecstatic experience." Similarly, Peter Furst counters Mircea Eliade's disparagement of intoxicant use for achieving ecstatic trances, observing that "it is difficult to distinguish phenomenologically between so-called spontaneous religious experiences . . . and those that are pharmacologically induced"; see Lewis, *Ecstatic Religion,* 28; Eliade, *Shamanism,* 401; Furst, "Introduction," ix. For related issues, see also Barbara G. Myerhoff, "Peyote and Huichol Worldview," 427, and Vincent J. Gianetti, "Religious Dimensions of Addiction," 187–97. The point here is not to make the case for drug taking as a means of spiritual illumination but to demonstrate the seriousness and significance of the chemical-spiritual connection as a subject of study—its "thickness," to use Gilbert Ryle's concept that Clifford Geertz made famous in his *Interpretation of Culture,* 6–7.

As far as James's own personal views of drinking are concerned, it is worth noting that, in an 1881 lecture to Harvard students, James favored teetotalism over moderate drinking from a medical perspective; see *The Works of William James,* 15:19–21. On James's views of drugs and consciousness expansion, see Lynda S. Boren, "William James, Theodore Dreiser, and the 'Anaesthetic Revelation.'"

26. Warner, "The Drunken Wife in Defoe's *Colonel Jack*"; commenting on the work of Robert Burns, Leopold Damrosch, Jr., observes that "the eighteenth century strove to be Apollonian; Burns proclaims the return of Dionysus the liberator"; see Damrosch, "Blake, Burns, and the Recovery of Lyric," 648.

27. See Nietzsche, *The Birth of Tragedy,* 34, 89. Also see note 6, above.

28. "Der Character des alten Dithyramben war frenlich eine rasende Begeisterung der Bacchanten, die vom Blitzstrahl des Weines getroffen, die Geburt und Taten seines Erfinders mit brausendem Munde sangen"; see Johann Gottfried Herder, *Sammtliche Werke,* 1:68.

29. The text of *A Midsummer's Night's Dream* is from *The Complete Pelican Shakespeare,* 169; for Spenser, see *The Poetical Works of Edmund Spenser,* 458; for Horace, see *The Complete Works of Horace,* 295.

30. In this regard it is important to note that Dionysos is both "most terrible" and "most gentle, to mankind" (*Bacchae,* 222). On the concept of sophrosyne and its relation to drink in Plato, see Elizabeth Belfiore's rigorous and no less vigorous article, "Wine and *Catharsis* of the Emotions in Plato's *Laws,*" 433.

31. The popular "Noctes Ambrosianae" contained regular literary "discussions" among characters whose capacity for learned punman-

ship was equaled only by their capacity for consuming and joking about alcohol and, on occasion, opium. Hence the apologetic tone of the 1843 American book edition of the "Noctes," where the "Advertisement" warns readers of the "savoury steams" with which the "pages of the Noctes occasionally reek"; but fortunately, the "Advertisement" goes on to say, "the nostrils of a more temperate generation need take no offense" at such follies, for the "garniture of hot dishes" (a euphemism for references to alcohol) is "quite harmless, especially in these days, when the spell which associated all good fellowship with excessive eating and drinking is broken never to be reunited." Thus did the future look to one prestigious American literary press in 1843; see *Noctes Ambrosianae*, 1:iii. Like the *Noctes, Cozzens' Wine-Press* and, to a lesser extent, *Knickerbocker* magazine, which occasionally featured the same writers (e.g., the witty John Waters), fostered the image of author as drinker.

32.   In his important recent study of antebellum literature, David S. Reynolds has rightly corrected the notion that major American writers inevitably rejected mainstream culture. But the fact remains that the split mentioned by Kazin and Ziff really did occur, and intoxicant use in particular often became the locus for adversarial relations between artist and society. In this regard, it is worth noting that Ziff's book is among those "historically oriented" studies that Reynolds actually praises for *not* minimizing authorial involvement in American society at large; see Reynolds, *Beneath the American Renaissance*, 571 n 13.

33.   Writing of the antebellum period, William Charvat has pointed out, "Like the poet, the tale writer felt himself to be a social deviate: from the point of view of the man of action, he was nonproductive, an idler," as Hawthorne imagined his Puritan forebears would have regarded him in "The Custom House" introduction to *The Scarlet Letter;* see Charvat, *Literary Publishing in America, 1790–1850,* 76. A striking instance of the marginalization of literary professionalism later in the nineteenth century is the case of John Hay, Lincoln's personal secretary during the Civil War and later a secretary of state. Hay initially hid his authorship of the novel *The Breadwinners* (1884–85), because the Republican party "still had some affinity for 'free labor,' and the writing of fiction was perhaps suspect for a man engaged seriously in politics and the evolution of public policy"; see Slotkin, *The Fatal Environment*, 512–13.

34.   According to Peter Furst, "The mystical and introspective aspects of drug use run counter to certain long-accepted values of Western culture, especially its action- and achievement-oriented North

American variant"; see Furst, "Introduction," vii; Stanton Peele makes a similar point in *Love and Addiction,* 16. See also Van Wyck Brooks's earlier attack on American rationalism and Puritanism (in both its upper- and lowercase senses) in *Wine of the Puritans,* 18, 29–33.

35. See also Ziff, *Literary Democracy,* 177–78.

36. Similarly, antebellum book reviewers often emphasized the dangers of novel reading by using metaphors of "physical stimulation, intoxication, and addiction"; see Baym, *Novels, Readers, and Reviewers,* 56. The association of intoxicants with literature and authors could also find its way into scientific studies; in 1828, for example, the prominent Scottish physician Robert Macnish, in the American edition of his study of alcohol abuse, wrote that "the pleasures of drinking [constituted] one of the most fertile themes of [the] poetry" of liquor-producing countries; see Macnish, *The Anatomy of Drunkenness,* 10.

37. Byron is, by the way, in very good company in Grindrod's list of dissolute literary figures, which includes Chaucer, Shakespeare, Ben Jonson, Addison, Goldsmith, and, of course, that infamous imbiber, Robert Burns (102–04, 110–12). For the similar albeit somewhat less intense tendency of English temperance supporters to associate writers with heavy drinking, see Brian Harrison, *Drink and the Victorians,* 351.

38. Letter of May 25, 1862, to Thomas Melville; see Herman Melville, *The Writings of Herman Melville,* 14:378.

39. Of course, the date of Legouis's article—1926, when prohibition, though not the law in England, was dominant in America and influential elsewhere—may have contributed to his tentativeness here.

40. Heath, "American Experiences with Alcohol," 478.

Chapter 2. God's Wine and Devil's Wine:
The Idea of Intoxication in Emerson

1. For a transcription and discussion of the song, see Tremaine McDowell, "A Freshman Poem by Emerson," 326–29.

2. On wine imagery in "Bacchus," see Bernard J. Paris, "Emerson's 'Bacchus.'" Other critics to discuss intoxication or wine in Emerson include Harold Bloom, *The Ringers in the Tower,* 225–28, 299–301; Hyatt Waggoner, *Emerson as Poet,* 66, 142–45; and R. A. Yoder, *Emerson and the Orphic Poet in America,* 97–104. In addition to his published poems, many passages in Emerson's manuscripts testify to his fascination with intoxication as topic and image; see Emerson, *Poetry Notebooks,* as well

as the recent *Collected Poems and Translations,* which includes manuscript poems.

3. Succinct accounts of the evolution of American temperance reform appear in Lender and Martin, 64–86, and in Rorabaugh, 187–221.

4. Hereafter the following abbreviations of the titles of editions of Emerson's works will be used: *CW, The Collected Works of Ralph Waldo Emerson; W, The Complete Works of Ralph Waldo Emerson* (Centenary Edition); *JMN, The Journals and Miscellaneous Notebooks of Ralph Waldo Emerson.* Quotations given here omit variants and cancellations given in these editions.

5. The traditional links between wine and poetic inspiration are ancient; as we have seen, Horace mentions the tradition that no poems written by water drinkers can achieve immortality (Horace, *Complete Works,* 295, *Epistles* I.xix.2–3), and it was the worship of Dionysos/Bacchus that traditionally gave birth to comedy and tragedy. In a journal entry of 1843, Emerson mentions his friend Samuel G. Ward's "Chinese book," with its "many sentences purporting that bards love wine" ( *JMN,* 8:378).

6. Not included in the Centenary Edition, this poem appeared in the first, 1847 edition of Emerson's verse; see Emerson, *Collected Poems and Translations,* 210. On Emerson's response to Persian poetry, see J. D. Yohannan, "The Influence of Persian Poetry upon Emerson's Works."

7. "Who but an American romantic?" Who indeed! Herman Melville apparently referred to Socrates' abilities with the bottle in "Marquis de Grandvin":

> On themes that under orchards old
> The chapleted Greek would frank unfold,
> And Socrates, a spirit divine,
> Not alien held to cheerful wine,
> That reassurer of the soul—

See Melville, *Collected Poems of Herman Melville,* 334.

8. Edward Waldo Emerson, in a note to the essay "On Persian Poetry," carefully distinguishes his father's attitudes from those of Hafiz: "Mr. Emerson felt no responsibility for the morals of this remote Oriental Pindar" (*W,* 8:241).

9. For an intriguing comparison of "Experience" to Keats's intoxication imagery in the "Ode to a Nightingale," see Joel Porte, *Representative Man,* 179.

10. Quoted in Tony Tanner, *The Reign of Wonder,* 8, where Tanner makes some insightful comparisons between American and European writers' attitudes to childhood. For the original context of Baudelaire's remark, see his *Oeuvres Complètes,* 880.

### Chapter 3. The Little Tippler's Discerning Eye:
### Dickinson and Visionary Drunkenness

1. All citations of Dickinson's poetry are from *The Poems of Emily Dickinson.*

2. See also the useful cataloging of drinking motifs in Scott Garrow, "Alcoholic Beverage Imagery in the Poems of Emily Dickinson," and David Luisi's discussion of drink as a metaphor of sustenance in his "Some Aspects of Emily Dickinson's Food and Liquor Poems."

3. Joanne Feit Diehl's *Dickinson and the Romantic Imagination* is the most thorough study to date of Dickinson's affinities with romanticism.

4. John Cody has argued that a "contradictory, though nonverbal, message must have been sent to the Dickinson children each time Edward, a militant prohibitionist and one-time member of the West Parish Temperance Association, served sherry and champagne at home," in his *After Great Pain,* 90. Cody's point, however, is necessarily no more than speculative without further evidence of the Dickinson children's views of their parents' relation to temperance. Moreover, *temperance* and *teetotalism* were not always synonymous in antebellum America, especially in upper-middle-class families.

5. On the relations between Emerson's work and "I taste a liquor never brewed," see Charles R. Anderson, *Emily Dickinson's Poetry,* 74–75; Jack L. Capps, *Emily Dickinson's Reading,* 115–16; and Karl Keller, *The Only Kangaroo Among the Beauty,* 155.

6. A thorough but largely noninterpretive cataloging of Dickinson's wine and drinking imagery is found in Garrow, "Alcoholic Beverage Imagery," which Bernice Slote has described as "a fairly elementary counting and cataloguing job (though it is interesting to see how pervasive is drink, and especially wine, in her poems)"; see Slote, "Whitman and Dickinson," 73.

7. Two passages from Jay Leyda's *The Years and Hours of Emily Dickinson* tellingly convey something of the temperance atmosphere of nineteenth-century Amherst. In September 1850, the Cold Water Army

of North Amherst held a "grand festival," including a parade of one hundred forty persons marching "with appropriate badges and banners"; Emily Dickinson's father was among the speakers. The following year Emily's father again spoke on temperance, claiming, "The public sentiment of Amherst was sound. . . . There was no Temperance Society here—none was needed—for the people had resolved themselves into a Committee of the Whole. They only wanted to be armed with the power of search." See Leyda, *Years,* 1:179, 199.

8. The Northampton *Courier* of April 19, 1842, reported that "the citizens of Amherst partook of a sumptuous dinner at Rockwood's 'Amherst House', last Wednesday, to congratulate him on his late removal of liquors from his *bar*" (italics mine); Dickinson's parents attended this event; see Leyda, *Years,* 1:73.

9. It is tempting to speculate on Dickinson's possible play not only on the idea of "pharmacy" as a remedy consisting of drugs, and thus obliquely echoing the previous phrase in the poem "No Drug for Consciousness," but also on the ambiguity of the root meaning of *pharmakon* as either remedy or poison. Jacques Derrida takes this ambiguity as his point of departure in discussing "la pharmacie du Platon" in *La Dissemination.*

Chapter 4. Beyond the Sober Eye of Reason:
Poe and the Paradoxes of Intoxication

1. Leslie Fiedler has eloquently explained the persistence of the popular myth of Poe: "the image of the *poet as drunkard,* the weak-stomached, will-less addict," is "necessary to us in a world of success and power"; thus it is that "the folk mind never wearies of crying, 'Let him die for the act we dream! Let him die the death we secretly desire!'" See Fiedler, *Love and Death in the American Novel,* 427–28. Balanced assessments of Poe's supposed alcohol and drug use may be found in Arthur Hobson Quinn, *Edgar Allan Poe;* Edward Wagenknecht, *Edgar Allan Poe,* 30–43; and Kenneth Silverman, *Edgar Allan Poe,* 183, 435. A desultory summary of earlier studies with some added speculations is the Poe chapter in Donald W. Goodwin's *Alcohol and the Writer,* 9–35. For intriguing contemporary accounts of Poe's supposed use of alcohol and opium, see Dwight Thomas and David K. Jackson, eds., *The Poe Log.* More recently, Dr. R. Michael Benitez has suggested that Poe's death may actually have been caused by rabies; see "Tale of Poe's Death

Rewritten to Blame Rabies, not Alcohol," *New York Times,* September 15, 1996, A18.

2. We can only guess at Poe's own reactions to intoxicants. Kenneth Silverman believes that the truth about Poe's drinking problem is that "after one drink he could not stop" (Silverman, 183). Another plausible explanation is that Poe suffered from "alcohol idiosyncratic intoxication," a condition in which "a marked behavioral change . . . is due to the recent ingestion of an amount of alcohol insufficient to induce intoxication in most people." See *Diagnostic and Statistical Manual of Mental Disorders (DSM-III),* 132. However, a more recent (1994 as opposed to 1980) edition of this standard psychiatric reference, *DSM-IV,* has deleted "alcohol idiosyncratic intoxication" from its list of disorders because of insufficient evidence to distinguish the condition from alcohol intoxication proper. See *DSM-IV,* 778.

3. Poe's wickedly witty reply to the temperance press attacks on his alleged intoxication includes the following:

> Repelled at these points the Frogpondian faction hire a thing they call the "Washingtonian Reformer" (or something of that kind) to insinuate that we must have been "intoxicated" to have become possessed of sufficient audacity to "deliver" such a poem to the Frogpondians.
>
> In the first place, why cannot these miserable hypocrites say "drunk" at once and be done with it? In the second place we are perfectly willing to admit either that we were drunk, or that we set fire to the Frog-pond, or that once upon a time we cut the throat of our grandmother. . . . We shall get drunk when we please. As for the editor of the "Jeffersonian Teetotaler" (or whatever it is) we advise her to get drunk, too, as soon as possible—for when sober she is a disgrace to the sex—on account of being so awfully stupid.

These passages, as well as a thorough, illuminating account of Poe's relations to the temperance movement, may be found in Pollin, "The Temperance Movement."

4. Rayburn S. Moore, "A Note on Poe and the Sons of Temperance," 359–60; on the details of Poe's death, see Quinn, *Edgar Allan Poe,* 637–41; Wagenknecht, *Edgar Allan Poe,* 20–22; and Thomas and Jackson, *The Poe Log,* 844–50.

5. Scholars who have devoted attention to Poe's intoxication motifs include Marie Bonaparte, *The Life and Works of Edgar Allan Poe,* 84–86, 390–93; Harry Levin, *The Power of Blackness,* 103–49; William

Bittner, "Poe and the 'Invisible Demon'" (mainly a discussion of Poe's poor wine connoisseurship); Hayter, *Opium and the Romantic Imagination,* 132–50 (a thorough discussion of opium in Poe, with particular reference to his biography); L. Moffitt Cecil, "Poe's Wine List"; Benjamin Franklin Fisher IV, *The Very Spirit of Cordiality,* a pamphlet concentrating on the humorous uses of alcohol (especially wordplay) in Poe's tales; and Pollin, "The Temperance Movement." More recently, T. J. Matheson has examined Poe's view of temperance fiction attitudes toward alcoholism in "The Black Cat" in his intriguing article, "Poe's 'The Black Cat' as a Critique of Temperance Literature." See also J. Gerald Kennedy, *Poe, Death, and the Life of Writing,* 41, and David S. Reynolds, *Beneath the American Renaissance,* 69–72, for brief but illuminating comments on "The Cask of Amontillado."

6. Poe, *The Collected Works of Edgar Allan Poe,* 2:671. All future quotations from Poe's tales and poetry are taken from this edition, hereafter referred to as *Works.* Other citations of Poe's works are indicated as follows: *Writings, Collected Writings of Edgar Allan Poe; Letters, The Letters of Edgar Allan Poe; Essays, Essays and Reviews.*

7. A handy compilation of "Noctes Ambrosianae" is to be found in the 1843 American edition cited in chapter 1, note 31. References to De Quincey and humorous references to drinking and opium occur passim. Rorabaugh, *The Alcoholic Republic,* 176–77.

8. Walter Colton, "Turkish Sketches," 421; for comparisons of opium to alcohol in the nineteenth-century American press, see H. Wayne Morgan, *Drugs in America,* 89–90; for Crane, see *The Works of Stephen Crane,* 1:365–70; for Francis Thompson, see Hayter, *Opium and the Romantic Imagination,* 282.

9. Sheila Shaw, "The Female Alcoholic in Victorian Fiction." For helpful assessments of the image of women in temperance literature and their role in the temperance movement as a whole, see Harry Gene Levine, "Temperance and Women in the United States," 25–65, and Ruth Bordin, *Woman and Temperance.*

10. Although not conclusively authenticated as Poe's, the "Lines on Ale" are accepted as authentic by the eminent Poe scholar and editor, T. O. Mabbott; see Poe, *The Collected Works,* 1:449.

11. Lawrence's memorable phrase dovetails neatly with other familiar formulations about Poe, for example, Charles B. Feidelson, Jr.'s comments about the conflict of reason and irrationality within Poe, in *Symbolism,* 35; and David Ketterer's description of Poe's fascination

with the apocalypse of consciousness, where an old world of mind disintegrates in making way for a new one, in *New Worlds for Old*, 13-14.

12. On Poe's blending of the serious and comic, see also G. R. Thompson, *Poe's Fiction*, 16, 105-09.

13. See Benjamin Rush, *An Enquiry into the Effects of Spiritous Liquors*, and Thomas Trotter, *An Essay*. On Poe's familiarity with contemporary studies of alcoholism, see Pollin's comments in *Collected Writings of Edgar Allan Poe*, 1:220. On the concept of alcoholism as a disease before the twentieth century, see Berton Roueché, *The Neutral Spirit*, 103-09; Roueché is particularly informative on the generally negative reaction, especially in the United States, to Trotter's medical approach to alcohol. See also George E. Vaillant, *The Natural History of Alcoholism*, 3; Mark Edward Lender and Karen R. Karnchanapee, "Temperance Tales"; and E. M. Jellinek, *The Disease Concept of Alcoholism*.

14. For a discussion of "The Black Cat" as a rebuttal to contemporary temperance fiction, see Matheson, "Poe's 'The Black Cat.'" While portions of Matheson's study anticipate my discussion of "The Black Cat" here, I differ from Matheson in my emphasis on "perverseness," and in my sense that the narrator's description of alcohol as a "disease" plausibly reflects Poe's own views.

15. A useful survey of recent research on the etiology of alcoholism may be found in Vaillant, *The Natural History of Alcoholism*, 45-106.

16. On hyperaesthesia and opium in Poe, see Hayter, *Opium and the Romantic Imagination*, 136-37.

17. Mabbott notes that the ruby drops are not poison but "a primary corporeal form attained by Ligeia's spirit; and in themselves the elixir of life"; see *Works*, 2:334. However, the description of these drops may have come to Poe from De Quincey's account, in *The Confessions of an English Opium-Eater*, of putting "a quart of ruby-coloured laudanum" into a glass receptacle "as much like a wine-decanter as possible." Considering the narrator's opium habit, it is not unlikely that the drops might be laudanum, as well as having the meaning assigned them by Mabbott. See De Quincey, *Collected Writings*, 3:410. On the influence of the *Confessions* on "Ligeia," as well as for a discussion of the opium motif in the story, see Clark Griffith, "Poe's 'Ligeia' and the English Romantics." For the view that Ligeia is herself an opium-induced hallucination, see Jack L. Davis and June H. Davis, "Poe's Ethereal Ligeia."

18. On a similar issue, Charles Segal notes that Poe, like De Quincey before and Carlos Castaneda after him, blurs the separation between

the "metaphorical opiate of fiction and the dreams stimulated by the real opium"; see Segal, *Dionysiac Poetics and Euripedes' "Bacchae,"* 227.

19. Similarly, Alice Fiola Berry has listed Poe among those (e.g., Orpheus, Dante, Rabelais, Baudelaire, and Rimbaud) who have traced "the same path downward into hell that great visionary poets have always traced, those who dared recognize the vortex in themselves and in the world"; see Berry, "Apollo vs. Bacchus," 93.

### Chapter 5. The Gentleman's Part: Drinking and Moral Style in Cooper

1. Maria Edgeworth's praise of Cooper's character drawing with Betty Flanagan may be found in George Dekker and John P. McWilliams, eds., *Fenimore Cooper*, 67.

2. The Falstaff parallel has been suggested by James Wallace: "behind the carousing of Lawton and Dunwoodie lies the carousing of Falstaff and Hal"; see Wallace, *Early Cooper and His Audience*, 105.

3. Increase Mather condemns not only drunkards but those who make others drunk, such as colonists who "have sold intoxicating Liquors to these poor Indians, whose Land we Possess, and have made them Drunk therewith"; see Mather, *Wo to Drunkards*, 35. For Margaret Fuller, see *The Writings of Margaret Fuller*, 81. For Red Jacket, see Alan R. Velie, ed., *American Indian Literature*, 256. A facsimile of a broadside containing Red Jacket's speech appears as illustration 3 in *The Last of the Mohicans*, ed. James Franklin Beard. Red Jacket's and Fuller's views are echoed in the statements of many other Native American observers; see, for example, Black Hawk's "Farewell" of 1832 and Chief Joseph's defense of Nez Perce Indians "driven to madness by whiskey sold to them by white men" in Thomas E. Sanders and Walter N. Peek, eds., *Literature of the American Indian*, 280, 303.

4. In a brief but incisive analysis, Jane Tompkins points out that the "first time he drinks the firewater, Magua loses his identity as a Huron. The second time he loses his status as a chief: 'the . . . chief was tied up before all the pale-faced warriors and whipped like a dog'. And as a result of the whipping, he damages his stature as an Indian male; to hide the signs of his shame, he must go about with his body covered 'like a squaw.'" See Tompkins, *Sensational Designs*, 105. An earlier study makes a similar observation about drinking and racial identity in the case of Chingachgook: "his lust for this white-man's-poison wars with

his knowledge that it unmans him, makes him unable to play the Indian's part of a hunter and warrior"; see Richard Slotkin, *Regeneration through Violence,* 487. With regard to Cooper's use of an alcoholic Indian as a heroic figure, Geoffrey Rans has observed how "astonishing" it is that Cooper "should choose the least admirable stereotype [of those available to him]—the Indian degraded by liquor—and use it to convey so searing a critique of the entire ethos upon which the novel is founded." See Rans, *Cooper's Leather-Stocking Novels,* 260 n. 28.

5. Cooper, *The Pioneers,* vol. 19 of *Cooper's Novels,* 202. Unless otherwise indicated, all further references to Cooper's works are from this, the so-called "Townsend" edition.

6. Craig MacAndrew and Robert B. Edgerton point out that "the literature on the fur trade abounds with instances in which every conceivable form of deceit and coercion was employed in forcing liquor upon the Indians" so as to give white traders the advantage in negotiations—a problem that an Abnakis chief already complained about in 1685; see MacAndrew's and Edgerton's now-classic study, *Drunken Comportment,* 115. The motif of alcohol as the tool of a genocidal agenda persists in twentieth-century American literature, for example, in the various works of, among many others, such prominent authors as Frank Waters, N. Scott Momaday, and Leslie Marmon Silko. As the contemporary Native American writer Simon Ortiz explains, with regard to the destruction of North American Indians, "Whiskey was only one way, and guns another"; see Ortiz, *From Sand Creek,* 48. Those wishing to explore further the relationship of drinking and American Indians should begin by consulting Jerrold Levy and Stephen Kunitz, *Indian Drinking,* and Joy Leland, *The Firewater Myths,* as well as a significant recent study, published in 1995: Peter Mancall, *Deadly Medicine.*

7. It is only fair to add that on a number of other occasions, Franklin lamented the decay of Native Americans attributable to drink and sympathized with those persecuted by whites. In 1764, for example, Franklin wrote his emotional "Narrative of the Late Massacres, in Lancaster County, of a Number of Indians," in which he mentions specific victims of a racist attack by name and condemns those whites "who would extenuate the enormous wickedness" of this massacre. Franklin goes on to assert that "the only crime of these poor wretches seems to have been that they had a reddish-brown skin and black hair, and some people, of that sort, had murdered some of our relations" (*Works,* 4:44). Without exaggerating Franklin's sensitivity to Indian suf-

fering, we should remember such accounts as a corrective to the racist straw man that Franklin becomes in D. H. Lawrence's *Studies in Classic American Literature,* a view implicitly echoed in Leslie Fiedler's *The Return of the Vanishing American,* 57.

8.   In calling Chingachgook a "beast," young Effingham echoes the convention of calling drunkards "brutes" or "beasts." The convention was sufficiently clichéd already in the eighteenth century for Benjamin Franklin to lampoon it in "The Drinker's Dictionary." At the end of his list of 225 synonyms for drunkenness, Franklin says that he thought of adding the word "Brutify'd," but decided against it for fear of "being guilty of injustice to the Brute Creation, if I represented Drunkenness as a beastly Vice, since, 'tis well-known that the Brutes are in general a very sober sort of People"; see *The Papers of Benjamin Franklin,* 2:178.

9.   Poe's comment is available in the reprint of his lengthy review of *Wyandotté* for *Graham's Magazine* found in Dekker and McWilliams, eds., *Fenimore Cooper,* 213.

10.   For a *nonfictional* account of alcoholism by Cooper, see his *Ned Myers,* a purportedly factual recounting and, even, a transcription of the reminiscences of an old naval comrade of Cooper's. The saga of Myers's alcoholic misadventures ends with his rejection of drink in favor of true personal, nonideological temperance. With a jab at the organized temperance movement, Myers proudly proclaims, "I knew nothing of temperance societies—had never heard that such things existed, or, if I had, forgot it as soon as heard; and yet, unknown to myself, had joined the most effective and most permanent of all these bodies" (meaning, presumably, his own private temperance society, rooted in religious faith and personal determination to be sober). See *Ned Myers,* 233. (The book is not available in the Townsend edition used elsewhere in this chapter.)

11.   Representative of the teetotal ban on any use of alcoholic beverages (with rare medicinal exceptions) is Edward Hitchcock, *An Essay on Alcoholic and Narcotic Substances;* for Macnish's warning against sudden and total abstinence from drinking, see his *Anatomy of Drunkenness,* 156.

12.   As Levine puts it, "This distinction [between desire and will] is important to much modern thought; it is also at the heart of the concept of addiction." See Levine, "The Discovery of Addiction," 149–50; Edwards is quoted on p. 150.

13.   On the appeal of temperance to the Federalist elite, the standard statement remains that of Gusfield in *Symbolic Crusade,* 42–44. On

the use of appeals to American independence in rebuttals to teetotalism, see Jill Siegel Dodd, "The Working Classes and the Temperance Movement." Reminiscent of Cooper's fulminations against the "*croquemitaine*" of temperance is the following excerpt from an antiteetotal statement appearing in the April 3, 1838, issue of the *Boston Post:* "The country is not yet ripe for slavery. The people have too much of the spirit of '75 in their bones to allow their mouths, tongues, consciences, wrists and ankles, and especially their stomachs, to be tied by *Societies,* Commissions, *Priests* or Legislatures. Our yeomanry will not yet wear flowery chains or handcuffs and fetters, even of gold" (Dodd, 517).

14.   See Walt Whitman, "You Cannot Legislate Men into Virtue!" (one of Whitman's editorials for the *Brooklyn Daily Eagle,* dated March 18, 1846) in *The Gathering of the Forces,* 1:59–61.

15.   For a wonderfully witty and detailed discussion of the concept of *poshlust,* see Vladimir Nabokov, *Nikolai Gogol,* 63–74.

16.   On drinking relations between employers and workmen, see Paul Johnson, *A Shopkeeper's Millennium,* 58–60. Cooper's father is quoted in James Grossman, *James Fenimore Cooper,* 11. Of course, for all his nostalgia for that earlier time, Cooper cannot have been unaware of its potential for the shocking and violent, for example, his own father's murder by a political enemy. A penetrating study of the milieu in which Cooper was raised is the historian Alan Taylor's recent book, *William Cooper's Town.*

17.   A representative sample of antebellum attacks on the "delusion" of moderate drinking is Grindrod's *Bacchus,* especially pp. 56–57; see chap. 1, n. 48. For similar views, see also Hitchcock, *An Essay on Alcoholic and Narcotic Substances.*

18.   For an elaboration of these metaphors in connection to drinking, see Gusfield, "Benevolent Repression."

### Chapter 6. From Conviviality to Vision: Intoxication in Hawthorne

1.   An incident from Hawthorne's own life amusingly suggests his ambivalence to drink and parallels the contradictoriness of his fictional presentation of it. In a letter to the publisher, William D. Ticknor, Hawthorne says, "I made a convert to total abstinence, yesterday. It was a sea-captain, who had fallen into dissipated habits: and I preached to him with such good effect that he asked me to draw up a pledge, which

he signed on the spot, and declared that he felt himself a new man. On the strength of this good deed, I thought myself entitled to drink an extra glass or two of wine in the evening, and so have got a little bit of a headache"; for the text of the August 31, 1855, letter, see Hawthorne, *The Centenary Edition of the Works of Nathaniel Hawthorne,* 17:379. Unless otherwise noted, all further citations of Hawthorne's works will come from this edition.

2. As Karen Sanchez-Eppler observes in a recent essay, David Reynolds's *Beneath the American Renaissance* "contains the most comprehensive discussion of temperance fiction to date." But Reynolds, whose work I have invoked earlier in these pages, also discusses such mainstream authors as Poe, Hawthorne, and Melville, especially in relation to the subversive mode that Reynolds labels "dark temperance"; see Sanchez-Eppler, "Temperance in the Bed of a Child," 28 n. 4. Two other scholars who have attended to drink and temperance in Hawthorne include Lawrence Sargent Hall, *Hawthorne,* and Joel Porte, *The Romance in America.* Hall makes occasional incisive comments on Hawthorne's attitudes toward drinking practices and temperance reform, but these topics are tangential to Hall's main concerns. Porte's brilliant analysis of Miles Coverdale's drinking (pp. 131–33) is, in my opinion, one of the best things ever written about alcohol and literature, although he seems unduly harsh on poor Coverdale because the latter merely "contents himself with 'devouring the grapes'" in a grape arbor, rather than pursuing a more "tempestuous" form of intoxication. We can't really blame Coverdale for the fact that there is no wet bar available in the Blithedale bushes—devouring the grapes and imagining the wine that they could yield is about as Dionysian as anyone could get in that particular situation.

3. The ideal reader I envision for the subtext of this tale would be one of Hawthorne's friends like James T. Fields, Franklin Pierce, or Zacharaiah Burchmore, with whom Hawthorne often adopted a jocular, ironic tone about drink in his letters. For a valuable critical perspective on this and other *Tanglewood Tales,* see Laura Laffrado, *Hawthorne's Literature for Children.*

4. Here, Hawthorne is close to Cooper's notion that an awareness of drink's evils need not blind us to its benefits. The broader philosophical position behind this view of drink, of course, informs the epigraph to my Cooper chapter from Aristotle's *Nichomachean Ethics.*

5. The gentle irony of "A Rill from the Town-Pump" leaves the

basic point of the tale elusive. A blunt satire of teetotalism would be far clearer than this story, where temperance statement and ironic counterstatement (or, more exactly, counterimplication) succeed one another in a tone of whimsical banter that seems far more to be the point of "A Rill from the Town-Pump" than is any definitive conclusion about temperance. The resulting indeterminacy of Hawthorne's treatment of temperance in "A Rill" fits a pattern described long ago by Frederick Crews, who observed of *The Blithedale Romance* that its irony is not "sufficiently ambiguous or sufficiently discernible to the reader; the most we can say is that it is consistently available to close scrutiny"; see Crews, *The Sins of the Fathers,* 196. Richard H. Millington makes a related observation about Hawthorne's elusiveness and mobility of perspective, pointing out that the narrator of *The Scarlet Letter* is "best understood, here as throughout Hawthorne's work, as an espouser of various cultural positions rather than a consistent voice"; see Millington, *Practicing Romance,* 67. As my own discussion indicates, however, I believe that, as far as drink and temperance are concerned, Hawthorne's work finally does achieve a certain consistency and clarity of view.

6. The notion of alcohol as a substitute for the kind of stimulation that higher culture affords was present in two other very different writers at work during Hawthorne's lifetime; in *Dred,* Harriet Beecher Stowe describes the lowlife drunkard, Cripps, and asks, with reference to his drinking, "Why not? He was uncomfortable—gloomy; and every one, under such circumstances, naturally inclines towards *some* source of consolation. He who is intellectual reads and studies; he who is industrious flies to business; he who is none of these—what has he but his whiskey?" And in William Gilmore Simms's novelette, *Paddy McGann,* the title character goes on at length about the same topic: "Yes, my friends, whiskey and tobacco may be curse enough, but them's pretty much a poor man's only consolation in his time of throuble.... You who have fine parlours, and fine society, big collections of books which you know how to read and onderstand—and some of you to write—who have da'ters who can play for you on the piana, and who kin intertain your friends in a hundred ways, to say nothing of a plenty to ate and drink—you kain't exactly onderstand the difficulties of a poor man in his hour of trouble." For Stowe, see *Writings,* 3:112; for Simm's *Paddy McGann,* see *The Writings of William Gilmore Simms,* 3:262.

7. Most of the anacreontic business in *Fanshawe* is limited to the novel's fifth chapter, but apart from a charming description of Fan-

shawe's drink-influenced speech ("his conversation was such as one might expect from a bottle of champagne, endowed by a fairy with the gift of speech"), the treatment of intoxication in this novel is pedestrian; see *Centenary Edition,* 3:386.

8.   Rita K. Gollin has pointed out that Etherege's spurious vision recalls at first a Poe character's awakening after death, but Etherege "reaches no new knowledge," only greater uncertainty and confusion; see Gollin, *Nathaniel Hawthorne and the Truth of Dreams,* 206. For a sympathetic, insightful discussion of Hawthorne's unfinished manuscripts in general, see Charles Swann, *Nathaniel Hawthorne.*

9.   In a letter of September 25, 1841, Hawthorne tells Sophia, "We found white and purple grapes, in great abundance, ripe, and gushing with rich juice when the hand pressed their clusters. Didst thou know what treasures of wild grapes there are in this land, if we dwell here, we will make our own wine—of which I know, my Dove will want a great quantity," Hawthorne's last comment obviously teasing the staunchly protemperance Sohpia (15:579).

10.   The blood/grape/wine connection is, of course, ancient (wine is called "the blood of grapes" in Gen. 49:11), but it is interesting to note its appearance in a passage by a contemporary of Hawthorne; in 1855, in a bon voyage poem entitled "Farewell" and addressed to J. R. Lowell, about to depart for Europe, Oliver Wendell Holmes wrote, "I give you one health in the juice of the vine, / The blood of the vineyard shall mingle with mine"; see *The Poetical Works of Oliver Wendell Holmes,* 97.

11.   The often-described link between spiritual and physical in Hawthorne has been captured with subtlety and precision by Leon Chai: "In Hawthorne the actual does not merely serve as a form of the temporal through which the eternal can shine forth in infinite splendor. Instead, the realm of the actual . . . possesses itself a kind of spiritual iridescence"; see Chai, *Romantic Foundations of the American Renaissance,* 39.

## Chapter 7. Too Sober or Too Drunken: Melville's Dialogics of Drink

1.   Miller's comment, made about Hawthorne, applies to Melville as well; see Miller, *Salem Is My Dwelling-Place,* 244–45.

2.   The fullest treatment of Melville's relationship with Hawthorne appears in James C. Wilson, ed., *The Hawthorne and Melville Friendship;*

see also Howard Vincent, *Melville and Hawthorne in the Berkshires*. Addressing Melville's personal drinking habits, a recent biography suggests that he may have been an abusive drinker, but the available evidence for this is inconclusive. See Laurie Robertson-Lorant, *Melville*, 370–71. For passing references to Melville's drinking, see Leon Howard, *Herman Melville*, 241–65, and Newton Arvin, *Herman Melville*, 135.

3. See Edward H. Rosenberry, *Melville and the Comic Spirit;* Jane Mushabac, *Melville's Humor;* William B. Dillingham, *Melville's Short Fiction, 1853–1856,* and *Melville's Later Novels;* William Bysshe Stein, *The Poetry of Melville's Late Years;* Dorothee Metlitsky Finkelstein, *Melville's Orienda;* David S. Reynolds, *Beneath the American Renaissance.* Also relevant here are two considerations of Melvillean "geniality": Merton M. Sealts, Jr., "Melville's Geniality," and Marjorie Dew, "Black-Hearted Melville." Sealts makes several interesting but passing references to drinking; Dew treats alcohol somewhat more fully, emphasizing wine as the accompaniment of a usually spurious geniality that, in her view, Melville condemns. However, although Melville does expose hypocrisy operating under the mask of the convivial, for example, in *The Confidence-Man,* his texts repeatedly betray a more unsettling (and unsettled) ambiguity regarding intoxication, in which drink is more than just an attribute of "geniality" and in which both geniality and drinking assume a host of shifting qualities and values. And, as my discussion will show, the permutations of Melville's various drink references involve much more than geniality, important as this theme is.

4. Herman Melville, *Writings,* 14:191. Future references to Melville's letters are drawn from this work. Melville's journal references come from *Journal of a Visit to London and the Continent by Herman Melville;* references to *Omoo, Mardi, Moby-Dick, Israel Potter,* and *The Confidence-Man* come from the Northwestern-Newberry editions of these texts, vols. 2, 3, 6, 8, and 10, respectively. Any references to Melville's marginalia come from Walker Cowen's "Melville's Marginalia."

5. Hazlitt, "Lord Byron," from *The Spirit of the Age,* in *The Complete Works of William Hazlitt,* 11:75.

6. In connection with the "dialogic," I have drawn mainly on Bakhtin's *Problems of Dostoevsky's Poetics,* ed. and trans. Caryl Emerson; on Gary Saul Morson and Caryl Emerson, *Mikhail Bakhtin,* 230–37; and, with specific regard to Melville, on Aaron Fogel's "Coerced Speech and the Oedipus Dialogue Complex."

7. Melville's fondness for tobacco is well known and appears throughout his fiction, where it is often linked with contentment and

solace. Ahab, of course, casts these qualities overboard with his pipe in a famously dramatic gesture in *Moby-Dick*. Melville's poetry also testifies to the value he placed on tobacco; in *Clarel*, for instance: "Wear and tear and jar / He met with coffee and cigar," or "Wine and the weed! blest innovations, / How welcome to the weary nations!" (this last couplet linking tobacco and liquor as sources of consolation); see Melville, *Clarel*, 155, 474.

8.   Elizabeth S. Foster has pointed out this frequency of Melville-Rabelais comparisons in the richly informative notes to her edition of *The Confidence-Man*, 330. On Melville's reading of Rabelais as the basis for the structure and themes of *Mardi*, see Merrell R. Davis, *Melville's "Mardi,"* 76–77. A wide-ranging discussion of the "Rabelaisian" in relation to Melville and, more particularly, the New York literary circles in which he moved is Perry Miller's *The Raven and the Whale*.

9.   Melville's blend of the farcical and the tragic recalls the interplay of the merry and the macabre on the sarcophagi described in *The Marble Faun*, as well as Hawthorne's idea in *The American Claimant* of the "bleakness and horror . . . underneath the story [being covered with] a frolic and dance of bacchanals all over the surface." See Hawthorne, *Centenary Edition*, 4:17–18 and 12:292.

10.   Melville's ironic stance toward temperance emerges amusingly in *Israel Potter*, where an annoyed Israel must put up with a meddling, morally solicitous Benjamin Franklin. Franklin first prevents Israel from drinking wine, then from enjoying Otard brandy, and finally urges him to ignore the blandishments of a coquettish French chambermaid. "Every time he comes in he robs me," complains Israel, adding that Franklin does so "with an air all the time, too, as if he were making me presents. If he thinks me such a very sensible young man, why not let me take care of myself? (*Writings*, 8:44). But in *Israel Potter*, as well as in other of Melville's novels considered here, Melville remains keenly aware of alcohol's double-edged qualities. Thus drink, so attractive in the Ben Franklin episodes, becomes a tool of vicious deceit when a British agent gets Israel drunk so as to impress him into the royal navy (8:83–84). (In a delightful irony, pointed out by Ann Douglas, an 1888 *McGuffey's Reader* "actually anthologized Melville's account of Benjamin Franklin's pro-temperance comments . . . for the edification of the American young"; see Douglas, *The Feminization of American Culture*, 314.)

11.   On the wine-blood link, see Jellinek, "The Symbolism of Drinking," 855–57.

Chapter 8. Forbidden Fruit:
Nineteenth-Century American Female Authorship
and the Discourses of Intoxication

The title of this chapter, and much of my thinking about its topic, have been inspired by Nina Auerbach's paper "Beaded Bubbles and Forbidden Fruit: Intoxicants and Gender," delivered at a panel I chaired at the 1981 Modern Language Association Convention.

1. On ambivalence and drinking, see chap. 1, n. 14.

2. Unlike Dickinson, most women poets scarcely touched the topic of intoxication, except for the numerous poetic effusions of temperance movement authors. Even in the work of such relatively bold poets as Ella Wheeler Wilcox and Elizabeth Oakes Smith, intoxication received less attention than it did in the work of prose authors. Typical of many female poets' treatment of intoxication is the fleeting reference in Smith's "The Sinless Child," where the poem's heroine leads a "reckless youth" away from "his former life / What once he called delight, / The goblet, oath, and stolen joy" (Smith, *The Sinless Child and Other Poems,* 121; the poem is not numbered by lines or stanzas). See also Emily Stipes Watts, *The Poetry of American Women,* 103.

3. At least two other authors deserve brief mention as well. Sarah Orne Jewett sets herself apart from the condemnatory, "coercive" mode of much temperance writing (see Lender and Karnchanapee, "Temperance Tales"), and of many women's writings on drink, in her open-minded, sympathetic references to the alcoholic mother in the novel, *A Country Doctor* (1884). And that professional Bohemian, Gertrude Atherton, echoes Mark Twain's call for "temperate temperance" in the following dialogue from *Patience Sparhawk and Her Times* (1897); taking on the temperance crusader, Miss Beale, Atherton's rebellious, eponymous protagonist declares,

> "If you really were temperance you might have more chance of success."
> "If we were what?"
> "Temperance in the actual meaning of the word. You're not, you know; you're teetotalists. That is the reason you antagonise so many thousands of men who might be glad to help you with their vote otherwise. The average gentleman—and there are thousands upon thousands of him—never gets drunk, and enjoys his wine at dinner and even his whiskey and water. He doesn't

see any reason why he should n't have it, and there isn't any. . . .
Those are the people that really represent Temperance, and naturally they have no sympathy with a movement that they consider narrow-minded and an unwarrantable intrusion." (281–82)

A year earlier (1896), Mark Twain made a similar point in the following
notebook entry: "Temperate temperance is best. Intemperate temperance injures the cause of temperance, while temperate temperance
helps it in its fight against intemperate intemperance. Fanatics will
never learn that, though it be written in letters of gold across the sky"
(Clemens, *Mark Twain's Notebook,* 310).

    4.    Marian Sandmaier, *The Invisible Alcoholics;* Gregory Austin, *Al-
cohol in Western Society from Antiquity to 1800;* Mark Edward Lender,
"A Special Stigma."

    Even in American colonial times, when drink was considered to be
a "good Creature of God," as Increase Mather called it in a phrase deriving ultimately from I Timothy 4:4 (see Mather, *Wo to Drunkards,* 7), and
when it was perfectly respectable for women as well as men to engage
in such practices as tavern ownership, a drunken woman seemed more
reprehensible than a drunken man. In 1626, for instance, a certain
Goodwife Fisher of the Virginia colony was observed reeling drunkenly
through the street. Her progress stopped only when she fell, according
to an eyewitness account, "on top of a cow." The court official who
hauled Goodwife Fisher before the authorities "testified that . . . his
companion at the time [of the incident] remarked that it was 'a great
shame to see a man drunk but more a shame to see a woman in that
case'" (Sandmaier, *The Invisible Alcoholics,* 35). On the relationship of
the saloon to shifting norms regarding male and female drinking, see
Roy Rosenzweig, "The Rise of the Saloon."

    5.    In connection with Lender's analysis of the emergent consen-
sus about what constitutes the ideal woman in Victorian America, it is
worth recalling that the nineteenth century in the United States was
generally more prudish than the eighteenth; see Ernest Earnest, *The
American Eve in Fact and Fiction,* 242.

    6.    Scott is quoted in Levine, "Temperance and Women," 33; see
also Storer, *Appendix* to Albert Day, *Methomania,* reprinted in Gerald
Grob, ed., *Nineteenth-Century Medical Attitudes,* 64–65, 62.

    7.    Reprinted in Gerald Grob's facsimile edition of addiction-
related materials, *American Perceptions of Drug Addiction,* 86.

8.  As her title indicates, Baym concentrates on pre-Civil War literature. However, constraints on women's writing persisted well past the surrender at Appomattox. As the century progressed, more and more women were practicing authors and important changes in women's educational and employment possibilities were taking place. Still, postbellum American women were obviously expected to conform to rigid notions of feminine propriety, and intellectualism in women, whether evidenced in work in the professions, in literature or elsewhere, was frequently frowned on. See Mark Edward Lender, "A Special Stigma"; Ann Douglas, *The Feminization of American Culture;* Susan Phinney Conrad, *Perish the Thought;* Margaret Gibbons Wilson, *The American Woman in Transition;* Barbara Bardes and Suzanne Gossett, *Declarations of Independence;* and Baym's other book-length study of American women's writing until just past the Civil War, *Woman's Fiction.* On the persistence of a double standard for female and male drinkers late into the twentieth century, see Thelma McCormack, "The 'Wets' and 'Drys.'"

9.  Unsigned review of Metta V. Fuller's novel, *Fashionable Dissipation,* in *Godey's Lady's Book,* 274.

10.  John S. Haller and Robin M. Haller give brief but incisive analyses of women's intoxicant use, as well as of the connections between gender and intoxicant choice, in *The Physician and Sexuality in Victorian America:* "A dark veil of obscurity shrouds the opium and alcohol inebriety of the Victorian Woman—a veil whose cloth had been woven by both the victim and the society alike to conceal the failures of those who did not survive the system and its principles" (274); in the wake of the industrial revolution and increased complexity of social life, alcohol "became a welcome stabilizer" for Victorian men.

> The laudanum vial and syringe, on the other hand, became the final resort of those who could not otherwise keep pace with the perilous social struggle. Among Victorian males, only the weakest turned to opiates, for among the physical outlets available to men, drug addiction was the least acceptable. Although momentary vices like the use of alcohol or prostitution might be tolerated without loss of standing, drug addiction, like homosexuality, was an anathema to the fittest man.
> Since the Victorian woman was unable to publicly consume alcohol without social censure, the shy sipping of nervines and tonics for 'medicinal' purposes became somehow more respectable. (302)

11.   Sheila Shaw's analysis of "Janet's Repentance" is a cogent one, although it perpetuates the mistaken notion that the disease concept of alcoholism arose only in the twentieth century. Admittedly, it was only in the 1860s and 1870s that American influence led to a more medical view of alcoholism in England, and "Janet's Repentance" was published earlier, in 1857. However, forms of the disease concept had been present in England at least since the work of Dr. Thomas Trotter in 1804; on medical models of alcoholism in the nineteenth century, see Brian Harrison, *Drink and the Victorians,* 22.

12.   See also Harry Gene Levine, "The Alcohol Problem in America," and Gusfield's *Symbolic Crusade.* Excellent historical discussions of women's relations to American drinking patterns and to temperance appear in Levine, "Women and Temperance"; Ian Tyrrell, *Sobering Up,* 181; and Ruth Bordin, *Woman and Temperance.* A temperance publication appearing in 1873, just a year before the founding of the WCTU, embodies the gender associations of drinking and temperance more memorably than any other single source I know. Authored by Silas Adams, the poetic pamphlet entitled *The Crisis; or, Women vs. Rum,* begins by saying that Adam and Eve were originally equals, with neither dominating the other. After eating the fatal fruit, however, Eve is told by God,

> The man, no more thy equal mate,
> Shall rule o'er thee in lordly state.
> To him henceforth shall be thy prayer
> For all things which thou may'st desire;
> And more than this, by doom divine,
> His appetite shall thirst for Wine!

Later, in a blithely revisionist account of the Fall, an angel appears to Eve and, like the good fairy in "Sleeping Beauty," softens the curse made earlier. The angel explains that, after a mere six thousand years, women shall cast off the chains of male domination and lead men away from intoxication:

> Though thy first born a drunkard prove,
> And wine his fiery passions move
> Him for to shed his brother's blood,
> Which from the ground shall cry to God. . . .
> Yet there shall come a joyful day,
> When men will turn from wine away.
>                                                     (Adams, 4, 8–9)

13. The names of Harriet Beecher Stowe and Frances Ellen Watkins Harper remind us of "the close relationship between the anti-slavery and anti-liquor movements" in nineteenth-century America; see Denise Herd, "Ambiguity in Black Drinking Norms." In *Uncle Tom's Cabin,* which we will examine in more detail shortly, the evils of drink are second only to those of slavery. In *Poems on Miscellaneous Subjects,* published in 1854 and reprinted twenty times over the following twenty years, Harper ardently advocated both temperance and abolition. Late in her career, Harper published a novel, *Iola Leroy* (1892), which depicts white liquor traffickers as but another form of slave drivers or slave hunters. Excoriating liquor-peddling whites, Aunt Linda tells her nephew, "Dem Yankees set me free, an' I thinks a powerful heap ob dem. But it does rile me ter see dese mean white men comin' down yere an' settin' up dere grog-shops, tryin' to fedder dere nests sellin' licker to pore culled people. Days de bery kine ob men dat used ter keep dorgs to ketch de runaways." Aunt Linda goes on to tell her nephew, "I beliebs we might be a people ef it warn't for dat mizzable drink'; see Harper, *Iola Leroy,* 159–60.

More explicit parallels between slavery and alcohol addiction were common in the nineteenth century. In 1842, for instance, Abraham Lincoln described his hope for a time "when there shall be neither a slave nor a drunkard on the earth" (see *Abraham Lincoln,* 140); in his autobiography, Frederick Douglass wrote, "It was about as well to be a slave to master, as to be a slave to whiskey and rum" (*The Life and Times of Frederick Douglass,* 148; Herd, "Ambiguity," 155); a widely used temperance pledge for freed blacks read in part, "Being mercifully redeemed from human slavery, we do pledge ourselves never to be brought into the slavery of the bottle" (Herd, " 'We Cannot Stagger to Freedom,'" 155). On the symbolic relations of race and alcohol in nineteenth-century America, see Herd, "The Paradox of Temperance."

14. Alcott helped to found a temperance society in Concord, while Harper was an important leader in the colored divisions of the WCTU; see *The Journals of Louisa May Alcott,* 233, and Hazel V. Carby, *Reconstructing Womanhood,* 68. The carefully maintained segregation within the WCTU fuels Carby's skepticism about "the existence of an American sisterhood between black and white women" (6); on Harper's involvement with the WCTU, see Carby, 68, 113–14.

15. On Holmes's fictional treatments of women and drinking, see Frances B. Cogan, *All-American Girl,* 137–38, 159–62.

16.   Holmes's text parallels the attitude mocked by Ernest Hemingway in one of the unused drafts for *The Sun Also Rises,* where Hemingway describes Jake's repulsion at the fanatical teetotalism of his aunt, who would rather see her husband, Jake's beloved uncle, dead (and hence abstinent) than alive and drinking, even moderately. See William Balassi, "Hemingway's Greatest Iceberg," 134. Of course, it was the temperance ethos represented by novels like *Meadow Brook* that held sway in the Prohibition era—when *The Sun Also Rises* was written.

17.   The admonition to parents not to let their children near alcohol was a popular motif in temperance-related writings, as in Julia A. J. Foote, *A Brand Plucked from the Fire,* 13.

18.   For Stowe's fiction, my source is *The Writings of Harriet Beecher Stowe,* in 16 volumes. For *Uncle Tom's Cabin,* see vols. 1–2; for *Dred,* vol. 3; for *My Wife and I* and *We and our Neighbors,* vols. 12 and 13, respectively.

19.   Along with many other nineteenth-century commentators, Stowe seems to have considered alcoholism a disease primarily of the will, but nonetheless as powerful as any purely physical disease. In *We and Our Neighbors,* Bolton's bouts of drunkenness are described as "lesions of the will that are no more to be considered subject to moral condemnation than a strain of the spinal column or a sudden fall from paralysis" (13:206). This raises the whole issue of just how we are to interpret nineteenth-century notions of alcoholism as a disease. As a modern scholar in alcohol studies has pointed out, "the disease model of Rush [which, as we saw in chapters 1 and 3, laid the foundation for the nineteenth-century disease concept of alcoholism] was defined not in terms of disease pathology as we know it today" but rather "as a 'disease of the will' and an addiction brought on by a gradual breaking down of moral willpower." See Genevieve M. Ames, "American Beliefs about Alcoholism," 30. For Stowe's personal experiences with and views of the temperance movement, see Joan D. Hedrick, *Harriet Beecher Stowe,* especially pp. 133–37.

20.   Similarly, Lyman Beecher wrote, "It is a matter of undoubted certainty, that habitual tippling is worse than periodical drunkenness"; see Beecher, *Six Sermons,* 9.

21.   The wonderfully named Audacia Dangyereyes, a caricature of the freethinking and free-drinking emancipated woman, embodies Stowe's sense of the impropriety of female drinking. Audacia is presumably based on the feminist Victoria Woodhull; see Johanna John-

ston, *Mrs. Satan,* 97–98. Bursting into the rooms of the earnest, complacent Harry Henderson, Audacia cries, "Now look here, bub!" and proceeds to "claim my right to smoke, if I please, and to drink if I please; and to come up into your room and make you a call, and have a good time with you, if I please" (*My Wife and I,* 12:241). In Stowe's hands, such a woman quickly becomes a degendered "it," as Henderson's friend Jim Fellows asks, with reference to Audacia, "Bless its little heart, has it got its rights yet? Does it want to drink and smoke? Come along with Jim, now, and let's have a social cocktail" (12:242). For the drinking heroines of dime-novel fiction, see for instance, Edward L. Wheeler, *Deadwood Dick on Deck,* originally published in 1885 in Beadle's half-dime library. See also Henry Nash Smith's comments on drinking heroines in his *Virgin Land,* 117. For the Susan Warner passage, see her *Wide, Wide World,* 2:271.

22.   Davis's *Life in the Iron Mills* was originally published in the *Atlantic Monthly* in April 1861. Future references to the book will be to the modern edition cited in the references. On Dickinson's request for *Life in the Iron Mills,* see Dickinson, *Letters,* 2:272–73.

23.   In asserting that intemperance was often the result of adverse social conditions, Willard was taking "a most heretical step for the advocate of Temperance"; see Gusfield's *Symbolic Crusade,* 92, and Clark's *Deliver Us from Evil,* 87–88. Paralleling Willard's view (and in distinct contrast to that of Stowe) is Charles Dickens's 1844 letter to Theodore Compton, protesting, "I can no more concur in the philosophy of reducing all mankind to one total abstainment level, than I can yield to that monstrous doctrine which sets down as the consequences of Drunkenness, fifty thousand miseries which are, as all reflective persons know, and daily see, the wretched causes of it"; see Dickens, *The Letters of Charles Dickens,* 1:563–64.

24.   Elizabeth Stuart Phelps's "Jack" originally appeared in the *Century Magazine* in June 1887. Subsequent references are to this edition.

25.   Phelps, *The Story of Avis,* was originally published in 1877, and has not, as far as I know, been republished since. Subsequent references are to this edition.

26.   Alfred Habegger notes the lack of realism in Phelps's account of Avis's hallucination in his *Gender, Fantasy and Realism in American Literature,* 314.

27.   Subsequent references to Stoddard's work are from Elizabeth Drew Stoddard, *"The Morgesons" and Other Writings.*

28. On the name Sairy Gamp, see Alcott, *Alternative Alcott,* 457; on Alcott's attitudes toward alcohol and temperance, see the informative comments of Charles Strickland, *Victorian Domesticity,* and Sarah Elbert, *A Hunger for Home.* One of the most representative examples of Alcott's fictional treatments of drinking is her novel *Rose in Bloom,* originally published in 1882.

29. On Alcott's drug tales, see the brief but useful comments of Madeline B. Stern in her "Writer's Progress," 248, and in her introduction to Alcott, *Plots and Counterplots,* 14–22.

30. "A Marble Woman" and "Perilous Play" appear on pp. 131–237 and 303–15, respectively, of *Plots and Counterplots. A Modern Mephistopheles* is reprinted in Alcott, *"A Modern Mephistopheles" and "Taming a Tartar".* Subsequent references are to these editions.

31. I am indebted for these observations on *Villette* to Nina Auerbach's "Beaded Bubbles and Forbidden Fruit," a paper presented at the annual meetings of the Modern Language Association, December 1981.

32. Intoxicated by love and hashish, Mark tells Rose that he longs to escape with her "anywhere, anywhere out of the world" (*Plots and Counterplots,* 312). This phrase strikingly recalls Baudelaire's famous prose poem, "N'importe ou hors du monde" (Anywhere Out of the World), which concludes, "Anywhere! anywhere! so long as it is out of this world" (my translation). The Baudelaire poem was published in 1867, two years before "Perilous Play," but Alcott's possible awareness of the poem must remain, at this time, a matter of (rather dubious) conjecture; see Charles Baudelaire, *Le Spleen de Paris,* 272.

33. See Alcott's diary-letter to her family, dated June 17, 1870, in Ednah D. Cheney, ed., *Louisa May Alcott,* 230.

34. This tension has become a commonplace of Alcott criticism but is nowhere more pithily expressed than by Elizabeth Janeway, who writes of *Little Women* that it is "as often smug as it is snug, and its highmindedness tends to be that peculiar sort that pays"; see Janeway, *Between Myth and Morning,* 234.

35. Dobson partly takes issue with Helen Waite Papashvily's earlier emphasis on the supposed bitter rebelliousness of much nineteenth-century women's fiction in her still-valuable *All the Happy Endings;* see also Susan K. Harris, "'But is it any *good?*'"

36. The phrase appears as the title of Barbara Welter's superb study, *Dimity Convictions,* and originates in Dickinson's poem 401:

What Soft—Cherubic Creatures—,
These Gentlewomen are—
One would as soon assault a Plush—
Or violate a Star—

Such Dimity Convictions—
A Horror so refined
Of freckled Human Nature—
Of Deity Ashamed—

It's such a common—Glory—
A Fisherman's-Degree—
Redemption—Brittle Lady—
Be so—ashamed of Thee—
                    (*Complete Poems*, 191)

37.  This 1909 publication's eminently respectable editorial board included Fannie Farmer of cookbook fame, as well as others from such reputable magazines as *Good Housekeeping* and *Ladies' Home Journal;* see Lender and Martin, *Drinking in America*, 98.

38.  Joan L. Silverman, "'I'll Never Touch Another Drop,'" 49.

39.  On American Bohemian attitudes toward Prohibition, see Andrew Sinclair, *Era of Excess*, and Robin Room, "A 'Reverence for Strong Drink.'"

## Conclusion

1.  Allowing for differences in tone and audience, we can detect a similar point about the relativity of such concepts as "problem drinking" or "drug abuse" in Dan Wakefield's 1991 interview with Allen Ginsberg. Asked about drug abuse among the Beats, Ginsberg replies, "Do you know the statistics? Between 20,000 and 35,000 people a year die of hard drugs, 100,000 of alcohol, and 400,000 die of nicotine or related causes, like heart failure, high blood pressure, and so on. So our eccentric use of recreational drugs was healthier than the average insurance salesman's casualty list"; see Wakefield, *New York in the Fifties*, 187.

2.  The views of Beecher and other proponents of the work ethic are found throughout my introduction; see also Joseph Gusfield's comments on alcohol's threat to notions of social hierarchy and worker productivity: "Precisely because it [drinking] possesses a meaning of contrast to organized work, it is a dissolver of hierarchy. In Victor Turner's term 'communitas', it is a contrast to structure, a commitment

to values of human similarity and anti-structure." As for the drinking laborer himself, Gusfield summarizes the conventional social perspective operative in nineteenth-century America: "Once let loose he may not show up for church on Sunday or for work on Monday"; see Gusfield, "Passage to Play," 79, 88.

3. For *Uncle Tom's Cabin,* see Stowe, *Writings,* 1:285; for Emerson, see *JMN,* 11:255; for Howells, see *The Landlord at Lion's Head,* 241; for Silko, see *Ceremony,* 40.

4. Of course, a more positive, celebratory dimension of the argument with reality was also prominent in many antebellum portrayals of intoxication. Following the Civil War, however, the visionary mode waned, as the more explicitly socioeconomic and biological concerns of realism and naturalism gained literary dominance. But the visionary/romantic mode of writing about intoxicants continued to find powerful new forms of expression in the twentieth century. The prohibition-defying "elevation of alcohol" in writing of the twenties and early thirties comes to mind, as does the drug- and liquor-related Dionysianism of the Beats, e.g., Ginsberg's poems produced after taking LSD or mescaline and the frequent hymning of quasi-mystical highs in Jack Kerouac's fiction.

On the "elevation of alcohol" in writers of the "lost generation," see Robin Room, "A 'Reverence for Strong Drink.'" Celebrations of intoxication in Kerouac's novels, such as *On the Road* or *The Dharma Bums,* are apparent to anyone who opens them. For representative Ginsberg poems dealing with or written on drugs (quite apart from the general hallucinatory exuberance of much of his work), see "Mescaline," "Lysergic Acid," and "Wales Visitation."

5. A notable and influential example of the broadening of the scope of addiction is Stanton Peele, with Archile Brodsky, *Love and Addiction.* In modern fiction, Thomas Pynchon has given memorably amusing expression to love's addictive power in *The Crying of Lot 49* through the man who says, "I'm a member of the IA. That's Inamorati Anonymous. An inamorato is somebody in love. That's the worst addiction of all"; *The Crying of Lot 49,* 112. Ironically, the inamorato's rejection of love as addiction has led to the emotional equivalent of a total abstinence position—his detachment is so great that he refuses Oedipa Maas's touchingly modest request for help (177). In a more recent work of fiction, Erica Jong's *Any Woman's Blues* (1990), the protagonist, Leila Sand, struggles with multiple, even intersecting addictions: to love, alcohol, sexual experimentation, and an irresistible but faithless man.

# References

Aaron, Paul, and David F. Musto. "Temperance and Prohibition in America: A Historical Overview." In *Alcohol and Public Policy: Beyond the Shadow of Prohibition,* edited by Mark H. Moore and Dean R. Gerstein, 127–81. Washington, D.C.: National Academy Press, 1981.

Adams, Silas. *The Crisis; or, Women vs. Rum.* Gardner, Mass.: A. G. Bushnell, 1873.

Alcott, Louisa May. *Alternative Alcott.* Edited by Elaine Showalter. New Brunswick: Rutgers University Press, 1988.

———. *The Journals of Louisa May Alcott.* Edited by Joel Myerson and Daniel Sheehy. Boston: Little, Brown, 1989.

———. *"A Modern Mephistopheles" and "Taming of a Tartar."* New York: Praeger, 1987.

———. *Plots and Counterplots: More Unknown Thrillers of Louisa May Alcott.* Edited by Madeline B. Stern. New York: Popular Press, 1978.

———. *Rose in Bloom.* Boston: Roberts Brothers, 1882.

Allen, Gay Wilson. *Waldo Emerson.* New York: Viking, 1981.

Ames, Genevieve M. "American Beliefs about Alcoholism: Historical Perspectives on the Medical-Moral Controversy." In *The American Experience with Alcohol: Contrasting Cultural Pespectives,* edited by Linda A. Bennett and Genevieve M. Ames, 23–29. New York: Plenum, 1985.

Anderson, Charles R. *Emily Dickinson's Poetry: Stairway of Surprise.* New York: Holt, Rinehart, and Winston, 1960.

Arvin, Newton. *Herman Melville.* New York: William Sloane Associates, 1950.

Atherton, Gertrude. *Patience Sparhawk and Her Times.* London: Bodley Head, 1897.

Auerbach, Nina. "Beaded Bubbles and Forbidden Fruit: Intoxicants and Gender." Paper presented at the annual meeting of the Modern Language Association, New York City, December 1981.

Austin, Gregory. *Alcohol in Western Society from Antiquity to 1800.* Santa Barbara, Calif.: ABC Clio, 1985.

Bakhtin, Mikhail. *Problems of Dostoevsky's Poetics.* Edited and translated by Caryl Emerson. Minneapolis: University of Minnesota Press, 1984.

Balassi, William. "Hemingway's Greatest Iceberg: The Composition of *The Sun Also Rises.*" In *Writing the American Classics,* edited by James Barbour and Tom Quirk, 125–55. Chapel Hill: University of North Carolina Press, 1990.

Bardes, Barbara, and Suzanne Gossett. *Declarations of Independence: Women and Political Power in Nineteenth-Century American Fiction.* New Brunswick: Rutgers University Press, 1990.

Barrows, Susanna, and Robin Room. "Introduction." In *Drinking: Behavior and Belief in Modern History,* edited by Susanna Barrows and Robin Room, 1–25. Berkeley and Los Angeles: University of California Press, 1991.

Barthes, Roland. "Wine and Milk." In his *Mythologies,* translated by Annette Lavers, 58–61. New York: Hill and Wang, 1972.

Baudelaire, Charles. *Oeuvres Complètes.* Paris: Pleiade, 1951.

———. *Le Spleen de Paris: Petits poèmes en prose.* Edited by Yves Florenne. Paris: Librairie Générale Française, 1972.

Baym, Nina. *Novels, Readers, and Reviewers: Responses to Fiction in Antebellum America.* Ithaca: Cornell University Press, 1984.

———. *The Shape of Hawthorne's Career.* Ithaca: Cornell University Press, 1976.

———. *Woman's Fiction: A Guide to Novels by and about Women in America, 1820–1870.* Ithaca: Cornell University Press, 1978.

Beecher, Lyman. *The Autobiography of Lyman Beecher.* Edited by Barbara Cross. 2 vols. Cambridge, Mass.: Harvard University Press, 1961.

———. *Six Sermons on Intemperance.* New York: American Tract Society, 1827.

Belfiore, Elizabeth. "Wine and *Catharsis* of the Emotions in Plato's *Laws.*" *Classical Quarterly* 36 (1986): 421–37.

Bernard, Joel. "From Fasting to Abstinence: The Origins of the American

Temperance Movement." In *Drinking,* edited by Susanna Barrows and Robin Room, 337–53. Berkeley and Los Angeles: University of California Press, 1991.

Berridge, Victoria, and Griffith Edwards. *Opium and the People: Opiate Use in Nineteenth-Century England.* New Haven: Yale University Press, 1987.

Berry, Alice Fiola. "Apollo vs. Bacchus: The Dynamics of Inspiration (Rabelais' Prologues to *Gargantua and to the Tiers Livre*)." *PMLA* 90 (1975): 88–95.

Bittner, William. "Poe and the 'Invisible Demon.'" *Georgia Review* 17 (1963): 134–38.

Blocker, Jack S., Jr. *American Temperance Movements: Cycles of Reform.* Boston: Twayne, 1989.

————. "Introduction." In *Reform and Society: The Liquor Issue in Social Context,* edited by Jack S. Blocker, Jr., 3–12. Westport, Conn.: Greenwood Press, 1979.

Bloom, Harold. *The Ringers in the Tower: Studies in Romantic Tradition.* Chicago: University of Chicago Press, 1971.

Bonaparte, Marie. *The Life and Works of Edgar Allan Poe: A Psycho-Analytic Interpretation.* Translated by John Rodker. London: Imago, 1949.

Bordin, Ruth. *Woman and Temperance: The Quest for Power and Liberty, 1873–1900.* Philadelphia: Temple University Press, 1981.

Boren, Lynda S. "William James, Theodore Dreiser, and the 'Anaesthetic Revelation.'" *American Studies* 24 (1983): 5–17.

Boynton, Henry Wolcott. *James Fenimore Cooper.* New York: Century Press, 1931.

Bradford, William. *Of Plymouth Plantation.* Edited by Samuel Eliot Morrison. New York: Knopf, 1963.

Bratanov, Dimitre. "Le problème de l'alcoolisme dans la littérature mondiale." *La revue de l'alcoolisme* 15 (1969): 215–32.

Brooks, Van Wyck. *Wine of the Puritans.* New York: Mitchell Kennerley, 1909.

Buell, Lawrence. *New England Literary Culture.* Cambridge: Cambridge University Press, 1986.

Burroughs, William S. "My Purpose Is to Write for the Space Age." *New York Times Book Review,* February 19, 1984, 9–10.

Capps, Jack L. *Emily Dickinson's Reading.* Cambridge, Mass.: Harvard University Press, 1966.

Carby, Hazel V. *Reconstructing Womanhood: The Emergence of the Afro-*

*American Woman Novelist.* New York: Oxford University Press, 1987.

Carpenter, Thomas H., and Christopher A. Farsone, eds. *Masks of Dionysos.* Ithaca: Cornell University Press, 1993.

Carter, Everett. *Wine and Poetry.* Davis: University of California Library, Davis, 1976.

Cather, Willa. *A Lost Lady.* New York: Vintage, 1972.

――――. "On the Divide." In Cather, *24 Stories,* selected and with an introduction by Sharon O'Brien, 35–49. New York: New American Library, 1987.

Cecil, L. Moffitt. "Poe's Wine List." *Poe Studies* 5 (1972): 41–42.

Chafetz, Morris. "Introduction." In *First Special Report to the United States Congress on Alcohol and Health,* 1–4. Washington, D.C.: National Institute on Alcohol Abuse and Alcoholism, 1971.

Chai, Leon. *The Romantic Foundations of the American Renaissance.* Ithaca: Cornell University Press, 1987.

Charvat, William. *Literary Publishing in America, 1790–1850.* Philadelphia: University of Pennsylvania Press, 1959.

Chase, Richard. *Emily Dickinson.* New York: William Sloane Associates, 1951.

Cheever, John. *Bullet Park.* New York: Alfred A. Knopf, 1969.

Cheney, Ednah D., ed. *Louisa May Alcott, Her Life, Letters, and Journals.* Boston: Roberts Brothers, 1890.

Chidsey, Donald Barr. *On and Off the Wagon: A Sober Analysis of the Temperance Movement from the Pilgrims through Prohibition.* New York: Cowles Book Co., 1969.

Chopin, Kate. *The Collected Works of Kate Chopin.* Edited by Per Seyersted. 2 vols. Baton Rouge: Louisiana State University Press, 1969.

Clark, Norman H. *Deliver Us from Evil: An Interpretation of American Prohibition.* New York: Norton, 1976.

Clavel, Marcel. *Fenimore Cooper: Sa vie et sonoeuvre.* Aix-en-Provence: Imprimérie Universitaire de Provence, 1938.

Clemens, Samuel L. *The Adventures of Huckleberry Finn.* Edited by Walter Blair and Victor Fischer. Berkeley and Los Angeles: University of California Press, 1985.

――――. *Mark Twain's Notebook.* Edited by Albert Bigelow Paine. New York: Harper, 1935.

Cody, John. *After Great Pain: The Inner Life of Emily Dickinson.* Cambridge, Mass.: Harvard University Press, 1971.

Cogan, Frances B. *All-American Girl: The Ideal of Real Womanhood in Mid-Nineteenth-Century America*. Athens: University of Georgia Press, 1989.

Coleridge, Samuel Taylor. *The Notebooks of Samuel Taylor Coleridge*. Edited by Kathleen Coburn. 3 vols. Princeton: Princeton University Press, 1973.

Colton, Walter. "Turkish Sketches: Effects of Opium." *Knickerbocker* 7 (1836): 421–25.

Conrad, Susan Phinney. *Perish the Thought: Intellectual Women in Romantic America, 1830–1860*. New York: Oxford University Press, 1976.

Cooper, James Fenimore. *Cooper's Novels*. 32 vols. New York: W. A. Townsend, 1857–1861.

———. *The Last of the Mohicans*. Edited by James Franklin Beard. Albany: State University of New York Press, 1983.

———. *Ned Myers, or a Life before the Mast*. New York: G. P. Putnam's Sons, 1900.

Courtwright, David T. *Dark Paradise: Opiate Addiction in America Before 1940*. Cambridge, Mass.: Harvard University Press, 1982.

Cowen, Walker. "Melville's Marginalia." Ph.D. dissertation, Harvard University, 1965.

Cozzens, Frederick Swartout, ed. *The Sayings of Dr. Bushwhacker*. New York: A. Simpson, 1867.

*Cozzens' Wine-Press: A Vinous, Vivacious Monthly*, 1854–61.

Crane, Jonathan Townley. *Popular Amusements*. Cincinnati: Hitchcock and Walden, 1869.

Crane, Stephen. *The Works of Stephen Crane*. Edited by Fredson Bowers. 10 vols. Charlottesville: University of Virginia Press, 1969.

Crews, Frederick. *The Sins of the Fathers: Hawthorne's Psychological Themes*. Oxford: Oxford University Press.

Crowley, John. *The White Logic: Alcoholism and Gender in American Modernist Fiction*. Amherst: University of Massachusetts Press, 1994.

Damrosch, Leopold, Jr. "Blake, Burns, and the Recovery of Lyric." *Studies in Romanticism* 21 (1982): 637–60.

Dana, Charles A., ed. *The Household Book of Poetry*. 4th ed. New York: D. Appleton, 1858.

Dana, Richard Henry. *Two Years Before the Mast*. Edited by Claude M. Friess. New York: Macmillan, 1926.

Dardis, Tom. *The Thirsty Muse: Alcohol and the American Writer.* New York: Ticknor and Fields, 1989.

Davidson, Edward H. *Poe: A Critical Study.* Cambridge, Mass.: Harvard University Press, 1957.

Davis, Jack L., and June H. Davis. "Poe's Ethereal Ligeia." *Bulletin of the Rocky Mountain MLA* 24 (1970): 170–76.

Davis, Merrell R. *Melville's "Mardi": A Chartless Voyage.* New Haven: Yale University Press, 1952.

Davis, Rebecca Harding. *Life in the Iron Mills.* Old Westbury, N.Y.: Feminist Press, 1981.

Davy, Mari-Madeleine. "La *Sobria ebrietas.*" *Corps Ecrit* 13 (1985): 111–19.

DeForest, John W. *Kate Beaumont.* State Park, Pa.: Bald Eagle Press, 1963.

Dekker, George, and John P. McWilliams, eds. *Fenimore Cooper: The Critical Heritage.* London: Routledge and Kegan Paul, 1973.

De Quincey, Thomas. *Collected Writings of Thomas De Quincey.* 14 vols. Edited by David Masson. Edinburgh: A. and C. Black, 1888–90.

Derrida, Jacques. *La Dissemination.* Paris: Editions Seuil, 1972.

Dew, Marjorie. "Black-Hearted Melville: 'Geniality' Reconsidered." In *Artful Thunder: Versions of the Romantic Tradition in American Literature in Honor of Howard Vincent,* edited by Robert J. DeMott and Sanford E. Marovitz, 177–94. Kent, Ohio: Kent State University Press, 1975.

*Diagnostic and Statistical Manual of Mental Disorders.* 3d ed. *(DSM-III.)* Washington, D.C.: American Psychiatric Association, 1980.

*Diagnostic and Statistical Manual of Mental Disorders.* 4th ed. *(DSM-IV.)* Washington, D.C.: American Psychiatric Association, 1994.

Dickens, Charles. *The Letters of Charles Dickens.* Edited by Walter Dexter. 3 vols. Bloomsbury: Nonesuch Press, 1938.

Dickinson, Emily. *The Letters of Emily Dickinson.* Edited by Thomas H. Johnson. 2 vols. Cambridge, Mass.: Harvard University Press, 1958.

———. *The Poems of Emily Dickinson.* Edited by Thomas H. Johnson. Cambridge, Mass.: Harvard University Press, 1955.

Dieckhoff, Reiner. "Literarische Avantgarde und Drogenkonsum von der Romantik bis zum Surrealismus." In *Rausch und Realitat: Drogen im Kulturvergleich,* edited by Gisela Volger, Karin von Welck, and Aldo Legnaro, 404–25. Cologne: Ethnologica, 1981.

Diehl, Joanne Feit. *Dickinson and the Romantic Imagination.* Princeton: Princeton University Press, 1981.

Dillingham, William B. *Melville's Later Novels.* Athens: University of Georgia Press, 1986.

———. *Melville's Short Fiction, 1853–1856.* Athens: University of Georgia Press, 1977.

Dobson, Joanne. "The Hidden Hand: Subversion of Cultural Ideology in Three Mid-Nineteenth-Century American Women's Novels." *American Quarterly* 38 (1985): 223–42.

Dodd, Jill Siegel. "The Working Classes and the Temperance Movement in Ante-Bellum Boston." *Labor History* 19 (1978): 511–31.

Dodds, E. R. "Introduction." In Euripides, *Bacchae,* edited by E. R. Dodds, xi–lix. 2d ed. Oxford: Clarendon Press, 1960.

Dorchester, Daniel. *The Liquor Problem in All Ages.* New York: Phillips and Hunt, 1884.

Dostoevsky, Feodor. *Crime and Punishment.* Translated by Jessie Coulson, edited and revised by George Gibian. New York: Norton, 1975.

Douglas, Ann. *The Feminization of American Culture.* New York: Knopf, 1977.

Douglass, Frederick. *The Life and Times of Frederick Douglass.* New York: Bonanza, 1967.

Durr, R. A. *Poetic Vision and the Psychedelic Experience.* Syracuse: Syracuse University Press, 1970.

Earnest, Ernest. *The American Eve in Fact and Fiction, 1775–1914.* Urbana: University of Illinois Press, 1974.

Eddins, Dwight. "Emily Dickinson and Nietzsche: The Rites of Dionysos." *Emerson Society Quarterly* 27 (1981): 96–107.

Elbert, Sarah. *A Hunger for Home: Louisa May Alcott's Place in American Culture.* New Brunswick: Rutgers University Press, 1987.

Eliade, Mircea. *Shamanism: Archaic Techniques of Ecstasy.* New York: Pantheon, 1964.

Emerson, Ralph Waldo. *Collected Poems and Translations.* Edited by Harold Bloom and Paul Kane. New York: Library of America, 1994.

———. *The Collected Works of Ralph Waldo Emerson.* Introduction and notes by Robert E. Spiller, text established by Alfred R. Ferguson and Jean Ferguson Carr. 5 vols. to date. Cambridge, Mass.: Harvard University Press, 1971–.

———. *The Complete Works of Ralph Waldo Emerson.* Edited by Edward W. Emerson. 12 vols. Boston: Houghton Mifflin, 1903–04.

————. *The Journals and Miscellaneous Notebooks of Ralph Waldo Emerson.* Edited by William H. Gilman et al. 17 vols. to date. Cambridge, Mass.: Harvard University Press. 1960–.

————. *Poems.* Boston: James Munroe and Co., 1847.

————. *The Poetry Notebooks of Ralph Waldo Emerson.* Edited by Ralph W. Orth et al. Columbia: University of Missouri Press, 1986.

Euripides. *Bacchae.* Translated by Philip Vellacott. Harmondsworth: Penguin, 1972.

"Fashionable Dissipation." Unsigned review of Metta V. Fuller, *Fashionable Dissipation. Godey's Lady's Book* (September 1854): 274.

Feder, Lillian. *Madness in Literature.* Princeton: Princeton University Press, 1980.

Feidelson, Charles, Jr. *Symbolism and American Literature.* Chicago: University of Chicago Press, 1953.

Fiedler, Leslie. *Love and Death in the American Novel.* Rev. ed. New York: Stein and Day, 1966.

————. *The Return of the Vanishing American.* New York: Stein and Day, 1968.

Filby, P. W., and Edward G. Howard. *Star-Spangled Books.* Baltimore: Maryland Historical Society, 1972.

Finkelstein, Dorothee Metlitsky. *Melville's Orienda.* New Haven: Yale University Press, 1961.

Fisher, Benjamin Franklin, IV. *The Very Spirit of Cordiality: The Literary Uses of Alcohol and Alcoholism in the Tales of Edgar Allan Poe.* Baltimore: Enoch Pratt Free Library, 1978.

Fogel, Aaron. "Coerced Speech and the Oedipus Dialogue Complex." In *Rethinking Bakhtin: Extensions and Challenges,* edited by Gary Saul Morson and Caryl Emerson, 173–96. Evanston: Northwestern University Press, 1989.

Foote, Julia A. J. *A Brand Plucked from the Fire; An Autobiographical Sketch by Mrs. Julia A. J. Foote.* In *Spiritual Narratives,* vol. 3 of the Schomburg Library of Nineteenth-Century Black Women Writers. General editor Henry Louis Gates, Jr. New York: Oxford University Press, 1988.

Forseth, Roger. "'Alcoholite at the Altar': Sinclair Lewis, Drink, and the Literary Imagination." *Modern Fiction Studies* 31 (1985): 581–607.

————. "Ambivalent Sensibilities: Alcohol in History and Literature." *American Quarterly* 42 (1990): 122–35.

Foucault, Michel. *Madness and Civilization: A History of Insanity in the*

*Age of Reason.* Translated by Richard Howard. New York: Random House, 1965.

Franklin, Benjamin. *The Papers of Benjamin Franklin.* Edited by Leonard W. Labaree. 31 vols. New Haven: Yale University Press, 1960.

————. *The Works of Benjamin Franklin.* Edited by John Bigelow. 12 vols. New York: G. P. Putnam's Sons, 1904.

Frye, Northrop. *Fables of Identity.* New York: Harcourt Brace Jovanovich, 1963.

Fuller, Margaret. *The Writings of Margaret Fuller.* Edited by Mason Wade. New York: Viking, 1941.

Furnas, J. C. *The Life and Times of the Late Demon Rum.* New York: G. P. Putnam's Sons, 1965.

Furst, Peter T. "Introduction." In *The Flesh of the Gods: The Ritual Use of Hallucinogens,* edited by Peter T. Furst, vii–xvi. New York: Praeger, 1972.

Gargano, James W. "The Distorted Perception of Poe's Comic Narrators." *Topic: 30* 16 (1976): 23–34.

Garrow, Scott. "Alcohol Beverage Imagery in the Poems of Emily Dickinson." *Markham Review* 2 (1969): 11–15.

Geertz, Clifford. *Interpretation of Culture.* New York: Basic Books, 1973.

Gelpi, Albert J. *Emily Dickinson: The Mind of the Poet.* New York: Norton, 1965.

Gerber, Gerald E. "Poe's Odd Angel." *Nineteenth-Century Fiction* 23 (1968): 88–93.

Gianetti, Vincent J. "Religious Dimensions of Addiction." *Studies in Formative Spirituality* 8 (1987): 187–97.

Gilmore, Thomas B., Jr. *Equivocal Spirits: Alcoholism and Drinking in Twentieth-Century Literature.* Chapel Hill: University of North Carolina Press, 1987.

Gollin, Rita K. *Nathaniel Hawthorne and the Truth of Dreams.* Baton Rouge: Louisiana State University Press, 1979.

Goode, Erich. *Drugs in American Society.* 2d ed. New York: Knopf, 1984.

Goodwin, Donald W. *Alcohol and the Writer.* Harmondsworth: Penguin, 1990.

Goshen, Charles E. *Drinks, Drugs, and Do-Gooders.* New York: Free Press, 1973.

Gossett, Thomas F. *"Uncle Tom's Cabin" and American Culture.* Dallas: Southern Methodist University Press, 1985.

Grenberg, Bruce L. *Some Other World to Find: Quest and Negation in the*

*Works of Herman Melville*. Urbana: University of Illinois Press, 1989.

Griffith, Clark. "Poe's 'Ligeia' and the English Romantics." *University of Toronto Quarterly* 24 (1954): 8–25.

Grindrod, Ralph Barnes. *Bacchus: An Essay on the Nature, Causes, Effects, and Cure of Intemperance*. 2d ed. London: William Brittain, 1843.

Grob, Gerald, ed. *American Perceptions of Drug Addiction*. New York: Arno Press, 1981.

———. *Nineteenth-Century Medical Attitudes toward Alcoholic Addiction*. New York: Arno Press, 1981.

Grossman, James. *James Fenimore Cooper*. New York: William Sloane Associates, 1949.

Gunderson, Robert G. *The Log Cabin Campaign*. Westport, Conn.: Greenwood Press, 1957.

Gusfield, Joseph. "Benevolent Repression: Popular Culture, Social Structure, and the Control of Drinking." In *Drinking,* edited by Susanna Barrows and Robin Room, 399–424. Berkeley and Los Angeles: University of California Press, 1991.

———. "Passage to Play: Rituals of Drinking Time in American Society." In *Constructive Drinking: Perspectives on Drink from Anthropology,* edited by Mary Douglas, 73–90. Cambridge: Cambridge University Press, 1987.

———. *Symbolic Crusade: Status Politics and the American Temperance Movement*. 2d ed. Urbana: University of Illinois Press, 1986.

Habegger, Alfred. *Gender, Fantasy, and Realism in American Literature*. New York: Columbia University Press, 1982.

Hall, Lawrence Sargent. *Hawthorne: Critic of Society*. New Haven: Yale University Press, 1944.

Haller, John S., and Robin M. Haller. *The Physician and Sexuality in Victorian America*. Urbana: University of Illinois Press, 1974.

Harper, Frances Ellen Watkins. *Iola Leroy, or Shadows Uplifted*. Vol. 17 of the Schomburg Library of Nineteenth-Century Black Women Writers. General editor Henry Louis Gates, Jr. New York: Oxford University Press, 1988.

———. "The Two Offers." In *Afro-American Women Writers 1746–1933: An Anthology and Critical Guide,* edited by Ann Allen Shockley, 61–70. Boston: G. K. Hall, 1988.

Harris, Susan K. "'But is it any *good?*' Evaluating Nineteenth-Century American Women's Fiction." *American Literature* 43 (1991): 43–61.

Harrison, Brian. *Drink and the Victorians.* Pittsburgh: University of Pittsburgh Press, 1971.

Hawthorne, Nathaniel. *The Centenary Edition of the Works of Nathaniel Hawthorne.* Edited by William Charvat et al. 23 vols. to date. Columbus: Ohio State University Press, 1962–.

Hayter, Alethea. *Opium and the Romantic Imagination.* Berkeley and Los Angeles: University of California Press, 1968.

Hazlitt, William. *The Complete Works of William Hazlitt.* Edited by P. Howe. 21 vols. London: J. M. Dent and Sons, 1930–34.

Heath, Dwight B. "American Experiences with Alcohol: Commonalities and Contrasts." In *The American Experience with Alcohol,* edited by Linda A. Bennett and Genevieve M. Ames, 461–80. New York: Plenum, 1985.

———. "The Sociocultural Model of Alcohol Use: Problems and Prospects." *Journal of Operational Psychiatry* 9 (1978): 55–66.

———. "Sociocultural Perspectives on Addiction." In *Etiologic Aspects of Drug Use,* edited by Edward Gottheil et al., 223–37. Springfield, Ill.: Charles C. Thomas, 1983.

Hedrick, Joan D. *Harriet Beecher Stowe: A Life.* New York: Oxford University Press, 1994.

Heilbronn, Lisa M. "What Does Alcohol Mean? Alcohol's Use as a Symbolic Code." *Contemporary Drug Problems* 15 (1988): 229–48.

Herd, Denise. "Ambiguity in Black Drinking Norms: An Ethnohistorical Interpretation." In *The American Experience with Alcohol,* edited by Linda A. Bennett and Genevieve M. Ames, 149–70. New York: Plenum, 1985.

———. "The Paradox of Temperance: Blacks and the Alcohol Question in Nineteenth-Century America." In *Drinking,* edited by Susanna Barrows and Robin Room, 354–75. Berkeley and Los Angeles: University of California Press, 1991.

———. "'We Cannot Stagger to Freedom': A History of Blacks and Alcohol in American Politics." In *Yearbook of Substance Abuse,* edited by L. Brill and C. Winick, 3:141–86. New York: Human Sciences Press, 1985.

Herder, Johann Gottfried. *Sammtliche Werke.* Edited by Bernhard Suphan. 33 vols. Berlin: Weidmanniche Buchandlung, 1877–1913.

Hinz, Evelyn J., ed. *Literature and Altered States of Consciousness. Mosaic* 19 (1986).

Hitchcock, Edward. *An Essay on Alcoholic and Narcotic Substances, as*

*Articles of Common Use, Addressed Particularly to Students.* Amherst: J. S. and C. Adams, 1830.

Hofstadter, Richard. *The Age of Reform: From Bryan to F.D.R.* New York: Vintage, 1955.

Holmes, Mary Jane. *Meadow Brook.* New York: Carleton, 1857.

Holmes, Oliver Wendell. *The Poetical Works of Oliver Wendell Holmes.* Edited by Eleanor M. Tilton. Boston: Houghton Mifflin, 1975.

Hoover, Suzanne R. "Coleridge, Humphry Davy, and Some Early Experiments with a Consciousness-Altering Drug." *Bulletin of Research in the Humanities* 81 (1978): 9–27.

Horace (Quintus Horatius Flaccus). *The Complete Works of Horace.* Translated by Charles E. Passage. New York: Frederick Ungar, 1983.

House, Kay S. *Cooper's Americans.* Columbus: Ohio State University Press, 1965.

Howard, Leon. *Herman Melville: A Biography.* Berkeley and Los Angeles: University of California Press, 1951.

Howells, William Dean. *The Landlord at Lion's Head.* New York: Harper and Brothers, 1896.

Huxley, Aldous. *The Doors of Perception and Heaven and Hell.* New York: Harper and Row, 1963.

James, William. *The Works of William James.* Edited by Frederick H. Burckhardt, Fredson Bowers, and Ignas K. Skrupskelis. 17 vols. Cambridge, Mass.: Harvard University Press, 1975–88.

Janeway, Elizabeth. *Between Myth and Morning: Women Awakening.* New York: William Morrow, 1974.

Jellinek, E. M. "Cultural Differences in the Meaning of Alcoholism." In *Society, Culture, and Drinking Problems,* edited by David J. Pittman and Charles R. Synder, 382–88. New York: John Wiley and Sons, 1962.

———. *The Disease Concept of Alcoholism.* New Brunswick: Hillhouse Press, 1960.

———. "The Symbolism of Drinking: A Culture-Historical Approach." Edited for publication by Robert E. Popham and Carole D. Yawney. *Journal of Studies on Alcohol* 38 (1977): 852–66.

Johnson, Paul. "Drinking, Temperance, and the Construction of Identity in Nineteenth-Century America." *Social Science Information* 25 (1986); 521–30.

———. *A Shopkeeper's Millennium: Society and Revivals in Rochester, New York, 1815–1837.* New York: Hill and Wang, 1978.

Johnston, Johanna. *Mrs. Satan: The Incredible Saga of Victoria Woodhull.* London: Macmillan, 1967.

Karoli, Christa. *Ideal und Krise: Enthusiastichen Kunstlertums in der deutschen Romantik.* Bonn: Bouvier Verlag, 1968.

Kazin, Alfred. "Giant-Killer: Drink and the American Writer." *Commentary* 61 (1976): 44–50.

———. *On Native Grounds.* New York: Harcourt Brace Jovanovich, 1942.

Keats, John. *The Poems of John Keats.* Edited by Miriam Allott. London: Longman, 1970.

Keller, Karl. *The Only Kangaroo Among the Beauty: Emily Dickinson and America.* Baltimore: Johns Hopkins University Press, 1979.

Kennedy, J. Gerald. *Poe, Death, and the Life of Writing.* New Haven: Yale University Press, 1987.

Ketterer, David. *New Worlds for Old: The Apocalyptic Imagination, Science Fiction, and American Literature.* Bloomington: Indiana University Press, 1974.

Krout, John Allen. *The Origins of Prohibition.* New York: Knopf, 1925.

Laffrado, Laura. *Hawthorne's Literature for Children.* Athens: University of Georgia Press, 1992.

Lawrence, D. H. *Studies in Classic American Literature.* Harmondsworth: Penguin, 1977. First published in 1923.

Legouis, Émile. "The Bacchic Element in Shakespeare's Plays." *Proceedings of the British Academy* 12 (1926): 115–32.

Leland, Joy. *The Firewater Myths.* New Brunswick: Rutgers University Press, 1976.

Lender, Mark Edward. "A Special Stigma: Women and Alcoholism in the Late 19th and Early 20th Centuries." In *Alcohol Interventions,* edited by David L. Strug, S. Priyadarsini, and Merton M. Hyman, 41–57. Binghamton, N.Y.: Haworth Press, 1986.

Lender, Mark Edward, and Karen Karnchanapee. "Temperance Tales: Antiliquor Fiction and American Attitudes toward Alcoholics in the Late 19th and Early 20th Centuries." *Journal of Studies on Alcohol* 38 (1977): 1347–70.

Lender, Mark Edward, and James Kirby Martin. *Drinking in America: A Social History.* New York: Free Press, 1982. Rev. ed., 1987.

Levin, Harry. *The Power of Blackness: Hawthorne, Poe, Melville.* New York: Knopf, 1958.

Levine, Harry Gene. "The Alcohol Problem in America: From Temperance to Alcoholism." *British Journal of Addiction* 79 (1984): 109–19.

————. "The Discovery of Addiction: Changing Conceptions of Habitual Drunkenness in America." *Journal of Studies on Alcohol* 39 (1978): 143–74.

————. "Temperance and Women in the United States." In *Alcohol and Drug Problems in Women,* edited by Oriana Josseau Kalant, 25–65. New York: Plenum, 1980.

Levine, Stuart. "Introduction." In *The Short Fiction of Edgar Allan Poe,* edited by Stuart Levine and Susan Levine, xv–xxxvii. Indianapolis: Bobbs-Merrill, 1976.

Levy, Jerrold, and Stephen Kunitz. *Indian Drinking.* New York: John Wiley and Sons, 1974.

Lewis, I. M. *Ecstatic Religion: An Anthropological Study of Spirit Possession and Shamanism.* Harmondsworth: Penguin, 1971.

Lewy, Hans. *Sobria Ebrietas: Geschichte der Antiken Mystik.* Gieben: Verlag von Alfred Topelmann, 1929.

Leyda, Jay. *The Years and Hours of Emily Dickinson.* 2 vols. New Haven: Yale University Press, 1960.

Lincoln, Abraham. *Abraham Lincoln: His Speeches and Writings.* Edited by Roy P. Basler. Cleveland: World Publishing Co., 1946.

Logan, John Frederick. "The Age of Intoxication." *Yale French Studies* 50 (1974): 81–94.

London, Jack. *John Barleycorn: Alcoholic Memoirs.* Santa Cruz, Calif.: Western Tanager Press, 1981.

————. *Martin Eden.* Vol. 3 of *The Bodley Head Jack London.* Edited by Arthur Calder-Marshall. London: Bodley Head, 1964–66.

Luisi, David. "Some Aspects of Emily Dickinson's Food and Liquor Poems." *English Studies* 52 (1971): 32–40.

Mabry, Marcus. "'You Have to Drink Wine.'" *Newsweek,* July 3, 1995, 33.

MacAndrew, Craig, and Robert B. Edgerton. *Drunken Comportment: A Social Explanation.* Chicago: Aldine, 1969.

McCormack, Thelma. "The 'Wets' and the 'Drys': Binary Images of Women and Alcohol in Popular Culture." *Communication* 9 (1986): 43–64.

McCormick, Mairi. "First Representations of the Gamma Alcoholic in the English Novel." *Quarterly Journal of Studies on Alcohol* 30 (1969): 957–80.

McDowell, Tremaine. "A Freshman Poem by Emerson." *PMLA* 45 (1930): 326–29.

Macnish, Robert. *The Anatomy of Drunkenness.* Philadelphia: Carey, Lea, and Carey, 1828.

Mailer, Norman. *Advertisements for Myself*. New York: New American Library, 1959.

Mancall, Peter. *Deadly Medicine: Indians and Alcohol in Early America*. Ithaca: Cornell University Press, 1995.

Mandel, George. *Flee the Angry Strangers*. Indianapolis: Bobbs-Merrill, 1952.

Mather, Cotton. *Magnalia Christi Americana*. Edited by Kenneth B. Murdock. Cambridge, Mass.: Harvard University Press, 1977.

Mather, Increase. *Wo to Drunkards*. 2d ed. Boston: Timothy Green, 1712.

Matheson, T. J. "Poe's 'The Black Cat' as a Critique of Temperance Literature." *Mosaic* 19 (1986): 69–81.

Melville, Herman. *Clarel*. Edited by Walter E. Bezanson. New York: Hendricks House, 1960.

———. *Collected Poems of Herman Melville*. Edited by Howard P. Vincent. Chicago: Hendricks House, 1947.

———. *The Confidence-Man*. Edited by Elizabeth S. Foster. New York: Hendricks House, 1954.

———. *Journal of a Visit to London and the Continent by Herman Melville, 1849–1850*. Edited by Eleanor Melville Metcalf. Cambridge, Mass.: Harvard University Press, 1948.

———. *The Writings of Herman Melville*. Edited by Harrison Hayford et al. 14 vols. to date. Evanston and Chicago: Northwestern University Press and Newberry Library, 1968–.

Miller, Edwin Haviland. *Salem Is My Dwelling-Place: A Life of Nathaniel Hawthorne*. Iowa City: University of Iowa Press, 1991.

Miller, Perry. *The Life of the Mind in America: From the Revolution to the Civil War*. New York: Harcourt, Brace and World, 1965.

———. *The Raven and the Whale: The War of Words and Wits in the Era of Poe and Melville*. New York: Harcourt, Brace, 1956.

Millington, Richard H. *Practicing Romance: Narrative Form and Cultural Engagement in Hawthorne's Fiction*. Princeton: Princeton University Press, 1992.

Mirsky, D. S. *A History of Russian Literature*. New York: Vintage, 1958.

Moore, Mark H., and Dean R. Gerstein. "Introduction." In *Alcohol and Public Policy: Beyond the Shadow of Prohibition,* edited by Mark H. Moore and Dean R. Gerstein, 3–5. Washington, D.C.: National Academy Press, 1981.

———. "The Nature of Alcohol Problems." In *Alcohol and Public Policy: Beyond the Shadow of Prohibition,* edited by Mark H. Moore and

Dean R. Gerstein, 16–47. Washington, D.C.: National Academy Press, 1981.

Moore, Rayburn S. "A Note on Poe and the Sons of Temperance." *American Literature* 30 (1958): 359–60.

Morgan, H. Wayne. *Drugs in America: A Social History, 1800–1980*. Syracuse: Syracuse University Press, 1981.

———. "Introduction." In *Yesterday's Addicts: American Society and Drug Abuse, 1865–1920*, edited by H. Wayne Morgan, 3–34. Norman: University of Oklahoma Press, 1973.

Morson, Gary Saul, and Caryl Emerson. *Mikhail Bakhtin: Creation of a Prosaics*. Stanford: Stanford University Press, 1990.

Morson, Gary Saul, and Caryl Emerson, eds. *Rethinking Bakhtin: Extensions and Challenges*. Evanston: Northwestern University Press, 1989.

Mushabac, Jane. *Melville's Humor: A Critical Study*. Hamden, Conn.: Archon, 1981.

Musto, David F. *The American Disease: Origins of Narcotic Control*. New Haven: Yale University Press, 1973.

Myerhoff, Barbara G. "Peyote and Huichol Worldview: The Structure of a Mystic Vision." In *Cannabis and Culture,* edited by Vera Rubin, 417–38. The Hague: Mouton, 1975.

Myerson, Abraham. "Alcohol: A Study of Social Ambivalence." *Quarterly Journal of Studies on Alcohol* 1 (1940): 13–20.

Nabokov, Vladimir. *Nikolai Gogol*. New York: New Directions, 1944.

Nietzsche, Friedrich. *The Birth of Tragedy*. Translated by Francis Golffing. New York: Doubleday, 1956.

O'Brien, John Maxwell. *Alexander the Great: The Invisible Enemy*. London: Routledge and Kegan Paul, 1992.

Ortiz, Simon. *From Sand Creek*. New York: Thunder's Mouth Press, 1981.

Papashvily, Helen Waite. *All the Happy Endings*. Port Washington, N.Y.: Kennikat, 1956.

Paris, Bernard J. "Emerson's 'Bacchus.'" *Modern Language Quarterly* 23 (1962): 150–59.

Pearce, Roy Harvey. *Savagism and Civilization*. Baltimore: Johns Hopkins University Press, 1953.

Peele, Stanton, with Archile Brodsky. *Love and Addiction*. New York: Taplinger, 1975.

Peschel, Enid Rhodes, ed. *Intoxication and Literature. Yale French Studies* 50 (1974).

Peterson, Norma Lois. *The Presidencies of William Henry Harrison and John Tyler.* Lawrence: University Press of Kansas, 1989.

Phelps, Elizabeth Stuart. "Jack." *Century Magazine* 34 (1887): 220–36.

———. *The Story of Avis.* Boston: Houghton Mifflin, 1877.

Philo Judaeus. *Allegorical Interpretation of Genesis.* In vol. 1 of *Philo.* Loeb Classical Library, 1929.

———. "On Drunkenness." In vol. 3 of *Philo.* Loeb Classical Library, 1954.

Pittman, David J. "International Overview: Social and Cultural Factors in Drinking Patterns, Pathological and Nonpathological." In *Alcoholism,* edited by David J. Pittman, 3–20. New York: Harper and Row, 1967.

Poe, Edgar Allan. *The Collected Works of Edgar Allan Poe.* Edited by T. O. Mabbott. 3 vols. Cambridge, Mass.: Harvard University Press, 1969–78.

———. *Collected Writings of Edgar Allan Poe.* Edited by Burton R. Pollin. 4 vols. Boston: Twayne; New York: Gordian Press, 1981–85.

———. *Doings of Gotham.* Edited by Jacob E. Spannuth and T. O. Mabbott. Pottsville, Pa.: Jacob E. Spannuth, 1929.

———. *Essays and Reviews.* Edited by G. R. Thompson. New York: Library of America, 1984.

———. *The Letters of Edgar Allan Poe.* Edited by John Ward Ostrom. 2 vols. Cambridge, Mass.: Harvard University Press, 1948.

Pollin, Burton R. "The Temperance Movement and Its Friends Look at Poe." *Costerus* 2 (1972): 119–44.

Porte, Joel. *Representative Man: Ralph Waldo Emerson in His Time.* New York: Oxford University Press, 1979.

———. *The Romance in America: Studies in Cooper, Poe, Hawthorne, Melville, and James.* Middletown: Wesleyan University Press, 1969.

Porter, Roy. "The Drinking Man's Disease: The 'Pre-History' of Alcoholism in Georgian Britain." *British Journal of Addiction* 80 (1985): 385–96.

Pynchon, Thomas. *The Crying of Lot 49.* Philadelphia: J. B. Lippincott, 1966.

Quinn, Arthur Hobson. *Edgar Allan Poe: A Critical Biography.* New York: Cooper Square, 1941.

Rans, Geoffrey. *Cooper's Leather-Stocking Novels.* Chapel Hill: University of North Carolina Press, 1991.

Reynolds, David S. *Beneath the American Renaissance: The Subversive*

*Imagination in the Age of Emerson and Melville.* New York: Knopf, 1988.

Robertson-Lorant, Laurie. *Melville: A Biography.* New York: Clarkson Potter, 1996.

Rohrer, James R. "The Origins of the Temperance Movement: A Reinterpretation." *Journal of American Studies* 24 (1990): 228–35.

Room, Robin. "Ambivalence as a Sociological Explanation: The Case of Cultural Explanations of Alcohol Problems." *American Sociological Review* 41 (1976): 1047–65.

———. "Discussion." In Abstracts of American Anthropological Association Meetings, *Drinking and Drug Practices Surveyor* 20 (1985): 52.

———. " 'A Reverence for Drink': The Lost Generation and the Elevation of Alcohol in American Culture." *Journal of Studies on Alcohol* 45 (1984): 540–46.

Rorabaugh, W. J. *The Alcoholic Republic: An American Tradition.* New York: Oxford University Press, 1979.

Rosenberry, Edward H. *Melville and the Comic Spirit.* Cambridge, Mass.: Harvard University Press, 1955.

———. "Melville's Comedy and Tragedy." In *A Companion to Melville Studies,* edited by John Bryant, 603–24. New York: Greenwood Press, 1986.

Rosenzweig, Roy. "The Rise of the Saloon." In *Rethinking Popular Culture: Contemporary Perspectives in Cultural Studies,* edited by Chandra Mukerji and Michael Schudson, 121–56. Berkeley and Los Angeles: University of California Press, 1991.

Roueché, Berton. *The Neutral Spirit: A Portrait of Alcohol.* Boston: Little, Brown, 1960.

Rush, Benjamin. *An Enquiry into the Effects of Spiritous Liquors upon the Human Body and Mind.* Philadelphia: Thomas Bradford, 1784.

Rusk, Ralph L. *The Life of Ralph Waldo Emerson.* New York: Charles Scribner and Sons, 1949.

Samson, G. W. *The Divine Law as to Wines.* New York: National Temperance Society, 1880.

Sanchez-Eppler, Karen. "Temperance in the Bed of a Child: Incest and Social Order in Nineteenth-Century America." *American Quarterly* 47 (1995): 1–33.

Sanders, Thomas E., and Walter N. Peek, eds. *Literature of the American Indian.* Beverly Hills: Glencoe Press, 1973.

Sandmaier, Marian. *The Invisible Alcoholics: Women and Alcohol Abuse in America.* New York: McGraw-Hill, 1980.

Schmidt, Laura. "'A Battle not Man's but God's': Origins of the American Temperance Movement in the Struggle for Religious Authority." *Journal of Studies on Alcohol* 56 (1995): 110–21.

Sealts, Merton M., Jr. "Melville's Geniality." In his *Pursuing Melville, 1940–1980,* 155–70. Madison: University of Wisconsin Press, 1982.

Segal, Boris M. *The Drunken Society: Alcohol Abuse and Alcoholism in the Soviet Union: A Comparative Study.* New York: Hippocrene Books, 1990.

Segal, Charles. *Dionysiac Poetics and Euripides' "Bacchae."* Princeton: Princeton University Press, 1982.

Sewall, Richard. *The Life of Emily Dickinson.* 2 vols. New York: Farrar, Straus, and Giroux, 1974.

Shakespeare, William. *The Complete Pelican Shakespeare.* Edited by Alfred Harbage. Baltimore: Penguin, 1969.

Shaw, Sheila. "The Female Alcoholic in Victorian Fiction: George Eliot's Unpoetic Heroine." In *Nineteenth-Century Women Writers of the English-Speaking World,* edited by Rhoda B. Nathan, 171–79. New York: Greenwood Press, 1986.

Siegel, Ronald K. *Intoxication: Life in Pursuit of Artificial Paradise.* New York: Dutton, 1989.

Silko, Leslie Marmon. *Ceremony.* New York: Viking, 1977.

Silverman, Joan L. "'I'll Never Touch Another Drop': Images of Alcoholism and Temperance in American Popular Culture, 1874–1919." Ph.D. dissertation, New York University, 1979.

Silverman, Kenneth. *Edgar Allan Poe: Mournful and Never-Ending Remembrance.* New York: HarperCollins, 1991.

Simms, William Gilmore. *The Writings of William Gilmore Simms.* Edited by John Caldwell Guilds et al. 18 vols. to date. Columbia: University of South Carolina Press, 1969–.

Sinclair, Andrew. *Era of Excess: A Social History of Prohibition.* New York: Harper and Row, 1962.

Slote, Bernice. "Whitman and Dickinson." In *American Literary Scholarship 1969,* edited by J. Albert Robbins, 56–76. Durham: University of North Carolina Press, 1971.

Slotkin, Richard. *The Fatal Environment: The Myth of the Frontier in the Age of Industrialization, 1800–1890.* New York: Athenaeum, 1985.

———. *Regeneration through Violence: The Mythology of the American*

*Frontier, 1600–1860.* Middletown: Wesleyan University Press, 1973.

Smith, Elizabeth Oakes. *The Sinless Child and Other Poems.* Edited by John Kuse. New York: Willey and Putnam, 1843.

Smith, Henry Nash. *Virgin Land: The American West as Myth and Symbol.* Cambridge, Mass.: Harvard University Press, 1950.

Southworth, E. D. E. N. *The Hidden Hand, or, Capitola the Madcap.* Edited by Joanne Dobson. New Brunswick: Rutgers University Press, 1988. First published in 1859.

Spenser, Edmund. *The Poetical Works of Edmund Spenser.* Edited by J. C. Smith and E. De Selincourt. London: Oxford University Press, 1924.

Stein, William Bysshe. *The Poetry of Melville's Late Years.* Albany: State University of New York Press, 1970.

Stern, Madeline B. "Introduction." In *Plots and Counterplots: More Unknown Thrillers of Louisa May Alcott,* edited by Madeline B. Stern, 7–25. New York: Popular Library, 1978.

———. "A Writer's Progress: Louisa May Alcott at 150." In *Critical Essays on Louisa May Alcott,* edited by Madeline B. Stern, 240–50. Boston: G. K. Hall, 1984.

Stern, Milton R. *The Fine Hammered Steel of Herman Melville.* Urbana: University of Illinois Press, 1957.

Stoddard, Elizabeth Drew. *"The Morgesons" and Other Writings.* Edited by Lawrence Buell and Sandra A. Zagarell. Philadelphia: University of Pennsylvania Press, 1984.

Storer, H. L. *Appendix* to Albert M. Day, *Methomania: A Treatise on Alcoholic Poisoning.* Boston: J. Campbell, 1867.

Stowe, Harriet Beecher. *The Writings of Harriet Beecher Stowe.* 16 vols. Boston: Houghton Mifflin, 1896.

Strickland, Charles. *Victorian Domesticity: Families in the Life and Art of Louisa May Alcott.* University: University of Alabama Press, 1985.

Swann, Charles. *Nathaniel Hawthorne: Tradition and Revolution.* Cambridge: Cambridge University Press, 1991.

Tanner, Tony. *The Reign of Wonder: Naivety and Reality in American Literature.* Cambridge: Cambridge University Press, 1965.

Taylor, Alan. *William Cooper's Town: Power and Persuasion on the Frontier of the Early American Republic.* New York: Knopf, 1995.

Thomas, Dwight, and David K. Jackson, eds. *The Poe Log: A Documentary Life of Edgar Allan Poe 1809–1849.* Boston: G. K. Hall, 1987.

Thompson, G. R. *Poe's Fiction: Romantic Irony in the Gothic Tales.* Madison: University of Wisconsin Press, 1973.

Thompson, Hunter S. *Fear and Loathing in Las Vegas.* New York: Vintage, 1971.

Tompkins, Jane. *Sensational Designs: The Cultural Work of American Fiction 1790-1860.* New York: Oxford University Press, 1985.

Trotter, Thomas. *An Essay Medical, Philosophical, and Chemical on Drunkenness.* London: Longman, 1804.

Tyler, Royall. *The Verse of Royall Tyler.* Edited by Marius B. Péladeau. Charlottesville: University of Virginia Press, 1968.

Tyrrell, Ian. *Sobering Up: From Temperance to Prohibition in Antebellum America, 1800-1860.* Westport, Conn.: Greenwood Press, 1979.

Vaillant, George E. *The Natural History of Alcoholism: Causes, Patterns, and Paths to Recovery.* Cambridge, Mass.: Harvard University Press, 1983.

Velie, Alan R., ed. *American Indian Literature.* Norman: University of Oklahoma Press, 1979.

Vincent, Howard. *Melville and Hawthorne in the Berkshires.* Kent, Ohio: Kent State University Press, 1968.

Wagenknecht, Edward. *Edgar Allan Poe: The Man Behind the Legend.* New York: Oxford University Press, 1963.

Waggoner, Hyatt. *Emerson as Poet.* Princeton: Princeton University Press, 1974.

Wakefield, Dan. *New York in the Fifties.* Boston: Houghton Mifflin, 1992.

Wallace, James. *Early Cooper and His Audience.* New York: Columbia University Press, 1986.

Warner, Jessica. "'Resolv'd to Drink No More': Addiction as a Preindustrial Concept." *Journal of Studies on Alcohol* 55 (1994): 685-91.

Warner, Nicholas O., ed. *Alcohol in Literature: Studies in Five Cultures. Contemporary Drug Problems* 13 (1986).

————. "The Drunken Wife in Defoe's *Colonel Jack:* An Early Description of Alcohol Addiction." *Dionysos* 1 (1989): 3-9.

Warner, Susan. *The Wide, Wide World.* 2 vols. New York: Putnam, 1853.

Watts, Emily Stipes. *The Poetry of American Women from 1632 to 1945.* Austin: University of Texas Press, 1977.

Weisbuch, Robert. *Emily Dickinson's Poetry.* Chicago: University of Chicago Press, 1975.

Welter, Barbara. *Dimity Convictions: The American Woman in the Nineteenth Century.* Athens: Ohio University Press, 1976.

Wheeler, Edward L. *Deadwood Dick on Deck; or, Calamity Jane, the Hero-ine of Whoop-Up.* In *"Seth Jones" by Edward Sylvester Ellis and "Deadwood Dick on Deck" by Edward L. Wheeler.* Edited by Philip Durham. New York: Odyssey Press, 1966.

Whipple, Edwin Percy. "Some Recollections of Ralph Waldo Emerson." In *Emerson Among His Contemporaries,* edited by Kenneth Walter Cameron, 240–47. Hartford: Transcendental Books, 1967.

Whitman, Walt. *The Early Poems and the Fiction.* Edited by Thomas L. Brasher. New York: New York University Press, 1963.

———. *The Gathering of the Forces.* Edited by Cleveland Rodgers and John Black. 2 vols. New York: George Putnam's Sons, 1920.

Wilson, James, C., ed. *The Hawthorne and Melville Friendship: An Anno-tated Bibliography, Biography, and Critical Essays, and Corre-spondence.* Jefferson, N.C.: McFarland, 1991.

Wilson, John. *The "Noctes Ambrosianae" of Blackwood.* 4 vols. Philadel-phia: Carey and Hart, 1843.

Wilson, Margaret Gibbons. *The American Woman in Transition: The Urban Influence, 1870–1920.* Westport, Conn.: Greenwood Press, 1979.

Winters, Yvor. *In Defense of Reason.* Chicago: Swallow Press, 1947.

Winthrop, John. "A Modell of Christian Charity." In Darrett B. Rutman, Jr., *Winthrop's Decision for America: 1629,* 94–101. Philadelphia: J. B. Lippincott, 1975.

Wolfson, Harry Austryn. *Philo: Foundations of Religious Philosophy in Judaism, Christianity, and Islam.* 2 vols. Cambridge, Mass.: Har-vard University Press, 1962.

*The Woman's Dictionary and Encyclopedia: Everything a Woman Wants to Know.* London: Munson Book Co., 1909.

Woodward, Samuel B. *Essays on Asylums for Inebriates.* Worcester, 1838.

Yetman, Michael G. "Emily Dickinson and English Romantic Tradition." *Texas Studies in Literature and Language* 15 (1973): 129–47.

Yoder, R. A. *Emerson and the Orphic Poet in America.* Berkeley and Los Angeles: University of California Press, 1978.

Yohannan, J. D. "The Influence of Persian Poetry upon Emerson's Works." *American Literature* 15 (1943): 25–41.

Zaehner, R. C. *Zen, Drugs and Mysticism.* New York: Pantheon, 1972.

Ziff, Larzer. *The American 1890's: Life and Times of a Lost Generation.* New York: Viking, 1966.

———. *Literary Democracy: The Declaration of Cultural Independence in America.* Harmondsworth: Penguin, 1982.

# Index